Architectural Hardware
Specifications Handbook

Architectural Hardware Specifications Handbook

Adon H. Brownell, H.A.H.C.

Chilton Book Company

Philadelphia   New York   London

Copyright © 1971 by Adon H. Brownell
First Edition   *All rights reserved*
Published in Philadelphia by Chilton Book Company
and simultaneously in Ontario, Canada,
by Thomas Nelson & Sons, Ltd.
ISBN   0–8019–5565–3
Library of Congress Catalog Card Number 74–148909
Designed by William E. Lickfield
Manufactured in the United States of America

PREFACE

The inspiration to prepare a book like this came about in the course of business visits to over three hundred architectural offices throughout the United States. At every call I asked the same question: "What is it that architects want from the manufacturers and distributors of architectural builders' hardware that they are not getting?"

Of the many different requests, two were made so often that they provided the challenge to do something about it. Thus, although the contents of this book are solely my responsibility, the book is not just "one man's opinion." The material presented here has been gathered from hundreds of active, participating members of the hardware industry, then interpreted, and in my best judgment expressed in common denominations.

The information contained here is intended to cover all areas of architectural builders' hardware that is used with regularity in all types of buildings, from the better residences to the largest buildings. To try to include hardware items of occasional special usage and those used in the lowest economy structures is not feasible, but the book does refer to three grades of many of the items shown.

The Two Requests Most Frequently Made

1. "Give us some basis for writing a hardware specification." As one architect put it: "Show us how to write a hardware specification that will be

(1) complete,
(2) competitive,
(3) reasonably restrictive,
(4) short,

and that will (5) protect the architect."

This book provides six ways of writing a specification. The fifth and sixth ways best incorporate all five objectives. The first method, although preferred, is often impossible to use on federal work or where use of federal funds is involved. In any case, the writing of a hardware specification is exhaustively covered.

2. "Give us an unbiased reference book that an architect can use to judge the equivalency of a product under an 'or equal' clause. We must either take the word of a salesman who has a commercial interest or spend much time going through hardware catalogues, and even then we cannot always get the right answers."

This book is such a reference. It is as unbiased and accurate as it was possible to make it. If any errors are reported, they will be verified and corrected in future printings.

It is said that ninety percent of man's knowledge has been gained in this century, and that fifty percent of that has been gained in the last decade. While change does not always indicate progress, we are undergoing continuous change to keep abreast of the astonishing technological advances being made around us. Despite a propensity to resist change, the builders' hardware industry is responding as it must. Distributors are investigating electronic data processing and are beginning to use it. They are debating such issues as whether the vertical or horizontal hardware schedule best fits today's needs. Manufacturers are building new facilities and improving production techniques, and others are merging.

The format of specification writing proposed in this book is an old system with some new features. It is recommended because it can be reused from project to project with a minimum of modification to make it adaptable. It is concise. Numbers are used so that no manufacturer's product will appear to be favored, and as a means of indicating the level of performance suggested, something that would not be possible using the present federal type numbers.

Some specifying agencies have little to work with except the Federal Supply Service specifications produced by the General Services Administration (G.S.A.). In some areas, these specifications have become outdated. Other agencies have prepared their own standards which complicate an already confused problem. Hardware samples on file with the Veterans Administration now affect only this one agency. There is no central authority

of the United States Government for specifying and listing builders hardware. The Veterans Administration, Public Buildings Service, Air Force, Bureau of Yards and Docks, and the Army all have their own hardware requirements. Recently the F.H.A. has investigated the idea of performance tests for hardware used in kitchen cabinets. State, county, and city government agencies have their own hardware specifications.

Unfortunately and with few exceptions, the only way that hardware could be evaluated was from examining samples, by studying catalogues, or by talking with a manufacturer's representative. In cooperation with an industry committee, G.S.A. made a significant step forward by establishing performance tests requirements for bored locks, series 159, 160, and 161. While all hardware products do not lend themselves to performance test requirements, the Builders Hardware Manufacturers Association (B.H.M.A.) has attempted to establish realistic tests for products that do. Since the hardware listed has been assigned a level of use, one can select the grade desired or evaluate a product being offered on the basis of the item having met the B.H.M.A. Product Standard requirements.

It is hoped that this book will contribute to the progress of the builders hardware industry.

Key to Preparation of a Hardware Specification

1. **Select System of Specification You Will Use**
   A   Hardware Allowance—Chapter 3, page 1
   B   Federal Specification Numbers—Chapter 3, page 2
   C   Descriptive Specification—Chapter 3, pages 3 and 4
   D   Hardware Set Numbers—Chapter 4, pages 1, 2, and 3
   E   Type Number System, Short Form, Chapter 5, pages 1 through 4
   F   Type Number System, Long Form, Chapter 6, pages 1 through 13

2. **Numbering System**
   With a number such as 10.5.1, the first number establishes the chapter and class of item (Chapter 10, Preassembled and Integral Locks). The second number indicates the particular article or function. The third number has several uses. In describing locks, for example, it identifies the grade. When an option or options are desired, they are coded with a digit following a hyphen after the number. For example, should hinge 7.5 be wanted streamlined, the number would read 7.5-1, and if Non-Removable also, it would read 7.5-1-5. Such a numbering system makes computing easy.

3. **Computer Numbering System**
   A   Where it is desired that no manufacturers' numbers be used, use those in this handbook.
   B   Under Specification Systems D, E, and F, when it is preferable to use the manufacturers' numbers, simply change handbook numbers to the manufacturers' numbers, but to make computerization possible, handbook numbers should also be shown.

4. **Other Suggestions**
   A   As is further explained in Chapter 5, page 2, further simplification of type numbers is recommended to save time. For example, to refer to Chapter 5, page 4, Door 6, simply designate the lock as Type 32, and the description of a Type 32 appears only once on page 3 as 11.36, which is the lock and function called for in Chapter 11, page 2.
   B   Do not overlook any and all options you may desire.
   C   One can always extend the description after a type number. For example, let us assume Chapter 12, page 2, Type 12.80.1 was wanted for a pair of U.L. Labeled Doors requiring a ¾″ throw latch and you wanted 3¾″ Backset. The description would read, "12.80.1-¾″ Throw Latch."

Hardware Associations

Builders Hardware Manufacturers Association (B.H.M.A.)

Many of the leading manufacturers and their associated companies comprise the membership of this organization. Membership is open to any individual, firm, or corporation in the manufacture of builders' hardware.

Its purposes are to advance the interests of all persons engaged in the industry, including employers and employees, in all lawful ways such as

1. Encouraging consumers to use better quality products.
2. Making technical and other cooperative efforts for improving the quality of products.
3. Collecting and disseminating accurate statistical information.

4. Studying and advancing benefits programs for members' employees.
5. Cooperating in efforts to secure and maintain adequate protective tariff legislation.
6. Conducting the usual association activities, such as the establishment of product standards.

The Association has sections dealing with various phases of the industry, such as hinges and locks. Many member firms are in several such sections. The Association Product Standards reflect the judgment and experience of all member firms who make the product.

Headquarters are at 60 East 42nd Street, New York City, New York 10017.

National Builders Hardware Association (N.B.H.A.)

This association is a trade association of some 500 leading hardware distributors throughout Canada and the United States. They publish "Doors and Hardware," a journal which is widely distributed to architects and the industry as a whole. Their national conventions have set a high standard of excellence in programs and exhibits and have proved to be an excellent means of introducing new products.

Membership is open only to those individuals, firms, and corporations who distribute builders' hardware. It is required that adequate stocks, sample rooms, com-

petent consultants be provided and that they must do their own estimating, detailing, scheduling, and servicing. Their code of ethics obligates them to maintain high ethical standards and to promote the advancement and distribution of quality contract hardware.

Local builders hardware clubs throughout the country, while not directly affiliated with the N.B.H.A., do add much to the overall objectives.

The N.B.H.A. headquarters is at 1290 Avenue of the Americas, New York City, New York 10019.

American Society of Architectural Hardware Consultants (A.S.A.H.C.)

This is a professional society of individuals, approaching 2000 in number. It was formed in 1940 to identify the profession. Its members are located widely around the United States and Canada. A candidate is required to have five years' experience in the trade before being eligible to take the rigid examinations prescribed by the Society. Upon satisfactorily passing, then accepting the Society's code of good business conduct, and having been approved by the membership committee, he is granted a membership certificate as a qualified Architectural Hardware Consultant (A.H.C.). Apprentice members are encouraged to join after two years' service in the trade, but they may not use the initials until they can qualify for regular membership.

The Society strongly assists and encourages the education of prospective members. It conducts an Architectural Institute offering six courses: First Year, Second Year, Third Year, Fourth Year, Management, and Professional Salesmanship. It also conducts a special course for the U.S. Army Corps of Engineers.

Its Code of Ethics calls for dedication to high ethical standards, integrity, fidelity, and fair play, sharing of experiences at conventions and local chapter meetings, and the promotion of quality hardware.

The A.S.A.H.C. address is P.O. Box 599, Mill Valley, California 94941.

Comments

A number of good hardware specifiers are not members of the A.S.A.H.C. Historically, we have always been rugged individualists and probably always will be. The non-conformists who for one reason or another have chosen not to become members of the Society are usually older men whose experience and knowledge may well be respected.

Quite a few women have successfully passed A.H.C. examinations and are accredited members, actively engaged in their profession and fully capable.

Conclusion

Architects who use products made by B.H.M.A. members and distributed by N.B.H.A. firms, and who depend for specifications, scheduling, and servicing by an A.H.C., can be confident that their hardware requirements are being handled competently.

CONTENTS

* Illustration(s), full page.

CONTENTS

* Illustration(s), full page.

* Illustration(s), full page.

CONTENTS

* Illustration(s), full page.

* Illustration(s), full page.

xv

Architectural Hardware
Specifications Handbook

CHAPTER 1
A Brief History of Locks

Locks in Ancient Times

Locks have been used since ancient times. The Old Testament has numerous references to locks and keys. The oldest known lock was used in about 4,000 B.C. on an old palace at Khorsabad near Nineveh. It was made of a set of wooden pins inside a wooden staple and was quite ornate. When a wooden bar was thrust into the staple, the pins dropped into a set of matching holes in the bolt. This wooden bar, therefore, was the key. Our very latest cylinder key construction works on that ancient principle.

The Greeks and other peoples of Asia Minor often relied on rope knots, often very intricate, to perform the function of a lock. This is reflected in the fable of the Gordion knot, which Alexander the Great is said to have severed with one stroke of his sword in 334 B.C. The Greeks of this time also used a bolt type lock. The bolt could be lifted through a specially placed opening by a sickle-shaped key of the proper length (see illustration, next page). The sickle key was carried over the shoulder.

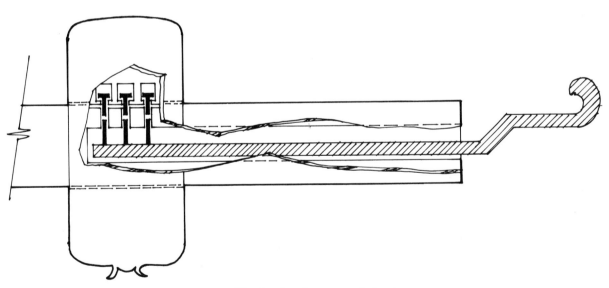

Wooden bar key as used about
4000 B.C. near Nineveh.

1

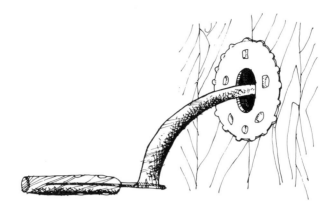

Sickle key operating a bolt inside a door.

The locks used by the Romans during the years of the Roman Empire were more ornate and somewhat more complex. The possessions they protected were similarly more numerous and valuable than those of earlier peoples. These locks, however, provided little real security.

One type of Roman key had a ring on the handle which could be worn on the finger (see illustration).

More Recent Locks

When the English of the eighteenth century began to become leaders in lock making, they had the advantage of know-ing all about Egyptian, Greek, Roman and Chinese puzzle locks, as well as French, German, Spanish and the Netherlands locksmithing. By the mid-1840's, with security becoming more and more important, English inventors came up with what they called "pick proof locks," and they offered substantial awards to anyone who could pick them. This was considered a major achievement in those days. At the London Exhibition of 1851, an American locksmith succeeded in picking such locks.

An interesting history of lockmaking is "Safe Bind, Safe Find: The Story of Locks, Bolts and Bars," by Garry Hogg, Criterion Books, Inc., New York City, 1968, $3.50.

Door key attached to finger ring,
used by the ancient Romans.

2

The Mortise Lock

American lock manufacturers until the early 1800's produced mostly rim (surface-applied) locks and padlocks. Mortise locks and latches were usually imported from England. (Strangely enough, many still are.) In the early 1800's an enterprising manufacturer in Nashua, New Hampshire, started producing American-made mortise locks. This proved quite successful, and other manufacturers in the United States, many still in business today, began to make mortise locks on a mass production basis. The illustrations show a simple mortise lock operated by a key with a wing bit.

Mortise locks operated by wing bit keys.

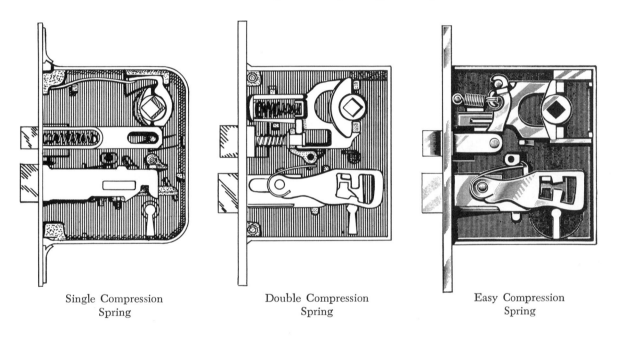

| Single Compression Spring | Double Compression Spring | Easy Compression Spring |

Yale's Cylinder Lock

In 1884 Linus Yale patented the cylinder lock, a lock with both keyhole and tumbler in a cylinder separate from the core. It was partly based on the pin system described earlier. It revolutionized the lock industry. One of its most important achievements was the use of a small key, easy to carry. An astronomical number of key pattern possibilities, depending on the number of pins, gave added security. (Security is covered in Chapter 23, page 4.)

With the cylinder lock, the principle of master keys had much greater application. Eventually all lock manufacturers started manufacturing cylinder mortise locks, and they still do. These locks and their functions are described and illustrated at length in Chapter 10.

A type of preassembled lock.

Phelps' Unit Lock

The unit lock was invented soon before the turn of the Century by the Honorable Byron Phelps, a former mayor of Seattle, Washington. In 1898 he came East and found a manufacturer for his product in New Britain, Connecticut.

The features which made this lock valuable were the ease of installation combined with the cylinder lock's key-in-knob principle. To install it, a notch is cut in the door and the lock is slipped in and bolted. Phelps patented the device and registered the name Unit Lock. In time a general term, preassembled lock, was used to refer to all locks of this type.

As first developed, it was distinguished by extra heavy construction and more expensive material. Because of its time-saving installation, long life, and useful function, architects came to specify it widely.

The less expensive cylinder lock for a time caused the preassembled lock to lose sales, and this in turn brought about its redesign and a simplification of the manufacturing process.

Just as happened with Yale's cylinder lock, when the patent expired nearly every major lock manufacturer produced preassembled locks with their own trade name.

The many versions of the cylinder lock now available are shown in Chapter 11, pages 1 through 4.

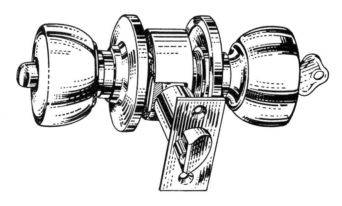

A type of cylindrical lock.

Schlage's Push Button

In the early 1920's Walter Schlage, a German inventor, migrated to the United States and settled in San Francisco. His push button lock evolved from his original idea of having a similar button in the knob turn on the room light. The push button lock was incorporated with the cylinder lock, together with the unit lock principle of the key in the knob. This is described in greater detail in Chapter 12.

Schlage's push button lock revolutionized the lock industry just as had Yale's cylinder lock, and similarly also, when Schlage's patent expired nearly all lock manufacturers produced competitive types.

The integral lock, developed by one manufacturer in the 1940s, also used the key-in-knob principle. It is described more fully in Chapter 11, pages 5, 6, and 7.

Integral lock applied on door.

Early Books Concerning Locks

"Locks & Hardware," by Henry R. Towne, was published in 1904. It has been out of print, but it was indeed a choice volume, measuring 4½″ by 6½″ by 2″ thick. Schools of lock design, important in those days, were heavily featured. With few exceptions it described only the products of Towne's manufacturer.

Towne's book contained a significant statement, which is as true today as it was then: "No lock having a key hole has ever been made or invented which is absolutely proof against picking, nor is it probable that one ever will or can be made."

A booklet, "Builders Hardware From the Ground Up," by W.N. Thomas, appeared in 1924, and his "Builders Hardware, Door by Door," came out in 1927. These booklets, like Towne's book, illustrated with few exceptions the products of one manufacturer. They also are out of print.

In 1935 the monthly trade journal

"Hardware Age," sensing the need in the business of builders hardware for more product information, authorized the author of the present book to write a series of articles covering the entire field of builders hardware, with the strict provision that it was to be non-partisan and unbiased. These articles were published serially every two weeks for two and a half years. The series was called, "Taking the Mystery out of Builders Hardware." At the conclusion of the series, hardware manufacturers strongly requested that the journal publish all of it as a book. "Hardware Age" was not a book publisher and at first refused, but it agreed when the manufacturers offered to finance the project. The book was published in 1940.

World War II interrupted the trend of education in builders hardware and greatly slowed the hardware manufacturing industry. Until the war was over, only black finish steel or iron could be used for hardware. With the end of the war, many new hardware products began to be introduced, some with merit, some without, and it was not until the mid-fifties that conditions had stabilized sufficiently to warrant a new hardware book.

Formal training for hardware personnel had regained and exceeded its former activity by the mid-fifties.

Hardware Training Classes

The National Builders' Hardware Association and the American Society of Architectural Hardware Consultants both took up the matter of industry education in earnest. Under their auspices, training classes were initiated in many areas, and many still are being conducted. Many of the large manufacturers also conduct classes periodically for their contract customers' employees.

The Architectural Hardware Institute, conducting annual classes in June at various universities throughout the nation, provides training in all phases of the industry, from basic information to management instruction. The Institute has contributed much to the qualifying of competent Architectural Hardware Consultants.

More Recent Hardware Literature

From his first book, "Taking the Mystery Out of Builders' Hardware," through the 1956 and 1961 editions of "Hardware Age Builders' Hardware Handbook," to the present handbook, the author has striven to be strictly impartial in his presentation.

The two editions of the "Builders' Hardware Handbook," directed toward formal training in the industry, have been much used by the Architectural Hardware Institute, in university courses in architecture, and in many other programs.

The National Builders' Hardware Association and the American Society of Architectural Hardware Consultants have augmented the available data for students of builders' hardware. These include the following books and brochures:

"Basic Builders' Hardware."
"Hardware for Labeled Fire Doors."

"Hardware for Hospitals."
"Hardware for Schools."
"Standardization for Terms and Nomenclature of Keying."
"Abbreviations and Symbols as Used in Builders' Hardware."
Builders' Hardware Manufacturers' "Product Standards." These are published in sections, some of which are available now.
"Education of a Consultant," by John R. Schoemer, D.A.H.C.
"Hardware Age Builders' Hardware Handbook" (1961), by Adon H. Brownell, H.A.H.C.

These can all be obtained from:

National Builders' Hardware Association
Suite 270
1290 Avenue of the Americas
New York, New York 10019

CHAPTER 2

The Hardware Specification

The Architectural Hardware Specification is a document that the architect, building owner, contractor and suppliers can use as their final authority concerning all questions pertaining to architectural hardware. It clearly establishes the quality and type of hardware desired for the project. It also clearly shows the conditions to which any bidder must adhere.

The most damaging mistake that the majority of specification writers make is to depend upon the use of the term "or equal" and to omit items that should be specified.

Use of the term "or equal" puts an unfair burden on the architect, who sometimes must decide, usually at awkward times, what is, indeed, equal. The same burden is put upon the general contractor who, occasionally, for competitive reasons, is tempted to interpret "or equal" a little more loosely than he should. The results are never too happy, and the most incredible thing of all usually happens: the consultant writing the specification, who bids the manufacturer's items he specified, more often than not loses the contract to the firm that figured the "or equal" so carefully inserted.

When a specific manufacturer's item is desired, such as a continuing master key system, it should be simply specified, without the use of unnecessary and sometimes seriously misleading phrases such as "or equal, subject to XYZ keyway." How to write a clear specification without an "or equal" phrase is explained in following chapters. It is the specification writer's responsibility not to name any combination of manufacturers that would tend to make the specification restrictive if open bidding is really wanted, yet completely restrictive in quality and performance standards.

A problem that has often been discussed, and one that perhaps tempts the specification writer to use the words "or equal," is lack of enforcement on the part of the architect. A clear understanding must exist between the consultant and the architect as to what products and procedures are acceptable. It would be reprehensible, for instance, for a consultant to specify that a key-control system be completely set up and indexed and the system explained to the owner or his agent, and then for the architect to permit the supplier to merely deliver the cabinet, the keys having been turned over to the owner by the contractor's agent. And for the architect to accept a product not named as an equal after bid opening and without having issued an addendum to that effect before bid opening, is equally reprehensible. The prudent consultant would refuse any future business with such an architect, just as a discreet architect would not engage for a second time the services of a consultant who had been in any way unethical.

It is the obligation of the specification writer to include all items to be furnished in their respective sections. For instance, if handrail brackets are to be furnished by the miscellaneous metal supplier, so state under hardware not included in hardware section.

The need for review cannot be over-emphasized. So often such items as hardware for aluminum doors are overlooked. See Chapter 6, page 1, "Work Not Included," as an example. Such a review and listing will prevent difficulties later on.

The Architect and the Hardware Consultant

Some architects agree to reimburse their consultant for his work if the consultant should lose the order. Others always pay a fee so that they can feel free of any obligation or bias. A few A.H.C.'s are full-time specification writers. They charge established fees and do not compete for business.

Any A.H.C. or other consultant who writes specifications has certain responsibilities. It is part of the code of ethics of the A.S.A.H.C. to accept specified obligations, which in part include—

(1) Whether paid or not, he will protect the architect in every way possible, because the specification when completed becomes the architect's responsibility.

(2) He will never overlook the four basics: Safety—Security—Stability—Service

(3) He will not resort to the giving of misleading information. In the latter category would be specifying Master Keying for systems that do not exist, while at the same time defending systems that are in existence that the owner wishes continued.

(4) He will not only prepare the specification, but he will check to see that the successful bidder keeps to the specification, and will even inspect hardware after installation, if necessary.

The following excerpts from "Hardware Age Builders' Hardware Handbook" discuss the roles of the architect and consultant.

Architect's Hardware Specifications
There are few architectural offices that write their own hardware specifications, but in those that do, usually there will be a competent hardware specification writer. It is only in a few large architectural firms [not more than a dozen] that such a man can be supported.

The usual architectural practice is to call in an architectural hardware consultant to write the specifications for the architect. This is a service, when properly done, that an architect deeply appreciates. Admittedly, it is one of the best ways to get the support and acceptance of your particular brand or brands. Such an opportunity is often solicited competitively.

Many firms write specifications free of charge to the architect, though it may take many painstaking and expensive hours of work.

While the majority of architects accepts this free service, there are two other practices sometimes followed. Some architects accept the free service if the hardware contract goes to the hardware firm that wrote the specification but insist on paying for the specification service if the hardware contract is awarded to a firm which did not write the specification. Other architects compensate the writer of the hardware specification in any case, feeling that in so doing they are without obligation and free to make the best deal for their client, the owner, who has to pay for the hardware wherever purchased.

The moral responsibility of the architectural hardware consultant should remain fixed regardless of the method of compensation.

Specification Responsibility

The ethical hardware practice is to write a clear, intelligent and fair specification that is competitive and honest. Any architect who permits the writing in of conditions to the unfair advantage of the hardware specification writer's firm, or any specification writer who does so unknown to the architect, is doing an injustice to all other bidders.

It is far more honest and honorable to give a hardware order outright to a given firm, no matter how disconcerting to competitors, than to ask competitors to spend time and money estimating a loaded specification just to keep the favored firm, which is going to get the order anyway, reasonably competitive.

The Architect's Place in the Picture

The architect is the owner's representative. He is paid by the owner to design the building, to supervise the work, and to see that the contractor lives up to the specifications. The architect also has a most important position in the selection of the materials such as the builders' hardware.

. . . The architect is interested and concerned that the hardware be in keeping with the rest of the building as to design and finish. He is greatly interested in those benefits that appeal to the owner . . . for he is the owner's representative. Many times the owner is not available, and everything is left to the architect. Cultivate him continuously.

Beginners in the business of selling builders' hardware to architects often are misled and make excuses for themselves through certain misconceptions.

One such misconception is that architects receive secret commissions for specifying certain brands of hardware. Long experience has proved that this is not so. Practically all architects are ethical, professional men who would not indulge in such a practice. They are paid by the owner to represent him and assure the owner of value received. To take money would be just the same as stealing it from the owner's pocket. As for the very few who do stoop to such practices, they only prove that architects, like all other men, are subject to human frailty.

Granted that architects are not influenced to specify certain brands because of personal financial gain, another misconception is that architects are unfair, biased, and arbitrary. This is an excuse the unsuccessful hardware man uses to ease his conscience. The real reason an architect favors your competitor is because he has confidence in that competitor or in the products that competitor sells. It is the consultant's responsibility to win the architect's confidence in a fair manner.

Remember that the builders' hardware order may be less than 1 percent but probably not over 2 percent of the cost of the building, but if the architect has difficulty with the hardware, it may be 10 percent or more of all the troubles he will experience on the entire job. Naturally, he favors the architectural hardware consultant who can eliminate difficulty. He is concerned with the interest of his client, the owner, as well as his own peace of mind.

When you get a contract from an architect, the very best way to win his confidence is to provide the highest quality service.

Labeled Openings

It was practically impossible to write a clear and accurate hardware specification for a fire door until the National Builders' Hardware Association began to distribute a series of booklets entitled, "Hardware for Labeled Fire Doors." A new edition is published every other year, and it is an asset for specification writers and A.H.C.'s.

The task is still difficult. The specifier may not know the specific brand of fire door to be used on a project, and there is the temptation to use the ambiguous "or equal" phrase. One manufacturer may use a lock with a ½″ throw on his A label door (so long as it is within a certain size) and another may not, and this does nothing to clarify the situation. Often we are tempted to cover all contingencies and specify hardware that will conform to all requirements. Sometimes we take the attitude that it is the door and frame supplier's responsibility to furnish doors that may be listed when the hardware we specified is used. This approach has some validity if the doors originally specified are correlated with the hardware specification. If they are not, the architect or the contractor is forced to act as arbitrator between the two suppliers. It is much easier and more efficient when the hardware supplier also supplies the doors and frames. Sometimes the hardware required for fire doors is specified in the door and frame section, which is a very poor solution to the problem. Different brands of hardware are often used by the two suppliers, resulting in a key system that often cannot be integrated and a divided responsibilty for the hardware in the building.

The all-inclusive approach to specifying hardware for fire doors is responsible for the needless use of many fusible link holder arms on door closers. The consultant must bear in mind that many fire doors are required to be merely self-closing and not automatic. When the automatic door is required, many codes now insist upon the use of electromagnetic or electromechanical door holder release devices in conjunction with door closers and do not allow the use of fusible link holder arms. This occurs where protection of human life is a more important factor than protection of the building. With more and more emphasis being placed on the use of heat rise, smoke detection, and alarm systems integrated with door control, we may expect that the fusible link door holder will be relegated to an occasional mechanical, boiler or storeroom door. See Chapter 22, page 2.

Attachment of Hardware

No matter how well any item of hardware may be specified, its stability and insurance of proper functioning depend on having proper attachments (screw and bolt fastenings). Page 10 of this chapter shows the ones in most common use.

The hardware consultant must be concerned not only with his own specification but also with those of other sections, which he should carefully check to guard against duplication and omissions.

The reuse of specifications is a major problem. Not only are items that should be specified sometimes overlooked, but unnecessary items are not taken out. We might wish it were common practice for consultants to be paid for writing specifications and for the specifications never to be reused. As it is, however, they are frequently written with no fee involved. This makes it most desirable to have standard formats which, if reused, will not be subject to complication and difficulty.

The preamble should be of a form that can be reused. The information that applies to all projects should be presented first, and the specific requirements that pertain to the particular job should follow somewhat in the order of individuality. Information that pertains to keying and finish should not precede the paragraph dealing with fastenings, for example. A preamble can be edited for reuse much more simply when there is a logical sequence of presentation. If the Hardware Type Number Systems E or F, Chapters 5 and 6, are used, even though some specific items unused in the project are not deleted, the nature of the system is such that the item of hardware still is not specified. All that really has happened is that an item has been described and assigned a number, but the number has not been used. While this is not a practice to be recommended, it does not create problems of omissions, nor does it result in unwanted hardware being furnished.

No harm is done even if all the items shown in Chapters 7 through 22 are mass produced so far as the type number descriptions are concerned. It is at the point of using given type numbers on specific doors that careful, individual attention in the use of type numbers becomes of utmost importance and must be tailored to the need of the opening in question.

Procedures Often Used in Preparing Hardware Specifications

Most architects call upon a hardware consultant (A.H.C.) or other competent hardware man they trust to work for them without fee. This service has proved, over the years, advantageous to the hardware distributor despite its cost, when the architect enforces the following three conditions:

(1) That the written specification is enforced.

(2) When other than his consultant's firm wins an order, that the architect will have his consultant review the successful bidder's proposed schedule without bias to see that the specifications have been met.

(3) The architect, realizing his obligation to his consultant, will use his influence with the owner and contractor, other things being equal, to enable his consultant's firm to secure the order.

Customary Procedure for Writing Hardware Specifications

Step 1

The architect selects an architectural hardware consultant, secures his acceptance, and provides sufficient time for the job to be done properly.

Step 2

Before the work of preparing the specification begins, it should be the architect's responsibility to make the following determinations with his consultant.

    (a) Decide the design or designs to be specified.

    (b) Specify the finishes wanted.

    (c) Select the appropriate system: A, B, C, D, E, or F (Chapters 3 through 6).

    (d) If System D, E, or F is selected, determine whether to use the manufacturers' product numbers or the numbers provided in this book.

    (e) When competition is desired, the architect should provide a list of the manufacturers he will accept, providing they meet the standard set under System D, E, or F.

Step 3

The architect should specify an individual in his organization who will be responsible for working with his hardware consultant on plans, details, etc. It should also be the responsibility of this appointee to keep the hardware consultant fully advised of changes and addenda.

Step 4

With the above three steps done, the hardware consultant can then proceed to prepare the architectural hardware specifications. Under Formats B, C, D, E, or F, the same general conditions are applicable, so they are outlined below and should proceed as a general preamble to any of the five formats.

Step 5

Practices of the American Institute of Architects and the Construction Specifications Institute may vary, but usually the procedures suggested below will be satisfactory.

    FURNISH all finish hardware, including all related items and appurtenances in strict accord with the requirements of applicable drawings of this specification and of the terms and conditions of the Contract Documents.

    WORK NOT INCLUDED in this section: Hardware for the following items and work is specified and required to be furnished as part of the work of other sections of the specification where noted.

NOTE

As omissions vary from job to job, no general listing can be made here, but, for explanation, such items as these might be included: Hand Rail Brackets, hardware for folding partitions, metal windows, wire mesh doors, etc.

    APPLICATION OF FINISH HARDWARE. All finish hardware is applied and/or installed by the appropriate trade, such as Finish Carpentry, Ornamental Metal Work, Hollow Metal Work, etc. It is the responsibility of the hardware supplier, however, for all material in this section, to prepay all delivery charges to the job site or other trades as specified by the contractor.

HARDWARE (GENERAL) The hardware supplier shall correlate and coordinate the manufacture and delivery of all hardware items with requirements of the contractor in such a manner that in no instance shall any portion or items of the contractor's work be delayed in completion or installation and/or application thereof as a result of delayed delivery. Included in above requirements shall be, without additional cost to owner, the delivery of all incidental hardware to various subcontractors requiring same to complete their portions of work.

All hardware items shall be neatly packaged in substantial and secure boxes, properly labeled and readily identifiable for individual locations and use. The general contractor shall acknowledge and give complete receipts for all hardware when and as delivered.

The hardware supplier shall furnish full and complete "Schedules" of all hardware as required for the use of the contractor. The furnishing of the above hardware items shall include all items of securement and fastening, such as screws, bolts, nuts, brackets, and the like; except where specifically required otherwise, all screws shall be Phillips head type screws.

The contractor shall provide one specific room, free of dampness and ventilated, with adequate shelving for the storing and laying out of all hardware as received. The room shall be provided with adequate security for the proper safe-keeping of all hardware so as to preclude delay on account of theft, and some one person of the contractor's staff shall be charged with the responsibility and/or accountability for the receipt and disposition, as needed, of all hardware items until all finished hardware has been installed or accounted for.

SAMPLES To be supplied to architect for approval in strict accord with the applicable requirements of the "General Conditions" of the contract relating to samples.

INSTALLATION, INSPECTION, AND ADJUSTMENT All finish hardware specified herein shall be installed by the contractor and/or various subcontractors whose items of work require finish hardware as directed by the contractor, who will be responsible for the correct application of all hardware. The hardware supplier shall likewise authorize his representative to be present when all finish hardware is delivered to the site and to check in each hardware item, turning over same to the contractor and seeing that same is stored in a secure place and under lock and key.

Prior to final inspection, the hardware manufacturer shall inspect and adjust all door closers and locks, and/or all items requiring close adjustment and/or regulation and check all keying. This shall be done at no additional charge. Cost of same to be included in hardware supplier's price.

HARDWARE (TYPE, KIND, AND QUALITY)

Materials: The catalogue plate numbers referred to hereinafter are the catalogue numbers of: (See instruction, page 6, Step 2(d) and insert the names of all manufacturers whose numbers are used.) These numbers are referenced to indicate characteristics and function and a general description of the type, approximate size, and suitability of all items otherwise.

The finish hardware listed below of comparable and/or equivalent items as manufactured by other hardware manufacturers, may be used as noted, provided the quality and type are equal to that specified. The architect shall be the sole judge as to kind, quality, function, and equivalency.

Butts and Hinges See instructions, Step 2(e), page 6, and insert the names of other acceptable manufacturers by product heading.

Exit Devices See instructions, Step 2(e), page 6, and insert the names of other acceptable manufacturers by product heading.

Locks See instructions, Step 2(e), page 6, and insert the names of other acceptable manufacturers by product heading.

Door Closing Devices See instructions, Step 2(e), page 6, and insert the names of other acceptable manufacturers by product heading.

Architectural Trim See instructions, Step 2(e), page 6, and insert the names of other acceptable manufacturers by product heading.

Cabinet Hardware See instructions, Step 2(e), page 6, and insert the names of other acceptable manufacturers by product heading.

Auxiliary Hardware See instructions, Step 2(e), page 6, and insert the names of other acceptable manufacturers by product heading.

Miscellaneous Items See instructions, Step 2(e), page 6, and insert the names of other acceptable manufacturers by product heading.

FINISH OF HARDWARE See instructions, Step 2(b), page 6, and insert finishes desired throughout. Examples:

"All hardware, except hinges and closers occurring in toilets and baths, shall be finished in polished chrome, #625."

"All hardware, except hinges and closers occurring in kitchens and food preparation rooms, shall be furnished in stainless steel, #630."

"Armor and kick plates, where specifically called for in steel in certain portions of building, are to be furnished in #626. All steel hinges are to be prime coat for painting, #600."

"All hardware for ornamental doors shall be in #628. All other hardware, including bronze hinges throughout building shall be of solid bronze metal in #612."

"Door closers shall be lacquer sprayed to match adjacent hardware."

"All lacquer shall be 'new type synthetic lacquer.' Supplier of the locks shall provide samples of the metal finishes selected as may be requested by architect or general contractor."

DESIGN All service portions of the building shall be _____.
Then specify all other designs wanted by area or rooms. See Step 2(a).

TEMPLATE HARDWARE The hardware supplier to furnish all necessary templates and samples of hardware to door and frame manufacturers so that doors and frames may be properly prepared to receive hardware to be furnished. Complete schedules of hardware for doors and frames shall also be furnished to various concerns to identify such templates and samples. Contractor shall arrange to ship prepaid all hardware for doors and frames which are to be applied at the plant of the door and frame manufacturers.

NOTE ON TEMPLATES

Increasingly, hardware manufacturers are providing metal door and frame manufacturers with complete template books of their products. This has proved highly beneficial to all concerned. It has speeded up production and eliminated endless correspondence.

The user of the template books should keep changes, that necessarily occur from time to time, immediately revised by inserting the new templates as received by the manufacturer.

The hardware distributor has a responsibility too in this regard, and that is to note in the template schedule he sends out the proper identifying manufacturer's number and date of issue. It is strongly recommended that such template list be sent to hardware manufacturers with purchase order so that all parties concerned are fully advised.

Attachments Commonly Used in Fastening Hardware

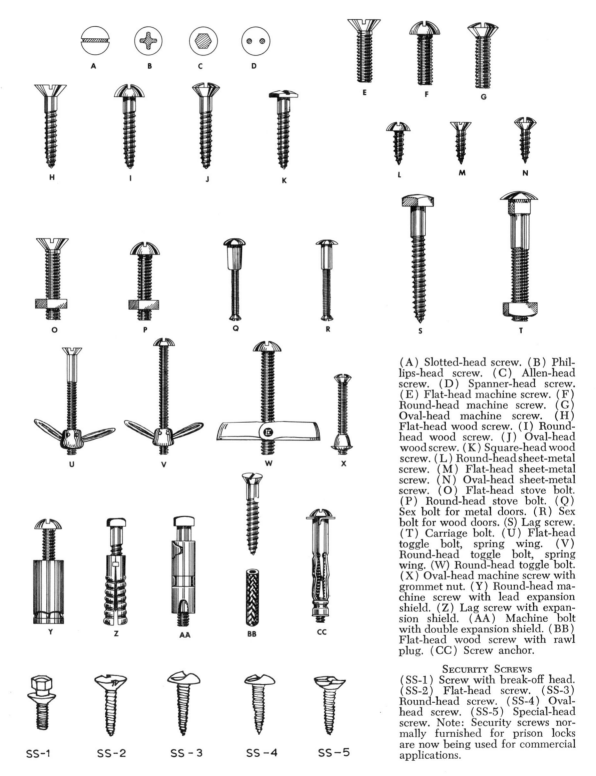

(A) Slotted-head screw. (B) Phillips-head screw. (C) Allen-head screw. (D) Spanner-head screw. (E) Flat-head machine screw. (F) Round-head machine screw. (G) Oval-head machine screw. (H) Flat-head wood screw. (I) Round-head wood screw. (J) Oval-head wood screw. (K) Square-head wood screw. (L) Round-head sheet-metal screw. (M) Flat-head sheet-metal screw. (N) Oval-head sheet-metal screw. (O) Flat-head stove bolt. (P) Round-head stove bolt. (Q) Sex bolt for metal doors. (R) Sex bolt for wood doors. (S) Lag screw. (T) Carriage bolt. (U) Flat-head toggle bolt, spring wing. (V) Round-head toggle bolt, spring wing. (W) Round-head toggle bolt. (X) Oval-head machine screw with grommet nut. (Y) Round-head machine screw with lead expansion shield. (Z) Lag screw with expansion shield. (AA) Machine bolt with double expansion shield. (BB) Flat-head wood screw with rawl plug. (CC) Screw anchor.

SECURITY SCREWS
(SS-1) Screw with break-off head. (SS-2) Flat-head screw. (SS-3) Round-head screw. (SS-4) Oval-head screw. (SS-5) Special-head screw. Note: Security screws normally furnished for prison locks are now being used for commercial applications.

CHAPTER 3

Specifications Systems A, B, and C

System A—Hardware Allowance

Purchase of the hardware under System A is the responsibility of the owner and the architect. Part of the contractor's responsibility is to pay for the allowance, as part of the general contract. It is also the contractor's duty to receive and install the hardware and service it, when necessary, prior to acceptance of the building.

The architect can establish the allowance price for good hardware by a rule of thumb at 2 percent of the cost of the building. This will usually prove adequate. The surer way would be to consult an A.H.C., give him a general idea of what is required, and let him establish the proper allowance price.

Even under an allowance, in justice to the contractor, there should be a descriptive list, especially so where concealed devices, panic bolts, or other high installation costs are involved.

The real benefits in using System A come from keeping the award under the control of the owner and architect, which avoids the unscrupulous practices of some contractors. Bid peddling, for instance, almost invariably results in attempts to cut corners and depart from the strict terms of the specifications.

Greater accuracy is assured, often resulting in substantial savings to the owner, because there is more time for careful selection when detailed drawings are further advanced than at the time of general contractor's bidding. This has often proved to work out more economically for the owner, because there is less guesswork by the hardware bidder and less chance for errors, extras, and delays.

Example of a Specification for a Hospital

The contractor shall include in his contract $10,000.00 for all finishing hardware not covered by other trades. The owner and architect reserve the right to select and purchase this hardware, which shall be paid for by the contractor. On receipt of the hardware, the contractor shall sign for the material, store it in a securely locked room, and be responsible for its distribution and installation.

For the contractor's guidance in estimating his cost of installation, the hardware requirements generally will be as follows:

Hinges for exterior and lead-lined doors will be floor pivot types; on wards and operating rooms swing-clear hinges; all other doors will be butt hung, three hinges to each door.

Closers, all other doors, modern surface closers.

Locks, other than those on special narrow-stile aluminum doors, will all be cylindrical or tubular type.

Door Holders and Door Stops generally will be surface-applied to floor or wall. There will be approximately 12 concealed in overhead door closers.

Exit Devices on aluminum exterior doors will be concealed type to be installed by the door manufacturer. All other hardware items such as kick plates, door silencers, thresholds, etc. will be surface applied as desired.

Should the hardware purchased exceed the allowance, the owner will pay the contractor the amount that the allowance covers and an extra order will be sent the contractor. Should it come to less than the allowance, the owner will deduct the difference from the contract price.

Since System B varies from Systems D and E in its use of Federal numbers, refer to either System D or E as preferred, and use Federal numbers as explained below.

System B—Federal Specifications

Where Federal funds are involved, it is sometimes necessary to use Federal numbers. These can be used under System C, D, E, or F in lieu of Product Standard numbers. Unfortunately, the Federal specifications often prove unwieldy and inadequate. Many of the sections have not been updated, so that new and better products now available are not shown. Other important hardware items are not even specified, and too often use of Federal numbers tends to downgrade rather than meet the basics of safety, security, and stability that good hardware provides.

Because of the limitations of the present Federal specifications where new products are wanted, it is generally acceptable to give a Federal number, mark it "modified," then describe the modification by giving a manufacturer's number, providing the hardware specification clearly includes these words:

> "Where Federal numbers given are noted as 'modified,' followed by a manufacturer's number, they are intended to be descriptive only, **not restrictive.** Any other manufacturer's product which meets the material, design, and function of these manufacturer's numbers, as approved by the architect, may be used."

Such modification will seldom be challenged. Should there be three manufacturers who can qualify, the author has never known it to be challenged by the government.

Note: Throughout this book no manufacturer's name is used. The following example shows that they are not necessary. The specification for Floor Hinges, Type #8, reads "3520A111 Modified." Three manufacturers make this item. Any hardware consultant would know who they are and can supply the name to specify the modification. This applies to all other numbers throughout this book that are marked "Modified."

Writing the Specification

Refer to Chapter 2, page 6, Step 5, and outline in the general preamble to the specification all matters noted from Step 5 through page 9. Then the following headings and type numbers will apply to System B. Section 1 is given here by way of example only. All other needed sections would be treated the same way by merely changing hardware numbers to Federal numbers.

> Section 1 BUTTS AND HINGES: Height as listed below; schedule proper width to suit details, using narrowest standard width; e.g., if a 4½" x 4" will clear and keep hinge knuckles closer to door than 4½" x 4½", so schedule. Where 6/1 or 3/3 is shown, this is to indicate 6 or 3 hinges of given type (not pairs).

Type	FFH	Height	Type	FFH	Height
#1	T2112S	5"	#5	T2127	3½"
#2	T2115	5"	#6	T2122	3½"
#3	T2106	4½"	#7	T2102	4½"
#4	T2127	4½"	#8	3520A-111 x FFH 3525B (Modified)	

System C—A Descriptive Specification

This example is based on a residence as shown on pages 5 and 6 of this chapter. The drawings were prepared with emphasis on hardware problems as are all other plans which follow. With that in mind, the reader will understand that in no way is there any intent to illustrate or to instruct anyone on layout or design. The sole purpose of every plan is to emphasize hardware problems and how to cover them in the hardware specification.

On page 5 is a plan of a residence, and on page 6 is a detail sheet containing door elevations and frame details. Listed below is a suggested door and window schedule. Such a schedule should appear on one of the drawings of a complete set of plans which, of course, this is not, or, if preferred, the schedule can be a page in the specifications.

DOOR TYPES AND DETAILS
(for Chapter 3, pages 5 and 6)

Door Number	Door Sizes	Door Type	Frame Type	Remarks
1	3′0″ x 7′0″ x 1¾″	A	A	Ornamental Door—Wood Door & Frame w. Cylinder Lock & Thumb Turn
2	3′0″ x 7′0″ x 1¾″	B	A	Flush Wood Door & Frame w. Cylinder Lock & Thumb Turn
3	Pr Drs 3′ x 7′0″ x 1¾″	E	B	Narrow Stile Wood Door & Frame. 5-Point Locks must be mounted at mill
4	2′6″ x 7′0″ x 1¾″	D	D	Double-Acting Wood Door & Frame
5	2′6″ x 6′8″ x 1⅜″	B	C	Flush Wood Door, Wood Frame
6	2′10″ x 6′8″ x 1⅜″	B	C	Flush Wood Door, Wood Frame
7	2′6″ x 6′8″ x 1⅜″	B	C	Flush Wood Door, Wood Frame w. Privacy Lock
8	2′10″ x 6′8″ x 1⅜″	B	C	Flush Wood Door, Wood Frame w. Privacy Lock
9	3′0″ x 7′0″ x 1¾″	C	C	Glass Panels, Wood Door, Wood Frame w. Cyl Lock & Push Button
10	3′0″ x 6′6″ x 1⅜″	B	C	Pr Bipassing Sliding Doors. Wood Doors & Frame
11	3′0″ x 7′0″ x 1¾″	B	A	Flush Wood Door, Wood Frame w. Cylinder Lock & Thumb Turn

WINDOW TYPES

Hinged Pr	2′0″ x 4′0″	Casements, Wood, Open Out
Sliding	3′0″ x 5′0″	Double-Hung Wood

Finish Hardware, System C

(for Chapter 3, Pages 5 and 6)

HINGES

Ext and bath doors—Bronze Metal—each 1¾″ Leaf ¾″, each 1⅜″, 3/3½″
Ext casement window each Leaf ⅔″ Galv Brass Pin
Folding shutters   each Leaf 2/2½″ Steel

LOCKS

Each Cylinder Lock—Hvy Duty Cylindrical—all Cylinders keyed alike
Each Privacy Lock—Standard Cylindrical—Push Button & Emergency Key
Pr doors #3—Provide 5-Point Latch Bolts & Custom Design Lever Hdle Operation
All other doors to have Standard Cylindrical Latches, Knobs both sides

MISCELLANEOUS

Furnish Bronze Wall or Base Stops as conditions require
At Door #1 provide Custom Design Knocker—Push Button—Letter Box Plate and Hood
At Door #4 provide Checking Floor Hinge—Design Push Plates—Kick Plate Kchn side
In each closet other than linen closets, provide Adj Hvy Closet Bar and C & H Hooks
At Doors #10 provide proper Fascia Track—Hangers—Guides—Pulls and Angle Stop

WINDOW HARDWARE

Casement fasts—Bolts and Casement Geared Operators, all Bronze Metal and provide Top Sash
   Snuggers each Leaf
D.H. windows—provide Crescent Sash Lock—Two 4″ Offset Bar Lifts and Adj Window Bead
   Screws

DESIGN

Kitchen, baths, utility room—Wrt Bronze Round 2″ Plain Knobs & Roses
Living & dining rooms, "XYZ" Custom Design—Cast Brze
Hall & bedrooms, "XYZ" Motif Design—Wrt Brze

FINISH

Kitchen & baths—Polished Chrome
Living & dining rooms—Dull Nickel oxidized and relieved
Hall & Bedrooms—Dull Brze oxidized and relieved

RESPONSIBILITY

It is the responsibility of the hardware supplier to furnish all finish hardware required by plans
   and specifications, and delivered to the job or millwork shop in the case of the 5 Pt Latch
   Set on Doors #3 (but not the Lever Hdles or Roses).

The hardware supplier must check details and be responsible for furnishing the proper hardware
   to suit. Note particularly that the hinges on doors #3 must be wide enough to clear the
   chair rail.

See Frame Detail B for 180° opening.

> NOTE: This sheet calls for Cylindrical (Bored) Sets. Should specifier
> want to use Mortise, Unit, or Integral Locks, refer to the section where
> such sets are described and change lock wording above.

Residence Floor Plan, System C

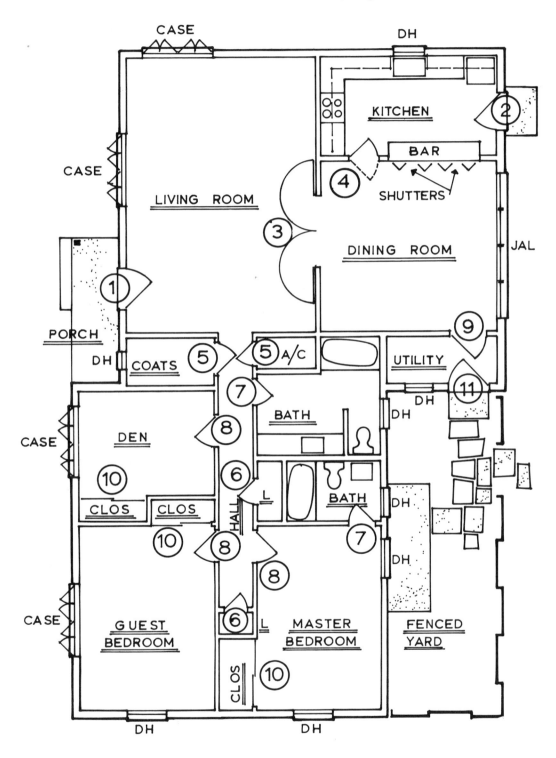

Door Types and Details, System C

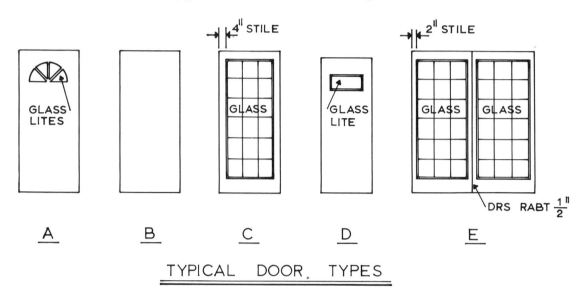

GLASS LITES

4" STILE

GLASS

2" STILE

GLASS LITE

GLASS　GLASS

DRS RABT $\frac{1}{2}$"

A　　B　　C　　D　　E

TYPICAL DOOR TYPES

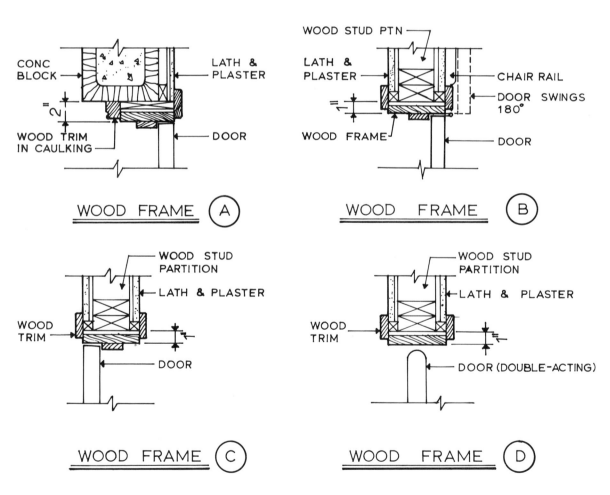

CONC BLOCK

LATH & PLASTER

2"

WOOD TRIM IN CAULKING

DOOR

WOOD FRAME Ⓐ

WOOD STUD PTN

LATH & PLASTER

CHAIR RAIL

DOOR SWINGS 180°

WOOD FRAME

DOOR

WOOD FRAME Ⓑ

WOOD STUD PARTITION

LATH & PLASTER

WOOD TRIM

DOOR

WOOD FRAME Ⓒ

WOOD STUD PARTITION

LATH & PLASTER

WOOD TRIM

DOOR (DOUBLE-ACTING)

WOOD FRAME Ⓓ

Specifications System D

System D—Set Numbers

This example is based on a portion of a school as shown on pages 4 and 5 of this chapter. On page 4 is the partial floor plan and on page 5 details to fit the door schedule.

The suggested door schedule below should appear on one of the drawings of a complete set of plans, which this, of course, is not, or, if preferred, the schedule can be incorporated in the specification.

DOOR TYPES AND DETAILS
(for Chapter 4, Pages 4 and 5)

Door Number	Door Sizes	Door Type	Frame Type	Remarks	Hdwe Set Number
1	3'0" x 7'6" x 1¾"	A	1	Pr Aluminum Custom-Made Doors, Threshold Type 6	1
2	3'0" x 7'0" x 1¾"	G	3	Pr Wood Doors, Threshold Type 7	2
3	3'0" x 7'0" x 1¾"	G	3	Pr Wood Doors, Threshold Type 8 by others	3
4	3'0" x 7'0" x 1¾"	G	3	Sgle Wood Door, Threshold Type 8 by others	4
5	2'8" x 7'0" x 1¾"	F	5	Sgle Wood Door, no Threshold	5
6	2'4" x 6'6" x 1⅜"	F	5	Sgle Wood Door, no Threshold	6
7	2'4" x 6'6" x 1⅜"	F	5	Sgle Wood Door, no Threshold	7
8	3'0" x 7'0" x 1¾"	F	2	Dble Smoke Screen H.M. Doors	8
9	3'0" x 7'0" x 1¾"	G	3	Sgle Wood Classroom Door, Threshold Type 8 by others	9
10	3'0" x 7'0" x 1¾"	G	3	Sgle Wood Door, Threshold Type 8 by others	10
11	2'8" x 7'0" x 1¾"	F	3	Sgle Wood Door, no Threshold	11
12	2'8" x 7'0" x 1¾"	F	3	Sgle Wood Doors, no Threshold	10
13	2'8" x 7'0" x 1¾"	F	5	Sgle Wood Door, no Threshold	12
14	3'6" x 7'0" x 1¾"	F	2	Sgle H.M. Door Exit Only, Threshold Type 6	13

General Procedure, System D

In a reference to the school floor plan and details on pages 4 and 5 of this chapter, the general procedure for specifying hardware under System D is as follows.

See Chapter 2, page 6, Step 5, and cover general conditions as there noted. Also work not included and application of hardware.

See Chapter 2, page 7, Step 5, and include HARDWARE (General) apropos to project. Samples, Installation, Inspection, etc.

See Chapter 2, page 7, Step 5, bottom paragraph. Particularly note that in case you elect to use the product type numbers in this book, then all the last paragraph need say is: "Type numbers used in this specification are taken from "Architectural Hardware Specifications Handbook." These numbers are referenced to indicate characteristics, functions, and general description of the type, approximate size, and suitability of all items otherwise. The architect shall be the sole judge as to kind, quality, function, and equivalency."

CAUTION

Should you elect instead to use manufacturers' numbers, then disregard the above paragraph and insert instead—from Chapter 2, page 7, bottom paragraph, "Materials"—the wording used there, including manufacturers' names, through the end of the paragraph beginning, "Finish hardware . . ." If you want a closed specification—no other manufacturers than those named—do not use this final paragraph at all.

Whenever reasonably restrictive competitive bidding is wanted, then include the paragraph at the top of page 8, and you get a reasonable restriction by naming only manufacturers which your experience has shown to be satisfactory. Name at least two in each category; e.g., HINGES: Manufacturer A (give name), Manufacturer B (give name), thus opening your bidding to three: A, B, and the manufacturer whose numbers you use. More manufacturers can be included if desired.

FINISH OF HARDWARE. See the procedure in Chapter 2, page 6, but make your own selection of finish hardware.

HARDWARE DESIGN. Space is provided under this heading for any special requirements of the architect. For example, he might specify "Wrought for service areas," when a more ornate, cast metal is being used in the main areas.

In addition to the hardware specified by set numbers on page 3, the following items are to be furnished by the hardware supplier:

3 Grand Master Keys—6 Master Keys each for 5 Master Key Systems.

4 Door Silencers, Type 21.64, for each pr Drs and 3 for each Sgle Dr in Metal Frame.

4 Door Silencers, Type 21.65 for each pr Drs and 3 for each Sgle Dr in Wood Frame.

1 Key Control Cabinet, Type 23.8 —1,200-key capacity, complete with Envelopes, Key Tags, Key Receipts, and Card Index.

It is the obligation of the hardware supplier to supervise the installation of the Key Control System, and when this is completed, the supplier shall carefully instruct, as to policing, distribution, and filing, the person designated by the school board to be responsible for operation of the system.

All interior doors are to have Door Silencers, Type 21.64 or 21.65, as required. (See Chapter 21, page 4.)

HARDWARE SETS FOR DOORS
(Page 4)

Hdwe Set 1—Each set to have
3 Pr Hinges, 2/7.50-4/7.1, 5"
2 Exit Devices, 14.7.4
2 Exit Devices, 14.8.4
1 Threshold, 9.40
2 Closers, 15.12
1 Stop, 21.42, stagger under rail
1 Stop, 21.44

Hdwe Set 2—Each set to have
3 Pr Hinges, 7.1-4½"
2 Closers, 15.5
2 Door Pulls, 16.31-3½" x 16"
2 Push Plates, 16.34-3½" x 16"
2 Door Holders, 21.22
2 Kick Plates, 16.13-10" height
1 Threshold, 16.49

Hdwe Set 3—Each set to have
3 Pr Hinges, 7.8-4½"
2 Flush Bolts, 21.8 & 21.13
1 Set Locks 10.20.1, w. Screwless Knobs, -07
2 Door Stops & Holders, 21.38

Hdwe Set 4—Each set to have
1½ Pr Hinges, 7.8-4½"
1 Closer, 15.3
1 Set Locks, 10.18.1, w. Screwless Knobs, -07
1 Door Stop, 21.61 (sec'y office)
1 Door Stop, 21.49 (custodian)

Hdwe Set 5—Each set to have
1½ Pr Hinges, 7.8-4½"
1 Closer, 15.3
1 Set Locks, 10.18.1 w. Screwless Knobs, -07
1 Door Stop, 21.54

Hdwe Set 6—Each set to have
1½ Pr Hinges, 7.10-3½"
1 Set Latches, 10.25.2 w. Screwless Knobs, -07
1 Door Stop, 21.40
4 C & H Hooks, 22.6
1 Closet Rod, 22.5

Hdwe Set 7—Each set to have
1½ Pr Hinges, 7.10-3½"
1 Set Privacy Locks, 10.27.2 w. Screwless Knobs, -07
1 Door Stop, 21.60
1 Robe Hook, 22.7

Hdwe Set 8—Each set to have
2 Floor Hinges, 9.15
2 Exit Devices for Dble Egress, 14.18
1 Smoke Detector, 22.10
2 Electromagnetic Holders, 22.11
2 Kick Plates, 16.13, 10" height

Hdwe Set 9—Each set to have
1½ Pr Hinges, 7.8-4½"
1 Closer, 15.7-Holder Arm, -3
1 Set Classroom Locks, 10.19.1 w. Screwless Knobs, -07
1 Door Stop, 21.50
1 Kick Plate 16.13, 10" height

Hdwe set 10—Each set to have
1½ Pr Hinges, 7.8, 4½"
1 Closer, 15.7
1 Cyl Deadlock, 13.10
1 Door Stop, 21.54
1 Kick Plate, 16.13, 10" height
1 Door Pull, 16.31, 3½" x 16"
1 Push Plate, 16.34, 3½" x 16"

Hdwe Set 11—Each set to have
1½ Pr Hinges, 7.12-4½"
1 Set Cyl Locks, 10.21.1 w. Screwless Knobs, -07
1 Stop, 21.49

Hdwe Set 12—Each set to have Same Hardware as Set 10 but omitting Cyl Deadlock

Hdwe Set 13—Each set to have
1½ Pr Hinges, 7.50 x 2/7.1, 5"
1 Exit Device, 14.1.1
1 Closer, 15.1
1 Corner Brkt, Option -12
1 Overhead Door Stop, 21.38
1 Threshold, 16.45

NOTE
This sheet calls for Mortise Locks. Should specifier want to use Unit, Integral or Bored Locks, refer to chapter where such sets are described and change lock numbers by same functions available in Chapters 11 and 12

School Floor Plan (Partial) and Door Types, System D

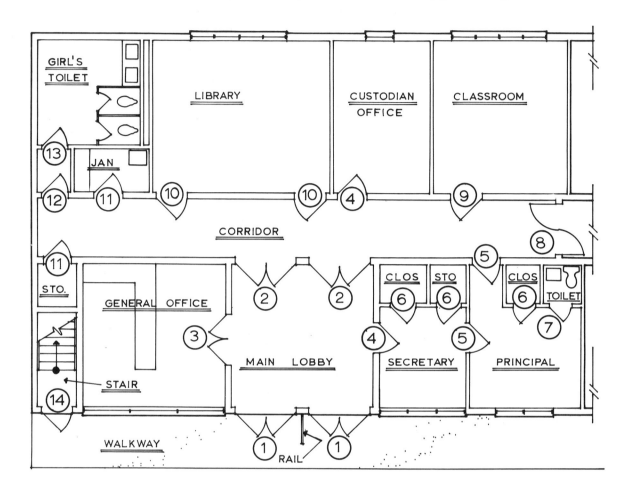

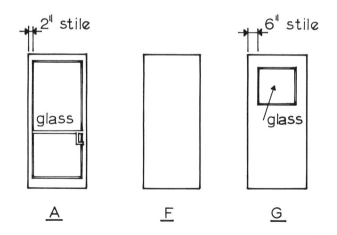

$\underline{A}$	$\underline{F}$	$\underline{G}$

Frame and Threshold Details, System D

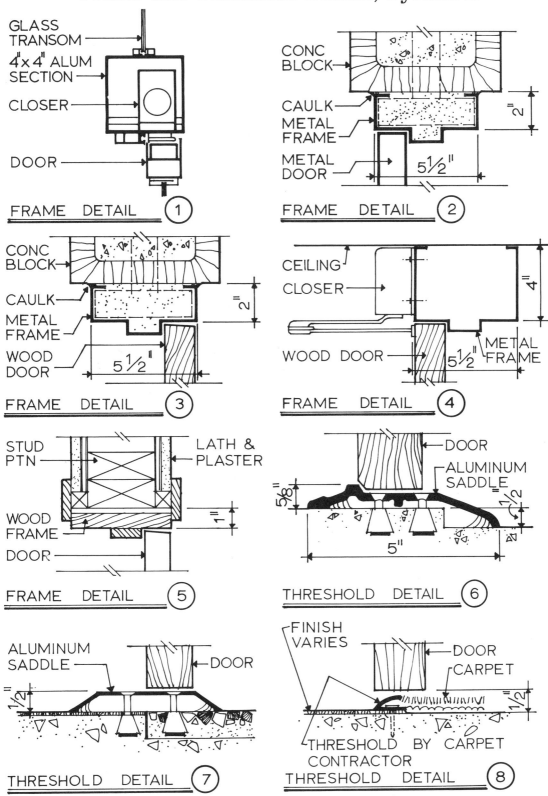

GLASS TRANSOM
4"x 4" ALUM SECTION
CLOSER
DOOR

FRAME DETAIL ①

CONC BLOCK
CAULK
METAL FRAME
METAL DOOR
2"
5½"

FRAME DETAIL ②

CONC BLOCK
CAULK
METAL FRAME
WOOD DOOR
2"
5½"

FRAME DETAIL ③

CEILING
CLOSER
WOOD DOOR
METAL FRAME
4"
5½"

FRAME DETAIL ④

STUD PTN
LATH & PLASTER
WOOD FRAME
DOOR
1"

FRAME DETAIL ⑤

DOOR
ALUMINUM SADDLE
5/8"
1/2"
5"

THRESHOLD DETAIL ⑥

ALUMINUM SADDLE
DOOR
1/2"

THRESHOLD DETAIL ⑦

FINISH VARIES
DOOR
CARPET
1/2"
THRESHOLD BY CARPET CONTRACTOR

THRESHOLD DETAIL ⑧

27

CHAPTER 5

Specifications System E

System E—Type Number, Short Form

Specifications System E has proved, after much use and comparison with Systems A through D, to be more complete and economical in time and money. Further, it answers the architect's need for a system that is competitive, reasonably restrictive, short, and protective of his interest in completing his assignment as he intended.

Here are seven specific advantages of System E.

1. It establishes what the responsibility of the hardware supplier will be at each section layout rather than in the general preamble.

2. The architect's inspector can see quickly whether all hardware called for has been furnished or not.

3. The product is identified by type number at the start. Then the type number is used throughout to refer to the product. This requires less typing, shortens the specification, and offers less chance of error.

4. Most architects prefer to identify type numbers in a table, as on page 4 of this chapter, especially for large projects. But for those who prefer other methods of preparing specifications, System E is adaptable.

5. If it should be necessary to modify specifications after they have been prepared, this can be done conveniently with System E. For example, if it should become necessary to cut costs, say by eliminating Door Closers or by assigning a lower grade to Hinges and Locks, the number of the eliminated item is simply deleted and that of the changed item is changed to the type number of a lower grade. In this example, all this could be done on page 4 of this chapter, the Door Hardware Form. Using System D, on the other hand, either new set numbers and new pages would have to be supplied or addenda would have to be issued.

6. Any hardware supplier who uses System E and is familiar with it can quote prices more quickly and accurately. This advantage often extends to the architect.

7. With the increasing use of computers in the hardware business, especially for the larger projects, the type numbers of System E make it possible to compute the hardware requirements.

General Procedure, System E

The general procedure for specifying hardware under System E is exemplified here in reference to the office plan on page 5 of this chapter, and to the door types and details on page 6.

GENERAL CONDITIONS. See Chapter 2, page 6, Step 5, and provide here the appropriate information.

HARDWARE NOT INCLUDED. See Chapter 2, page 6, Step 5, and provide here the appropriate information.

HARDWARE—General Clauses. See Chapter 2, pages 5 through 8, and provide here the appropriate information.

DESIGN. See Chapter 2, page 6, Step 2(a).

LOCKS

All Locks occurring in service areas to be . . . (Design is specified.)

All Locks throughout building other than service areas to be . . . (Design is specified.)

FINISH

All Steel Hinges with prime coat for painting.

All other hardware in service areas: Fin #600.

All Surface Closers spray painted to harmonize with Locks.

All hardware throughout balance of building: Fin #613, including all Bronze Metal Hinges where called for.

Numbering System

This example applies to all hardware type numbers for all hardware items.

In the first column on page 4 appears the door number keyed to the door plan on page 5.

These first-column numbers are followed first by the chapter number of this handbook in which the particular item of hardware appears. Then follows the number assigned the item within that chapter, but they do not appear on Door Schedule.

BUTTS AND HINGES

Hinge height as listed. Furnish proper width to suit details, using the narrowest standard width; e.g., if a 4½″ x 4″ will clear door and keep Hinge Knuckles closer to door, so schedule. The first number before slash indicates quantity of hinges per opening; after slash is the type required, e.g., 3/1, 6/5.

Type #1	7.1	5″
#2	7.5	4″
#3	7.9	4½″
#4	7.12	4″
#5	7.12	4½″
#6	17.1	Lavatory
#7	8.29	Gate Pivot

EXIT DEVICES AND THRESHOLDS

Type #10 Bolt 14.6 x G.M.K. Cylinder to Keying System

#12 Bolt 14.1. No Hardware Outside

#13 Threshold 16.43—Full Width Opening

#14 Threshold 16.44—Full Width Opening

General Procedure, System E (Continued)

Office Plan, Page 5
Door Types and Details
(Page 6)

DOOR CLOSING DEVICES

It is the responsibility of the hardware supplier to furnish the proper size recommended by the manufacturer for each condition.

Type #20　15.12
　　#21　15.5
　　#22　15.2
　　#23　15.3
　　#24　15.3　with Holder Arm, -3
　　#25　15.1　for doors opening in, 15.2
　　　　　　　for doors opening out

LOCKS

All Locks to have beveled fronts and Wrt Box Strikes. Lip of Strikes shall be of proper length to protect door trim but no longer than ⅛″ beyond and curved where necessary.

Type #30　11.38　(if Integral, 11.63)
　　#31　10.5.1　Architect's selection of Handle design
　　#32　11.36　(if Integral, 11.60)
　　#33　11.37　(if Integral, 11.65)
　　#34　11.46　(if Integral, 11.72)
　　#35　11.49　(if Integral, 11.75)

KEYING

All Locks and Cylinders shall be Master and Grand Master Keyed as later directed by owner and/or architect.

Locks Type #31 shall be operated by all Tenant Keys; Doors #5 and #6 keyed alike in their respective tenant spaces but not to each other; Doors #7 shall operate Doors #6 in their respective offices but not to each other.

ARMOR, KICK, AND MOP PLATES

Armor, Kick, and Mop Plates, where called for, shall be beveled three sides—16 gauge metal.
Full width of door less 2″ for stops and beveling.

Type #40　Height　4″　16.20
　　#41　Height　8″　16.13
　　#42　Height 10″　16.13
　　#43　Height 48″　16.6

DOOR STOPS AND DOOR HOLDERS

It is the responsibility of the hardware supplier to furnish these items of type and quality specified, but details must be checked and items furnished to meet conditions when necessary.

Type #50　21.43
　　#51　21.48
　　#52　21.49
　　#53　21.58

All interior doors are to have Door Silencers 21.64 or 21.65 as required. (See Chapter 21, page 4.)

General Procedure, System E (Continued)

AUXILIARY ITEMS (Miscellaneous)

Type #60 Mailbox Plate 22.24
#61 Secret Gate Latch
#62 Lava Bolt and Strike 17.68 x 17.52
#63 Lava Hook 17.76
#64 Lava Pull 17.74
#65 Exit Alarm 13.23 (Inoperative during day)
#66 Exit Alarm 13.23 (Always operative)

DOOR TYPES AND DETAILS
(For Chapter 5, Pages 5 and 6)

CAUTION: Door Numbers need to be changed only where hardware or other conditions do.

Door Number	Door Size	Door Type	Frame Type	Remarks	Hardware Type Numbers
1	3'6" x 7'6" x 1¾"	A	1	Heavy Traffic Custom Made Drs & Frames	3/1-10-13-20-42-50
2	3'2" x 7'0" x 1¾"	B	2	B Label with Alarm System	3/1-10-13-21-43-50-65
3	3'2" x 7'0" x 1¾"	B	2	B Label with Alarm System	3/1-12-13-22-50-66
4	2'6" x 7'0" x 1¾"	C	3		3/2-23-30-41-52
5	3'2" x 7'0" x 1¾"	D	6		3/1-14-23-31-42-52
6	3'0" x 7'0" x 1¾"	E	3		3/3-23-32-42-52-60
7	2'8" x 7'0" x 1¾"	C	3		3/4-33-53
8	3'0" x 7'0" x 1¾"	C	3		3/5-25-30-52
9	2'0" x 5'0" x 1¼"	F	5	Lavatory Dwarf Door	2/6-62-63-64
10	2'6" x 3'0" x 1⅜"	G	4	Gate	7-61
11	3'0" x 7'0" x 1¾"	B	2	B Label	3/3-25-34-52
12	2'6" x 7'0" x 1¾"	C	3	Communicating	3/4-35-52

NOTE: This sheet calls for unit locks with alternative numbers in brackets. Should integral lock specification be desired, functions of both are similar. Should cylindrical locks be wanted, see Chapter 12 and use those symbols. Should mortise locks be wanted, see Chapter 10 and use those symbols. The type of locks used do not reflect a recommendation for any particular type of building; they only demonstrate how to specify all types of locks.

Office Building Floor Plan (Partial), System E

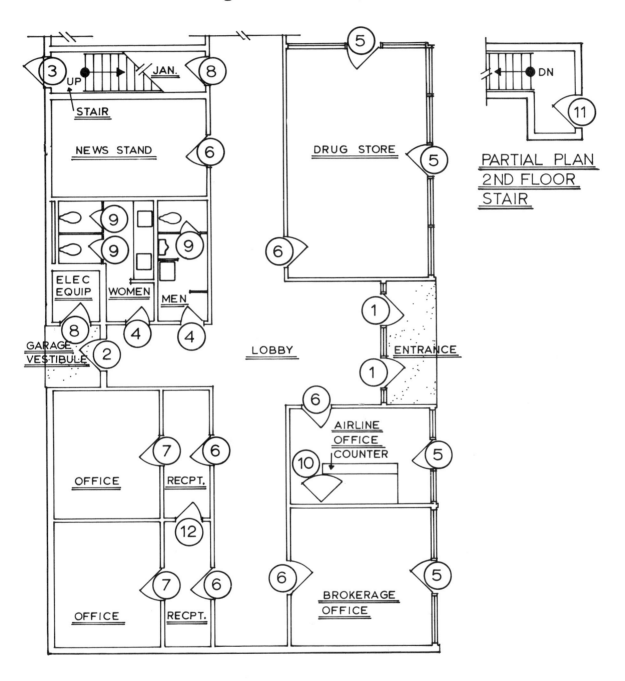

Door Types and Details, System E

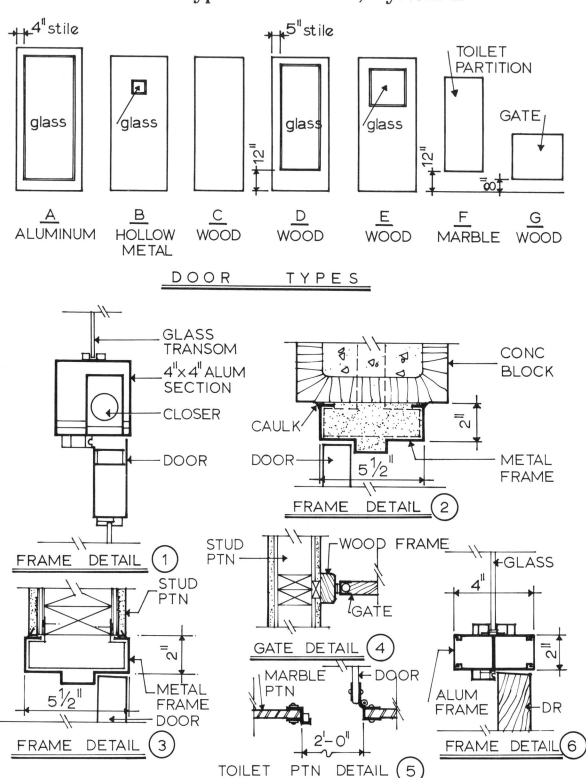

DOOR TYPES

CHAPTER 6

Specifications System F

System F—Type Number, Long Form

With the long form of specification by type number, it is possible to write a complete hardware specification for a large building in full detail without referring to Steps 1 through 5 in Chapter 2.

The example used to demonstrate System F considers the typical floor plan (partial), doors, and details shown on pages 10 and 11 of this chapter. They describe a hotel with 1,000 guest rooms, basement, lobby, ballroom floors, and restaurants.

As with Systems C through E, there is no attempt to show how plans should be drawn, but only to exemplify hardware specification. All the plans are typical of what might be found in a building of their respective types.

Although the floor plans used to illustrate the systems are partial, the specifications for these parts are intended to be as complete as possible, as shown on the Door Schedule Sheets.

FINISH HARDWARE

1. THIS SECTION covers the furnishing of all Finish Hardware, including delivery to Contractor at building, and/or as required otherwise, to fabricators requiring application of builders hardware to their work, complete in every respect, including all related items and appurtenances in strict accord with requirements of applicable drawings of this specification and with the terms and conditions of the Contract Documents.

2. WORK NOT INCLUDED
   (a) Hardware for the following items and work is specified and required to be furnished as part of the work of other sections of the Specifications where so noted:
   Elevator Shaft Enclosure Doors
   Automatic Fire Doors
   Letter Box and Mail Chute
   Hand Rail Brackets
   Metal Trap Doors
   Laundry and Rubbish Chutes (Night Latch Type Locks only, by Hardware Supplier)
   Sliding Doors, unless hardware is specifically called for on drawings under "Hardware Notes"
   Metal Windows
   Refrigerator Doors
   Metal Roof Scuttles
   Wire Mesh Doors (except cylinders, by Hardware Supplier)
   Metal Access Doors
   Room Numbers
   Folding Partitions (except cylinders, by Hardware Supplier)

(b) Hardware for telephone booths will be furnished and installed by the Telephone Company.

(c) Application of Finish Hardware: All Finish Hardware is to be applied and/or installed under work of respective trades; e.g., Finish Carpentry Trades, Ornamental Metal Work Trades, Hollow Metal Work Trades, etc.

3. HARDWARE (General). Hardware Contractor shall correlate and coordinate the manufacture and delivery of all hardware items with requirements of General Contractor, in such a manner that in no instance shall any portion or items of General Contractor's work be delayed in completion or installation and/or application thereof, as a result of delayed delivery. Included in the above requirements shall be the delivery of all incidental hardware to various subcontractors requiring same to complete their portions of work.

All hardware items are to be neatly packaged in substantial and secure boxes, properly labeled and readily identifiable for individual locations and use. General Contractor shall acknowledge and give complete receipts for all hardware when and as delivered.

Hardware Contractor shall furnish full and complete "Schedules" of all hardware in triplicate and/or as required otherwise, for the use of the General Contractor. The furnishings of the above hardware items shall include all items of securement and fastening, such as screws, bolts, nuts, brackets, and the like. Except where specifically required otherwise, all exposed screws shall be Phillips Head Screws.

General Contractor shall provide one specific room, free of dampness and ventilated, with adequate shelving, for the storing and laying out of all hardware as received. Room shall be provided with adequate security for the proper safekeeping of all hardware so as to preclude delay on account of theft, and some one person of the General Contractor's staff shall be charged with the responsibility and/or accountability for the receipt and disposition, as needed, of all hardware items until all finished hardware has been installed or accounted for.

4. SAMPLES are to be supplied to Architect for approval in strict accord with the applicable requirements of the "General Conditions" of the contract relating to samples.

5. INSTALLATION, INSPECTION, AND ADJUSTMENT. All Finish Hardware specified herein shall be installed by the General Contractor (carpentry, mill, and cabinet work), and/or by various subcontractors whose items of work require Finish Hardware as directed by General Contractor, who will be responsible for the correct application of all hardware. Hardware Contractor shall likewise authorize his representative to be present when all Finish Hardware is delivered to the site and check in each hardware item, turning over same to the Contractor and seeing that same is stored in a secure place.

Prior to final inspection, Hardware Manufacturer shall inspect and adjust all door closers and locks and/or all items requiring close adjustment and/or regulation and check all keying. This shall be done at no additional charge. Cost of same to be included in Hardware Supplier's bid.

Explanation to Architect
  (not part of specification)

In the sample specification of item 6 below, manufacturers are designated merely by letter. In an actual specification, the preferred manufacturers are given in Column A, an acceptable alternative in column B, and a second acceptable alternative in Column C. As many more manufacturer alternatives may be listed as desired, but Federal specifications generally require a total of three manufacturers.

For a specification completely unrestricted in regard to choice of manufacturer, item 6 is simply omitted.

Conversely, when only those manufacturers are wanted which experience has proved as being acceptable, item 6 expressly provides for this while allowing for competition.

   6. HARDWARE TYPE, KIND, AND QUALITY
     MATERIALS: The catalog numbers referred to hereinafter indicate characteristics, function, general description, and approximate size and suitability of all items, together with a list of the manufacturers under the various hardware categories acceptable. The manufacturer listed first under each category is the one whose numbers have been used. Then follow the names of other manufacturers in each category whose products may be used provided the quality, function, type, size and suitability are equal to that specified. The architect shall be the sole judge as to kind, quality, function, and equivalency.

Product	Types	Mfr.		
Hinges	#1 thru #19	A	B	C
Closing Devices	#20 thru #29	A	B	C
Locks	#30 thru #49	A	B	C
Exit Devices	#50 thru #59	A	B	C
Pull & Push Plates	#60 thru #69	A	B	C
Armor, Kick, Mop Plates	#70 thru #79	A	B	C
Auxiliary Hdwe Items	#80 thru #89	A	B	C
Miscellaneous Items	#90 to as far as needed	A	B	C

Notes: Keys and Keying are covered as to requirements immediately preceding the Lock specifications and shall be of one manufacturer.

All Lock Cylinders shall have Key change number stamped thereon, and the Key Code Chart shall be given the owner prior to opening of the building.

Special Conditions

Certain circumstances may make it advisable to provide for special conditions in specifications. One such circumstance might be specifying for a ballroom, when it is possible that the design for it will be submitted late or be changed.

For such conditions, it is recommended that hardware type numbers be used starting with #200 and that an allowance price be set for all such hardware. Special wording may be necessary in order to take precautions, such as those provided for in System A (Chapter 3).

7. FINISH OF HARDWARE. Hinges in non-ferrous metal shall be finished to match finish of Locks in respective openings. Ferrous Hinges shall be prime coated; Closers spray-painted to harmonize with balance of hardware on door. All other hardware in kitchens, food preparation rooms, Stainless Steel Fin. 630. All other hardware for ornamental doors shall be Alum. Fin. 628. Armor or Kick Plates calling for steel plates shall be Black, Fin. 622. All other hardware in public areas shall be Bronze, Fin. 616. All other hardware in service areas shall be Dull Brass, Fin. 606.

Manufacturer of the Locks shall provide samples of finish for other trades as may be requested by the Architect or Contractor.

8. DESIGN. (Architect to decide design and describe it here. Letters in the following examples are codes for specified designs.)

    Lobbies, ballrooms, meeting rooms, restaurants, use Design A-B-C.

    Guestroom entrance doors, Cast Bronze both sides, Design D-E-F.

    Interior doors of guest rooms, Wrought Bronze both sides, Design G-H-I.

    Service areas throughout, Cast Bronze both sides, Design J-K-L.

Caution to Hardware Specifier (not part of specification)

When you elect to use Mortise Lock, Chapter 10, add to design description: "Knobs shall be screwless, Option -7, in service areas. All Turn Pieces Cast Bronze. Should Lever Handles be required, use Options -25 or -26."

9. TEMPLATES. The Hardware Supplier is responsible for furnishing promptly a Template Schedule to Metal Door Manufacturer to guide him in his preparation of shop drawings. On receipt of approved shop drawings, the Supplier shall then correct his temporary template schedule and then immediately provide all necessary templates. He should never place orders with his manufacturers until the revised template schedule is approved. It is the Hardware Supplier's responsibility in placing his orders to clearly specify what templates have been used.

10. BUTTS AND HINGES. In all cases, these shall be wide enough to give proper clearance. Quantities of hinges per opening are indicated as shown on Door Schedule; e.g., 3/5 indicates three hinges per opening, 6/5 indicates 6. Proper screws for wood or metal doors and frames is the Hardware Supplier's full responsibility.

Note

Very few projects require the large number of type numbers called for in the specifications of a large hotel such as this. To conserve space here, as with System E, only the indicated type numbers under each category will be furnished.

Similarly, in writing an actual specification, unneeded type numbers should be eliminated. Even if they are not eliminated, if they are not called for on the Door Hardware Schedule, they will not be furnished.

Butt and Hinge Type Numbers
Described From Chapter Numbers

#1 Hinge,	Type 7.1,	5″
#2 Hinge,	Type 7.2,	4½″
#3 Hinge,	Type 7.4,	5″
#4 Hinge,	Type 7.4,	4½″
#5 Hinge,	Type 7.9,	5″
#6 Hinge,	Type 7.9,	4½″
#7 Hinge,	Type 7.9,	4″
#8 Hinge,	Type 7.12,	5″
#9 Hinge,	Type 7.12,	4½″
#10 Hinge,	Type 7.12,	4″
#11 Hinge,	Type 7.12,	3½″
#12 Hinge,	Type 7.5,	4½″

Note

If options are desired, see Chapter 7, page 1. For example, -1 is the option number for Modern Streamlined Hinges. For #8 Hinge, the type number would be 7.12-1.

11. DOOR CLOSING DEVICES. All shall be of size recommended by Manufacturer for the various size doors shown and conditions under which devices must function.

Brackets shall be included where needed. All Closers shall have Key Valves. Floor Closers shall be center or offset, as desired by Architects.

#20 Closer, Type 15.1
#21 Closer, Type 15.2
#22 Closer, Type 15.3
#23 Closer, Type 15.5
#24 Closer, Type 15.10
#25 Floor Hinge, Type 9.1
#26 Floor Hinge, Type 9.14
#27 Floor Hinge, Type 9.16
#28 Floor Hinge, Type 9.19

12. LOCKS AND LATCHES. Keying: All Cylinder Locks shall be Grand Master Keyed, Master Keyed, Keyed Different, or where desired, Keyed Alike in sets.

Before Locks are ordered from the Manufacturer, Hardware Supplier shall prepare keying chart layout in consultation with the hotel management, then submit chart to the Architect, etc. for final approval.

In general, the keying layout will follow the example of a good keying practice in a modern hotel (as shown on page 6 of this chapter).

All Lock Cylinders shall have change number stamped thereon in a concealed location. All guest room keys to be stamped with room number on large bow keys, as shall all Master, Grand Master, Display, and Emergency Keys. Furnish 3 Emergency, 12 Grand Master, and 6 Master Keys for each different Master Key System; also 10 Guest Room Keys for each guest room and 3 Display Keys for a total of 10 display rooms.

All Cylinders are to have construction keying. Furnish 25 Construction Keys and three Knockout Keys to destroy usefulness of Construction Keys when building is completed.

Example of Good Keying Practice in a Modern Hotel

(Laid out, for illustration, as a 1,000-room hotel with 100 rooms on each of 10 floors.)

Key No. 1—Emergency Key

Made to operate all of the 1000 guestroom locks. This key will open any guestroom lock even though the door is locked from the inside. This key will also act as a lock-out key, making all keys (G.G.M.K., G.M.K., M.K., and G.K.) inoperative.

NOTE: It is strongly recommended that a rigid control be maintained by top management offices or by a duly authorized person or persons for use of this key.

Key No. 2—Display Key

Made to operate only one room, such as display, sample, or permanent guestroom door. It operates exactly the same as the emergency key, except that it passes but one room instead of 1000.

Key No. 3—Privacy Key

One or more keys that operate desired locks that must not be passed by any key other than its own. Example: liquor storage, bar, etc. They should be set so that no other keys (even G.G.M.K., G.M.K., and M.K.) will operate such locks.

Most manufacturers make keyways that can be used in such cases so that key blanks to cut a sample are not available for general locksmith distribution and are sold only to the owners on duly authorized orders.

Key No. 4—Great Grand Master Key

A key that will operate all locks throughout the entire hotel with the following exceptions:

A. It will not operate locks set to privacy key No. 3.
B. It will not operate guestroom doors when doors are:
    1. Locked by guest from inside.
    2. Locked by emergency key No. 1 or display key No. 2.
C. It will not operate the inside cylinder of a guestroom lock.

Such a key is necessary only when there are two or more grand master key systems involved.

NOTE: Wherever possible, avoid the use of a Great Grand Master Key. Such an additional series of passkey work definitely limits the mathematically possible individual key changes. It necessitates the use of thinner pins in the cylinders, causing increased wear and decreased protection against picking of the cylinder. Better results will be obtained by the use of two or more Grand Master Keys, even though a few people are inconvenienced by having to carry an extra Grand Master Key.

Key No. 5—Grand Master Key

Its description and use are identical with that of key No. 4 except that, if there are two or more Grand Master Key systems, one Grand Master Key should not operate the locks of another Grand Master Key System. It will operate all of the locks under its own system, within the limitations outlined under key No. 4.

Key No. 6—Guestroom Key

It will operate only the lock to its individual room, and none of the other 999 rooms in the hotel. If the guestroom lock is a two-cylinder type, this key operates both the outside and the inside cylinders. It is recommended that, in the case of the inside cylinder, the key be locked into the cylinder while the door is locked, thus insuring immediate use in case of emergency, such as fire.

Should the hotel be equipped with locks on the guest-room closet door, it is customary to key the closet lock to the same key change as the individual guestroom door.

The Guestroom Key will not operate the guestroom lock outside if the door has been locked from the inside or by the emergency key outside.

Key No. 7—Engineer's Master Key

This key operates all locks under the direct supervision of the engineer, such as engineer's office doors, entire maintenance section, janitor's closets, wire and pipeshaft doors.

NOTE: It is customary to key these latter doors alike on all floors so that the electrician can use one change key but the engineer can also use his master key.

The Grand Master Key, of course, also operates all these locks.

Key No. 8—Steward's Master Key

This key operates all locks under the direct supervision of the steward, such as kitchens, banquet rooms, food storage, dining rooms, steward's offices.

The Grand Master Key, of course, also operates all these doors.

Key No. 9—Housekeeper's Master Key

This key operates all locks under the direct supervision of the housekeeper, such as housekeeper's office door, lockers, linen closets, maids' toilets, and all guestroom doors if not locked inside by key or outside by emergency key or display key.

The Grand Master Key, of course, also operates all these doors.

Key No. 10—Laundry Master Key

This key operates all doors in the laundry section, the linen rooms on each floor, and the laundry chutes. It is customary to key all locks alike on all floors for the linen room and the laundry-chute doors so that the laundry men can use one change key for delivery or dispersal of linen, but the Laundry Master Key also passes all these locks.

Key No. 11—Cleaning Master Key

This key operates all locks in the offices and the public rooms on the main floors that customarily are cleaned by the usual cleaning personnel.

Key No. 12—Maid's Master Key

These keys control a given group of guestrooms as determined by management—this might be 20 rooms or a whole floor. If 20 doors, the Maid's Master Key will operate the 20 locks but none of the other 980 rooms in the hotel with the following exceptions:

A. It will not operate guestroom doors when doors are locked by guest from inside or locked by emergency No. 1 or display key No. 2 outside.
B. It will not operate the inside cylinder of a guestroom lock. *NOTE:* It is desirable to use this feature so that, for several reasons, a maid cannot lock the door with her key from the inside. While she is in the room, therefore, access is possible by Guest Key, Master Key, or Grand Master Key.
C. When guestroom closet doors are equipped with cylinder locks, it is also recommended that the Maid's Key not operate such locks so that guests, when they desire, may lock up their closet doors against the Maid's Master Key.

It is customary to have the Maid's Master Key operate designated doors on her own floor, such as laundry chutes, linen rooms, slop sinks, maids' toilets, etc.

Comparison of Lock Type Numbers

Table comparing type numbers of hotel Locks in Chapters 10, 11, and 12 for each function. Hotel lock types of all manufacturers are represented as best as possible. For mortise locks, chapter 10, the final digit 1 stands for heavy duty, 2 for standard duty, 3 for economy grade. Economy grade availability is shown in the chapters on locks.

Number	Description of Function	Mortise Lock	Preassembled (Unit) Lock	Integral Lock	Cylinder or Tubular Locks
30	Guestroom Foyer Entry Dr	10.23.1	11.55	11.67	12.96.1
31	Guestroom Entry Door	10.23.1 10.23.2	11.55		12.83.1 12.83.2
32	Guestroom Entry From Foyer	10.23.1 10.23.2 Stps in face	11.55 Adapt to suit	11.67 Adapt to suit	12.96.1 Adapt to suit
33	Utility Door	10.21.1 10.21.2	11.45	11.64	12.79.1 12.79.2
34	Office Door	10.18.1 10.18.2	11.36	11.65	12.80.1 12.80.2
35	Store or Utility Door, 2 Cylinders	10.15.1 10.15.2	11.52	11.61	12.78.1
36	Store or Utility Door, 1 Cylinder	10.16.1 10.16.2	11.44	11.69	12.79.1 12.79.2
37	Classroom Door	10.19.1 10.19.2	11.42	11.66	12.82.1 12.82.2
38	Communicating Door	10.28.1 10.28.2	11.49	11.75	12.91.1 12.91.2
38A	Twin Communicating Doors	Special lock, 23.1, 23.2, for Drs. No. 5, page 11			
39	Passage Latch, No Locking	10.25.1 10.25.2	11.46	11.72	12.88.1 12.88.2
40	Bath or Privacy Lock	10.27.1 10.27.2	11.47	11.74	12.89.1 12.89.2
41	Extra Hvy Duty Deadlock. State Backset & Function	13.9.1-1			
42	Std Duty Deadlock. State Backset & Function	13.9.2 13.9.3			
43	Deadlock Narrow Stile Dr. State Desired BS & Functn.	As 13.9.2 but short backset			
44	Sliding Door Lock, 2 Cyl	13.12.1 13.12.2			
45	Mortise Cylinder Only x Special Cam				
46	Rim Cylinder Only, Tailpiece to Suit				
47	Rim Night Latch, Gen. Purpose Use	13.13.1 13.13.2			
48	Rubbish or Linen Chute Dr, Latch Only, No Slide or Knob on Case	As #47 ex. as noted			
49	Padlock, Gen. Purpose. Chain Optional: Add -C to Number	13.16.1 13.16.1-C			

13. EXIT DEVICES. Requirements vary according to State and local codes. Devices requiring cylinders must be furnished to job Grand Master Key Systems. While all numbers listed below will not be used further in this chapter, they are shown here for hardware specifier's use as may be needed. Refer to Chapter 14 for type number desired.

Number	Description and Function
50	Rim Device, no hardware outside
51	Rim Device, Cyl x Pull outside
52	Vert. Device, no hardware outside
53	Vert. Device, Pull outside but no Cyl
54	Mortise Device, Cyl and Thumb Latch Hdle outside
55	Concealed Device, no hardware outside
56	Concealed Device, Pull outside, no Cyl
57	Concealed Device, Cylinder only outside
58	Concealed Device, Cyl and Pull outside
59	Removable Mullion

14. ARCHITECTURAL TRIM PULLS AND PUSH PLATES. Note particularly that Nos. 66 through 69 are all to be 12″ high, beveled on 4 sides, and all except #68 to be 16 gauge. Specify size and material for #64 and #68.

Number	Description
60	Surface Pull, Plain, Type 16.32
61	Surface Pull, Design, Type 16.31
62	Special Design Pull & Push Plates, Type #200
63	Push Plate, Plain, Type 16.33
64	Push Plate, Plastic, Type 16.33
65	Push Plate, Design, Type 16.34
66	Push Plate, Stainless Steel, Type 16.35
67	Push Plate, Bronze, Type 16.35
68	Push Plate, Plastic, Type 16.35
69	Push Plate, Steel, Type 16.35

15. ARMOR, KICK, AND MOP PLATES. Heights can be modified as for Types 16.6 through 16.12, Chapter 16, page 1. When more than one of a type is wanted (as for both sides of a door), the quantity required for each opening is indicated by the number followed by a slash preceding the type number; e.g., 2/74. Specify size and material for Types 16.11, 16.18, 16.25.

Number	Description
70	Armor Plate, 48″ high, Type 16.8
71	Armor Plate, 48″ high, Type 16.6
72	Armor Plate, 48″ high, Type 16.12
73	Armor Plate, 48″ high, Type 16.11
74	Kick Plate, 12″ high, Type 16.15
75	Kick Plate, 12″ high, Type 16.13
76	Kick Plate, 12″ high, Type 16.18
77	Mop Plate, 4″ high, Type 16.22
78	Mop Plate, 4″ high, Type 16.20
79	Mop Plate, 4″ high, Type 16.25

16. DOOR HOLDERS AND DOOR STOPS. Specify exact type required according to description in handbook. For example, #80 refers to Chain Stops with No Cover (Type 21.66) and to Rubber Covered (Type 21.67).

Number	Description
80	Chain Stop, Extra Heavy, w. Spring, Types 21.66 and 21.67
81	Door Stop w. Holder, Types 21.42 and 21.43
82	Overhead Concealed Holder, Types 21.22 through 21.25
83	Overhead Surface Holder, Types 21.26, 21.27, and 21.28
84	Roller Stop, Types 21.60 through 21.63
85	Dome Stop, Types 21.49 and 21.50
86	Wall Stop, Concave, Types 21.56 and 21.57
87	Wall Stop, Convex, Types 21.54 and 21.55
88	Floor Stop, Type 21.24
89	Base Stop, Type 21.51 for 1¾" Dr, Type 21.52 for 1⅜" Dr

17. AUXILIARY AND MISCELLANEOUS HARDWARE ITEMS. Flush Bolt #91 is for inactive door of a pair of doors. For #95 and 96, provide three each Sgle Dr; four each Pr Drs. Place as near center as possible. For #97, #98, and #99, further specification is required; consult manufacturers' catalogues.

Number	Description
90	Dutch Door Bolt, Type 12.11
91	Flush Extension Bolt, Types 21.8 (2/91) and 21.9 (1/91)
92	Automatic Dr Deadener, width of Doorless Stops
93	Robe Hook, Types 22.7 and 22.8

Number	Description
94	C & H Hook, Type 22.6
95	Door Silencer, Type 21.64
96	Door Silencers, Type 21.65
97	Alarm Lock System, Types 13.23 through 13.29
98	Smoke Control Devices, Types 22.10 through 22.14
99	Visible Key Control Cabinet with full installation, Types 23.7, 23.8, 23.9

Note

Any auxiliary items may be added as individual job requires. The numbering system used leaves #100 to #199 open to permit more types as needed.

18. SPECIAL HARDWARE CONDITIONS requiring later decisions, unusual designs, etc. often arise on a large hotel. The best way to handle this in order to be able to secure firm prices at general bid time is to set up a hardware allowance and indicate Type #200 in Door Schedule. This will show those items to be included under the hardware allowance. Follow recommended System A, Chapter 3, page 1.

To explain this more fully, assume that the ballrooms are to have special design hardware. We set an allowance of $2,000, which the hardware supplier must include in his quotation on the job. Then take, say, #62 on the preceding page, or any other items such as #97 or #98 this page, and put them into the allowance.

Interior decorators frequently decide the designs. The hardware supplier may not get all or even part of Type #200 items, but he has to pay up to $2,000 or credit the contractor to purchase the items separately.

Typical Hotel Floor, Partial Plan

From this partial plan of a typical hotel floor it is possible to visualize what a complete layout for a door schedule would be. The next three pages describe the seven types of doors on the plan below, other typical hotel doors, and details of frame thresholds, and hardware.

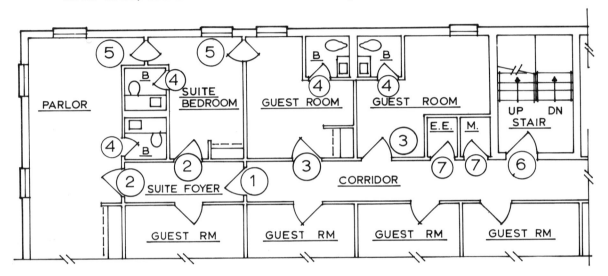

Door Types

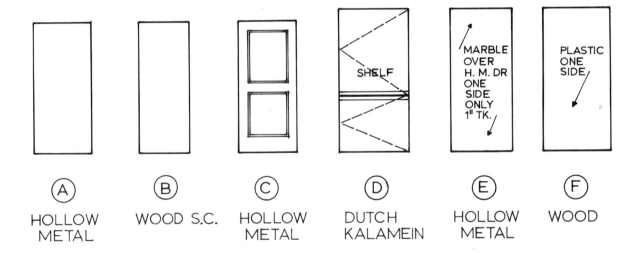

DOOR TYPES AND DETAILS
(For Chapter 6, Page 10)

Recommended type numbers given, but higher or lower grades can be specified

Door Number	Door Type	Door Size	Material	Thresh-old	Frame Number	Remarks	Hardware Type Numbers, Pages 5–8
1	A	2′10″ x 6′8″ x 1¾″	H.M.	1	2	Corridor to Suite Foyer	3/4-30-41, one cylinder 2¾″ BS, which locks into floor to hold Dr open -85
2	B	2′10″ x 6′8″ x 1¾″	Wood	—	2	Foyer to Bedroom	3/4-32-85
3	B	2′10″ x 6′8″ x 1¾″	Wood	1	2	Corridor to Guest-room	3/4-30-85
4	B	2′10″ x 6′8″ x 1⅜″	Wood	2	1	Private Bath in Guest room	3/11-40-89-93
5	B	2 Doors 2′0″ x 6′8″ x 1⅜″	Wood	4	3	Twin Communi-cating Doors	6/11-1/23.1-2/89-2/92
6	A	3′0″ x 6′8″ x 1¾″	H.M.	3	4	Corridor to Stairs, "B" Label	3/6-20-39 Hvy Duty 75-85
7	A	2′8″ x 6′8″ x 1¾″	H.M.	—	4	Electric & Meter Closets	3/9-33 Hvy Duty -85

DOOR FRAME DETAILS

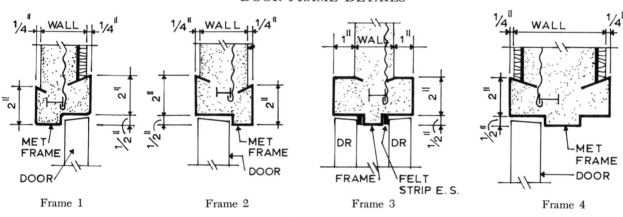

Frame 1   Frame 2   Frame 3   Frame 4

THRESHOLD DETAILS

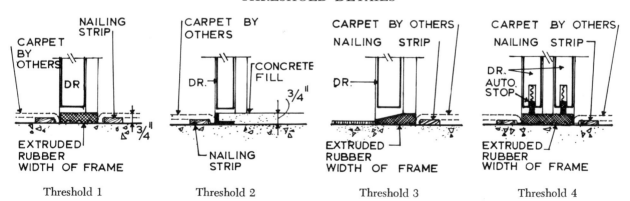

Threshold 1   Threshold 2   Threshold 3   Threshold 4

Additional Hotel Doors

Listed below are additional hotel doors found in many hotels. For an actual specification, they would be keyed to a floor plan as on page 10, and other data would be listed as on page 11.

Door Number	Door Function	Hardware Types
8	Office Entrance Door	3/7-22-34.1-75-86-95
9	Inner Office Door	3/10-34.1-86-95
10	Utility Room Door	3/10-33.1-85-95
11	Corridor Door to Shops	3/6-22-1-35.1-95, Option -97
12	Corridor Door to Public Toilets	3/12-22-42 (2 Cyl, 2¾″ BS) -61-65-75-85-95
13	Toilet Vestibule Door to Toilet	3/12-22-61-65-75-85-95
14	Exterior Stairs Door	3/1-21-50-75-80-97
15	Corridor Smoke Detector Doors (Pair)	6/6-2/22-2/61-2/65-2/75-2/98-96
16	Basement Service Corridor Doors (Pair)	2/6-2/21-6/60-2/63-2/72-2/85-96
17	Service Door, e.g., to Paint Shop	3/3-20, Option -1-36.1-72-85-95
18	Janitor's Closet Door	3/10-33.1-85-95
19	Linen or Rubbish Chute Door	Locks only, -48
20	Other Doors—Alum, Sliding, Partitions	-45-46, or as required
21	Refrigerator Door or other doors requiring Padlock	-49C
22	Metal Exit Doors (Pair)	2/26-56-58-2/75-2/82
23	Service Entrance Doors, Exterior (Pair)	3/1-21-35-75-83-97
24	Door to Roof	3/1-21-35-80

Note

This is only a partial list of typical hotel doors. Seven special types are described on the next page in more detail.

The suggested hardware trim is all listed for Grade 1 Locks.

For economy jobs, the type number is easily changed to Grade 2, as from 10.34.1 to 10.34.2. Some locks are available in Grade 3, but they are definitely not recommended.

Special Door Types

Door 25: Dutch Door (Door Type D, page 10). Often used for Check room, Laundry, and Valet Drs. Hardware recommended: 4/7.12-4½″, 10.36.1, 21.11, 21.27, 21.50.

Door 26: Two In & Out Serving Drs, Kit. to Restaurant. Hdwe recommended: 6/3.4, 2/13.9.1, 6/21.64, 3/16.35 (12″ x 36″), 3/16.18 (12″ x 36″).

NOTE: Kick and Push Plates on entrance side only of respective doors.

Door 27: This is an enlarged view of Door 5, Twin Communicating, to emphasize need for a minimum of ⅞″ space between the two doors, thus more fully explaining the Hdwe called for Drs 5 on Page 11.

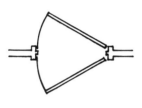

Door 28: Door from stairs to lobby. One-way door, exit from stairs. Lobby side of door marble-covered like walls. See detail below.

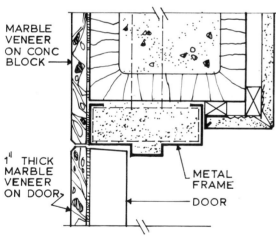

MARBLE VENEER ON CONC BLOCK

1″ THICK MARBLE VENEER ON DOOR

METAL FRAME

DOOR

Hardware for Door 28

Floor Hinge 9.14 in Threshold 9.27 and Intermediate Pivot 9.50

Exit Device 14.1 (no Hdwe on Lobby side)

Door Stop 21.38 (no hold-open feature).

Exit Alarm 13.23, since this door is to be used only in an emergency.

Door 29: Pr of Drs between Ballroom and Lobby. Fire law requires H.M. Dr. Architect requires wood on ballroom side and plastic veneer on lobby side to match decor.

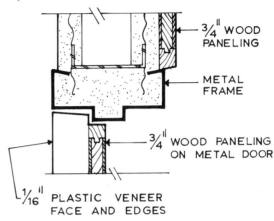

¾″ WOOD PANELING

METAL FRAME

¾″ WOOD PANELING ON METAL DOOR

1/16″ PLASTIC VENEER FACE AND EDGES

Hardware for Door 29

Floor Hinge 9.14, 2 Sets, in Threshold 9.27 and Intermediate Pivots 9.48.

Pr Automatic Bolts. Doors rabbeted.

Lock 10.31, 1 Set, rabbeted front.

Knobs & Roses, 1 set, Special Design.

Cyl Collar Type 200.

Dummy Trim, 1 Set, to match Type 200.

2 Dr Holders, Type 21.22

Specially made Spindle for Knobs (see position of lock in center of metal door).

Concealed Exit Devices required in most areas.

CHAPTER 7

Standard Hinges

The importance of selecting the correct hinge type and then having the door hung correctly cannot be overemphasized. When a door is hung correctly, difficulties that arise with Locks, Exit Devices, and other operative trim, as well as damage to doors and frames, are largely eliminated.

Specification Notes

1. The number preceding the slash mark indicates the number of Hinges required; e.g., 3/7.1 for 3 Hinges (Single Dr), 6/7.1 for 6 Hinges (Pr of Drs), 10/7.1 for 10 Hinges.

2. When pertinent, specify type of bearing: ball, Oilite, nylon.

3. Specify Hinge width when it is not standard; e.g., 5″ x 4½″, 5″ x 6″.

4. Width of Hinge should be minimum. The closer the pin to the frame, the less the strain on the screws.

Hinge Nomenclature

Full Mortise Hinge One Hinge leaf mortised into Dr; other mortised into Frame.

Half Mortise Hinge One leaf mortised into Dr, narrower leaf surface-applied to jamb.

Full Surface Hinge Both leaves applied to surfaces.

Half Surface Hinge One leaf mortised into Jamb; other leaf surface-applied to Dr.

Anchor Hinge The top hinge of a set having one or two anchor straps that fasten to top of door and/or to head of door frame for reinforcement.

NOTE: When Door is to be equipped with Door Closer, always specify Hinges with anti-friction bearings, such as oil-impregnated or ball bearings.

Grades

1. Heavy Duty, High Frequency.
2. Standard Duty, Average Frequency.
3. Light Duty, Low Frequency.

Non-ferrous Hinges recommended for all exteriors, kitchen areas, toilets, baths, etc.

Exceptions: When U.L. requires Steel Hinges for such areas, specify a rust-resistant surface over steel.

Index of Hinge Types

Designs

Conventional: Square Edges
Optional: Rounded Corners
Modern: Streamline or Slim Line

NOTE: Consult manufacturers' catalogues to specify exact design required.

Options

Add option number to type number according to key below; e.g., 7.1-2-8 for a Type 7.1 with Rounded Corners and Special Fastenings. If other or more specific options are desired, add catalogue number of article of preferred manufacturer.

Option Key

-1 Modern Streamlined	-6 Slide-In Hinge for
-2 Rounded Corners	aluminum
-3 Hospital Tips	-7 Special Swaging
-4 Ornamental Tips	-8 Special Fastenings
-5 Non-removable Pin or Stud feature	

Important Factors in Selecting a Hinge

1. Material. See Appendix 4.

2. Finish. See Appendix 5.

3. Size and Grade. These factors together may be considered the most important ones. Installation of the wrong size or grade hinge can lead to major difficulty. The three tables below provide basic information in selection of hinge size and grade.

TABLE 1: *Minimum Hinge Height*

(From "Basic Builders' Hardware," published by the American Society of Architectural Hardware Consultants and the National Builders Hardware Association and used by permission).

Door Thickness (in.)	Door Width (in.)	Minimum Hinge Height (in.)
⅞ or 1	Any	2½
1⅛	To 36"	3
1⅜	To 36"	3½
1⅜	Over 36"	4
1¾	To 41"	4½
1¾	Over 41"	4½ Heavy
1¾ to 2¼	Any	5 Heavy*

* Heavy-duty 5"-high Hinge for heavy Doors with high-frequency use or unusual stress.

Proper Hinge width is important when trim clearance is required. Heavy doors and those that get high-frequency use (see Table 3) should be equipped with heavy grade hinges. For all exterior doors opening out and interior doors with reverse bevel and locks, specify a pin which cannot be removed when door is closed or an interlocking leaf feature.

Author's Note: Without wishing to disagree with the authorities noted above, the writer believes that doors over 36" wide and 1¾" thick of high frequency use should have heavy hinges with four bearings.

4. Type of Bearing—oil-impregnated, ball, or nylon; also, whether visible or concealed.

5. Type of Tip—button, ball, flat, ornamental, hospital—and type of design.

6. Type of Pin—loose, fast, non-rising. Specify N.R.P. (Option -5) as a security measure for exterior doors.

General Information: When two hinge dimensions are given, the first is the height, not including tips, and the second is the width with leaves fully open.

Table 2 gives clearances for regular stock size hinges. The clearances are for hinges set back ¼" for doors from 1⅜" through 2¼" thick and ¾" for doors 2½" through 3" thick.

TABLE 2: *Maximum Hinge Clearance*

Door Thickness (in.)	Hinge Dimensions (in.)	Maximum Clearance (in.)
1⅜	3 x 3	¾
	3½ x 3½	1¼
	4 x 4	1¾
1¾	4 x 4	1
	4½ x 4½	1½
	5 x 5	2
	6 x 6	3
2	4½ x 4½	1
	5 x 5	1½
	6 x 6	2
2¼	5 x 5	1
	6 x 6	2
2½	5 x 5	¾
	6 x 6	1¾
3	6 x 6	¾
	6 x 8	2¾
	8 x 8	2¾
	8 x 10	4¾

TABLE 3: *Type of Door and Frequency of Use**

Building and Door Type	Daily	Yearly	
Large department store entrance	5,000	1,500,000	High frequency
Large office building entrance	4,000	1,200,000	
Theater entrance	1,000	450,000	
Schoolhouse entrance	1,250	225,000	
Schoolhouse toilet door	1,250	225,000	
Store or bank entrance	500	150,000	
Office-building toilet door	400	118,000	
Schoolhouse corridor door	80	15,000	
Office-building corridor door	75	22,000	
Store toilet door	60	18,000	
Dwelling-house entrance	40	15,000	
Dwelling-house toilet door	25	9,000	
Dwelling-house corridor door	10	3,600	
Dwelling-house closet door	6	2,200	

* Number of cycles of door; opening and closing = 1 cycle.

Full Mortise (Butt) Hinges

Type 7.1.

Heavy Duty, Non-Ferrous, 4 Bearings, High Polish, Inner Leaf Beveled. Stainless Steel Pins.

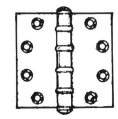

Type 7.2.

Same as 7.1 but Stainless Steel.

Type 7.3.

Same as 7.1 but Extruded Aluminum.

Type 7.4.

Same as 7.1 but Wrt Steel, and Pins Ferrous (Not Stainless Steel).

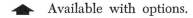 Available with options.

For doors over 3 ft. wide and receiving high frequency use.

Type 7.5.

Standard Duty, Non-ferrous, 2 Bearings, High Polish, Inner Leaf Beveled.

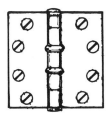

Type 7.6.

Same as 7.5 but Stainless Steel.

Type 7.7.

Same as 7.5 but Extruded Aluminum. Stainless Steel Pins.

Type 7.8.

Same as 7.5 but Wrt Steel, and Pins Ferrous (Not Stainless Steel).

Type 7.9.

Same as 7.8 but Planished and Leaf Not Beveled.

Available with options.

For doors up to 3 ft. wide and receiving medium or high frequency use.

NOTE: Always use bearing hinges when door closers are specified.

Type 7.10.

Standard Duty, Non-ferrous, No Bearings, High Polish, Inner Leaf Beveled.

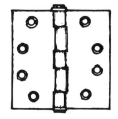

Type 7.11.

Same as 7.10 but Wrt Steel, Machine Polish.

Type 7.12.

Same as 7.10 but Wrt Steel, Planished, and Leaf Not Beveled.

Available with options.

For light frequency use when door closers are not specified.

Type 7.13.

Heavy Wrt Steel, Friction Bearings, High Polish, Leaf Beveled.

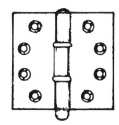

Type 7.14.

Same as 7.13 but Planished, Leaf Not Beveled.

Recommended only where it is necessary for reasons of economy. These hinges act as door stays. Tension can be adjusted as required.

NOTE: When this type hinge is specified, door frame must be securely anchored, and hinge screws must be such that they can carry the strain of the pull created by the friction.

Half Mortise and Half Surface Hinges

Type 7.15.
Half Mortise, Heavy Duty, Nonferrous, 4 Bearings, High Polish, Inner Leaf Beveled. Stainless Steel Pins.

Type 7.16.
Same as 7.15 but Stainless Steel.

Type 7.17.
Same as 7.15 but Wrt Steel. Pins All Ferrous (Not Stainless Steel).

 Available with options.

For doors over 3 ft wide and for high frequency use.

Type 7.18.
Half Mortise, Standard Duty, Nonferrous, 2 Bearings, High Polish, Inner Leaf Beveled.

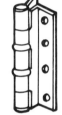

Type 7.19.
Same as 7.18 but all Stainless Steel.

Type 7.20.
Same as 7.18 but Wrt Steel. Pins All Ferrous (Not Stainless Steel).

Type 7.21.
Same as 7.20 but Planished (Not Polished).

 Available with options.

For doors up to 3 ft. wide and for either medium or high frequency use.

Type 7.22.
Half Mortise, Light Duty, Ferrous (All Steel), No Bearings, Planished, Leaf Not Beveled.

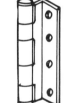

Available with options.
NOTE: Hinges with no bearings

should not be specified for doors that require door closers.

Type 7.23.
Half Surface, Heavy Duty, Nonferrous, 4 Bearings, High Polish. Stainless Steel Pins.

Type 7.24.
Same as 7.23 but All Stainless Steel.

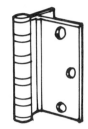

Type 7.25.
Same as 7.23 but All Steel. Ferrous Pins are not Stainless Steel.

Available with options.
For doors over 3 ft. wide and any high frequency use.

Type 7.26.
Half Surface, Standard Duty, Non-ferrous, 2 Bearings, High Polish. Stainless Steel Pins.

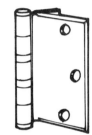

Type 7.27.
Same as 7.26 but All Stainless Steel.

Type 7.28.
Same as 7.26 but All Steel.

Type 7.29.
Same as 7.28 but Planished (Not Polished).

Available with options.
For doors up to 3 ft. wide for either medium or high frequency use.

Type 7.30.
Half Surface, Light Duty, All Steel, No Bearings, Planished, Leaf Not Beveled.

Available with options.

NOTE: Not for use with doors with door closers.

Full Surface, Transom and Continuous Hinges

Type 7.31.
Full Surface, for Kalamein Doors w. Channel Frames, Heavy Duty, Non-ferrous, 4 Bearings, Door Leaf with Through Bolts. Stainless Steel Pins.

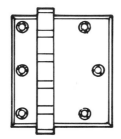

Types 7.32.
Same as 7.31 but All Stainless Steel.

Type 7.33.
Same as 7.31 but All Steel, Planished. Pins Steel (Not Stainless).

Type 7.34.
Same as 7.31 except: for Tubular Steel Doors.

Type 7.35.
Same as 7.32 except: for Tubular Steel Doors.

Type 7.36.
Same as 7.33 except: for Tubular Steel Doors.

Type 7.37.
Full Surface, Standard Duty, Non-ferrous, 2 Bearings, Polished. Stainless Steel Pins. For Kalamein Doors w. Channel Frames. Door Leaf w. Through Bolts.

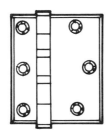

Type 7.38.
Same as 7.37 but All Stainless Steel.

Type 7.39.
Same as 7.37 but All Steel, Planished, and Pins Steel (Not Stainless).

◆ NOTE: For doors over 3 ft wide, use Heavy Duty Hinges, such as Types 7.31 through 7.36.

Type 7.40.
Mortise (Butt), Light Commercial Duty, Wrt (Non-ferrous), No Bearings, Planished. Largely used in speculative bldgs with Ready-Hung Doors. For use on Exterior, Bath, or Kitchen Doors where rusting is a problem.

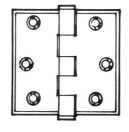

Type 7.41.
Same as 7.40 but Wrt Steel, Square Corners.

Type 7.42.
Same as 7.41 except with rounded corners, as usually demanded for Ready-Hung Doors.

Type 7.43.
Transom Hinge. Full Mortise, Standard Duty Available, Non-ferrous, Planished. Removable Pin.

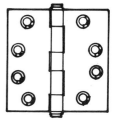

Type 7.44.
Same as 7.43 but Steel.

Type 7.45.
Same as 7.44 but with Tight, Non-Removable Pins.

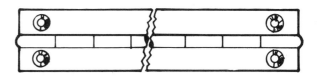

Continuous Hinge. Light, Standard, and Heavy Duty, lengths optional. Available in widths ¾" to 3". Consult manufacturers' catalogues.

Type 7.46.
Continuous Hinge, Stainless Steel. Stainless Steel Pin.

Type 7.47.
Continuous Hinge, Wrt Brass (Non-ferrous). Brass Pin.

Type 7.48.
Continuous Hinge, Wrt Alum (Non-ferrous). Aluminum or Stainless Steel Pin.

Type 7.49.
Continuous Hinge, Wrt Steel (Ferrous). Steel or Brass Pin.

Anchor Hinges

Anchor hinges are highly recommended for doors receiving high-frequency use, such as office building exterior doors and school doors that can expect hard use.

They are available only for use with Hinge Types 7.1 through 7.4. Since they are only used as the top hinge, the specification for one door set would read, for example, 1/7.50 w. 2/7.1.

Type 7.50.
Heavy Duty, Non-ferrous, 4 Bearings, High Polish, Inner Leaf Beveled.

NOTE: Left-hand or right-hand use must be specified.

Type 7.51.
Same as 7.50 but All Stainless Steel.

Type 7.52.
Same as 7.50 but All Steel.

Type 7.53.
Same as 7.50 but shorter Door Plate, where a concealed holder is used.

Type 7.54.
Same as 7.53 but All Stainless Steel.

Type 7.55.
Same as 7.53 but All Steel.

Type 7.56.
Same as 7.50 but No Door Plate for mortising at top of door.

Type 7.57.
Same as 7.56 but All Stainless Steel.

Type 7.58.
Same as 7.56 but All Steel.

Type 7.59.
Inner Leaf Beveled, 4 Bearings, Heavy Duty. Door Plate made for doors with hinge side beveled. Non-ferrous, high polish.

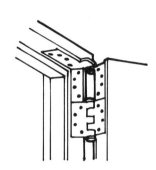

NOTE: Left-hand or right-hand use must be specified.

Type 7.60.
Same as 7.59 but All Stainless Steel.

Type 7.61.
Same as 7.59 but All Steel.

Swing-Clear, Invisible, and Pivot Hinges

Type 7.62.

Swing clear to 95°, Full Mortise, Heavy Duty, Non-ferrous, 4 Bearings, Polished, Inner Leaf Beveled. For doors over 3 ft wide.

Type 7.63.

Same as 7.62 but Ferrous, Planished, and Inner Leaf Not Beveled. Usually used in prime coat for painting.

NOTE: Do not use on doors that must swing more than 95°.

Type 7.64.

Same as 7.62 but Swing Clear and Half Mortise.

Type 7.65.

Same as 7.64 but Steel, Planished, and Inner Leaf Not Beveled. Usually used in prime coat for painting.

Type 7.66.

Same as 7.62 but Swing Clear and Full Surface.

Type 7.67.

Same as 7.66 but Steel, Planished, Inner Leaf Not Beveled. Usually used in prime coat for painting.

Type 7.68.

Same as 7.62 but Swing Clear and Half Surface.

Type 7.69.

Same as 7.68 but Steel, Planished, and Inner Leaf Not Beveled. Usually used in prime coat for painting.

Type 7.70.

Full Surface, Triple Weight, 2 Bearings Concealed. For extra heavy doors up to 2,000 lb. Many Variations. See manufacturers' catalogues.

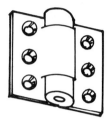

Type 7.71.

Full Surface, Double Weight, 2 Bearings Concealed. For heavy doors up to 800 lb. Many variations. Consult manufacturers' catalogues.

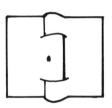

Type 7.72.

Invisible Hinge, Full Mortise. Specifying this number should suffice. They are available in many sizes, but the supplier is responsible for furnishing the proper hinge in accord with manufacturer's recommendation.

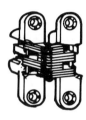

Type 7.73.

Pivot Hinges for Double-Acting Doors w. No Stop. Non-ferrous.

Type 7.74.

Iron.

Type 7.75.

Steel.

Some of the special uses of pivot hinges are described on the next page. Type 7.76, Emergency Stop, is used w. Pivot 7.75, which is usually specified for private bath doors to provide for emergency release.

Rescue, Special, and Olive Knuckle Hinges

Type 7.76.
Emergency Stop, Non-ferrous. Use w. Pivot Type 7.75, preceding page. Stop permits emergency release as illustrated at left, permitting quick rescue. This is in addition to the usual bath privacy locks, Chapters 10, 11, and 12.

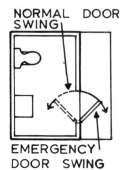

Type 7.77.
Emergency Stop-Release Hinge. Height, 4½". One hinge in set has spring tension against frame. Same purpose as 7.75–7.76 but limited to specific conditions.

Type 7.78.
Pivot Hinge (left) permits 180° opening. Nylon Bushing, Ferrous. For Flush Doors w. No Stile. See also Chapter 23, page 5.
A Set comprises 1 top pivot and 1 bottom pivot. A pair of doors requires 2 Sets.

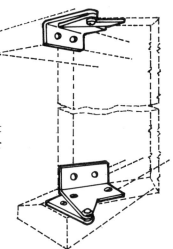

Type 7.79.
Heavy Duty, Non-ferrous, 1 Bearing. Stainless Steel Pin.

Type 7.80.
Same as 7.79 but Steel.

Type 7.81.
Same as 7.80 but Standard Duty and with Nylon Bushing.

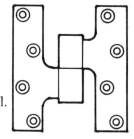

Consult manufacturers' catalogues for size. These Full Mortise Pivots are preferred by some Architects and Hardware Consultants in lieu of the conventional Full Mortise (Butt) Hinges.

OLIVE KNUCKLE HINGES

Olive Knuckle Hinges are strongly preferred by many architects, especially for fine residences and offices. Admittedly, they make a much more decorative appearance, but be sure to compare their cost of installation with that of other types before specifying them.

Type 7.82.
Full Mortise, Heavy Duty available, Non-ferrous, 1 Bearing, High Polish. Height, 6". Widths, 4", 4½", 5".

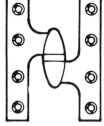

Type 7.83.
Same as 7.82 but Steel available. Plated and Polished. Prime coated for painting.

Type 7.84.
Same as 7.82 but Standard Duty, for doors of medium or light use.

Type 7.85.
Same as 7.83 but Standard Duty.

Type 7.86.
Full Mortise, Light Duty available, Non-ferrous, 1 Bronze Bushing, Polished. Height, 3"–3½". Width, 2¼"–3¼". For cabinets and other light doors only.

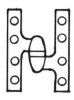

Type 7.87.
Same as 7.86 but Steel Ferrous.

Type 7.88.
Same as 7.86 but Zinc.

Details of Doors and Frames

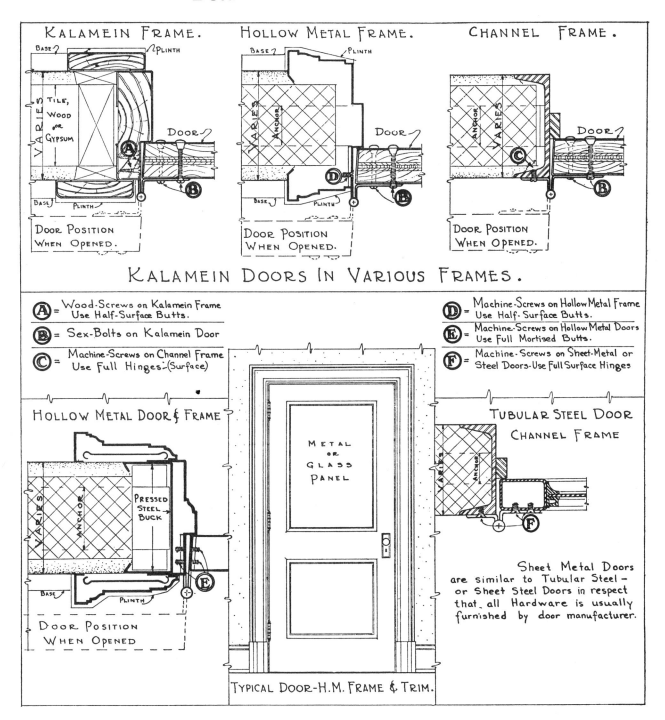

KALAMEIN FRAME.   HOLLOW METAL FRAME.   CHANNEL FRAME.

KALAMEIN DOORS IN VARIOUS FRAMES.

Ⓐ = Wood-Screws on Kalamein Frame Use Half-Surface Butts.

Ⓑ = Sex-Bolts on Kalamein Door

Ⓒ = Machine-Screws on Channel Frame Use Full Hinges-(Surface)

Ⓓ = Machine-Screws on Hollow Metal Frame Use Half-Surface Butts.

Ⓔ = Machine-Screws on Hollow Metal Doors Use Full Mortised Butts.

Ⓕ = Machine-Screws on Sheet-Metal or Steel Doors-Use Full Surface Hinges

HOLLOW METAL DOOR & FRAME

METAL OR GLASS PANEL

TUBULAR STEEL DOOR CHANNEL FRAME

Sheet Metal Doors are similar to Tubular Steel — or Sheet Steel Doors in respect that all Hardware is usually furnished by door manufacturer.

TYPICAL DOOR-H.M. FRAME & TRIM.

The door manufacturer is responsible for producing doors sufficiently reinforced to accept hardware.

The hardware consultant is responsible for furnishing all the hardware for metal doors, including proper templates, screws, and bolts.

Throw of Hinges

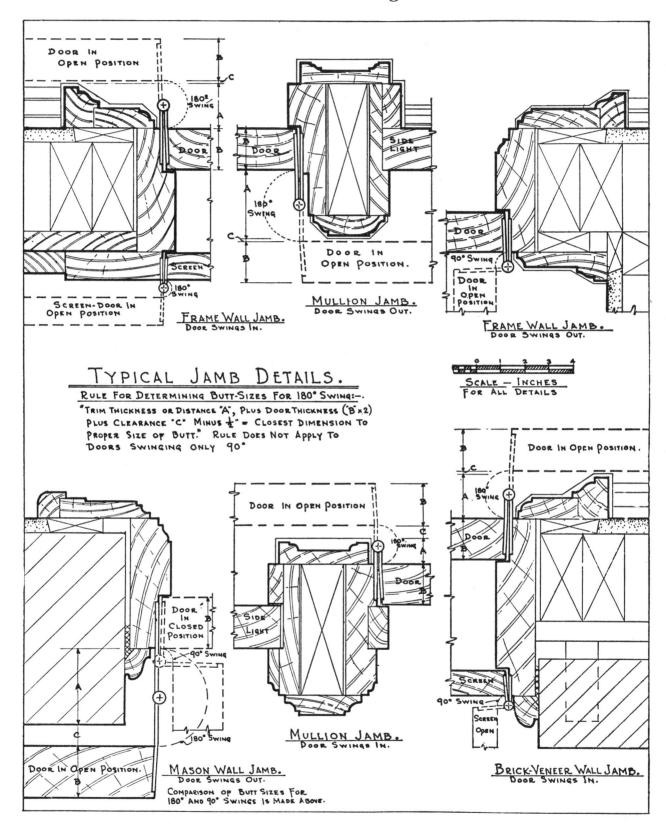

Door In Open Position

180° Swing

Door

Door B

Screen

180° Swing

Screen-Door In Open Position

FRAME WALL JAMB.
Door Swings In.

B
C
A
B

Door

180° Swing

A

180° Swing

C

B

Door In Open Position.

Side Light

MULLION JAMB.
Door Swings Out.

Door

90° Swing

Door In Open Position

FRAME WALL JAMB.
Door Swings Out.

SCALE — INCHES
FOR ALL DETAILS

TYPICAL JAMB DETAILS.

RULE FOR DETERMINING BUTT-SIZES FOR 180° SWING:—

"TRIM THICKNESS OR DISTANCE "A", PLUS DOOR THICKNESS ("B" x 2) PLUS CLEARANCE "C" MINUS $\frac{1}{2}$" = CLOSEST DIMENSION TO PROPER SIZE OF BUTT." RULE DOES NOT APPLY TO DOORS SWINGING ONLY 90°

Door In Closed Position

B

90° Swing

180° Swing

C

Door In Open Position.

B

MASON WALL JAMB.
Door Swings Out.

COMPARISON OF BUTT SIZES FOR 180° AND 90° SWINGS IS MADE ABOVE.

Door In Open Position

B
C
A

180° Swing

Door

B

Side Light

MULLION JAMB.
Door Swings In.

B
C

180° Swing

A

Door

B

Door In Open Position.

Screen

90° Swing

Screen Open

BRICK-VENEER WALL JAMB.
Door Swings In.

CHAPTER 8

Door-Closing Hinges and Pivots, Non-Checking

Screen door hinges are listed in Chapter 20

1. The use of spring hinges on labeled doors that must be self-closing is permissible in many cases. Consult your local codes where economy is important.

2. Where doors are extra heavy, or receive high frequency use, three hinges per door should be specified. The middle hinge should be installed nearer the top hinge for greater efficiency.

3. Select hinges listed for non-hanging strip or with hanging strip as noted.

4. No options have been listed, but if special fastening is required, add Option 8, as in Chapter 7, page 1.

5. Single-acting hinges can be furnished with reverse springs to hold door open instead of closed.

If so desired, add R.S. to the hinge type; e.g., 8.1-R.S.

6. Use of spring hinges with 3½″ or 4½″ jamb flange to fit standard cutouts of mortise hinges, listed as Types 8.9 through 8.11, has received popularity. This is especially important in replacement work where mortise hinges had been used.

7. As all spring hinge manufacturers recommend in their catalogues the proper size for any given door, it should become the responsibility of the hardware supplier to furnish the proper size recommended and is so considered in these specifications, thus simplifying the work.

8. All spring hinges have steel springs; other hinges are non-ferrous.

9. Dimensions in inches show available heights.

Spring Hinge. Full Mortise, Single-Acting, Adjustable Tension. 3″ to 10″.

Type 8.1.
Non-ferrous. For use on Frames with Hanging Strip.

Type 8.2.
Steel. For use on Frames with Hanging Strip.

Type 8.3.
Non-ferrous. For Frames without Hanging Strip.

Type 8.4.
Steel. For use on Frames without Hanging Strip.

Spring Hinge. Full Mortise, Double-Acting, Adjustable Tension. 3″ to 10″.

Type 8.5.
Non-ferrous. For use on Frames with Hanging Strip.

Type 8.6.
Steel. For use on Frames with Hanging Strip.

Type 8.7.
Non-ferrous. For Frames without Hanging Strip.

Type 8.8.
Steel. For use on Frames without Hanging Strip.

Spring Hinge. Full Mortise, Single-Acting, Adjustable Tension. 3½″ and 4½″ only. Fits same mortise as a butt hinge. See Note 5 above.

Type 8.9. Non-ferrous.

Type 8.10. Steel.

Type 8.11.
Steel. For use in conjunction with a Door Closer.

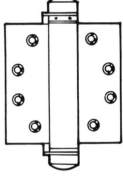

Spring Hinge. Double-Acting on Jamb, Full Mortise. No hanging strip required. Available with or without Hold-Open feature.
NOTE: Do not use on a door weighing over 18 lb.

Type 8.12.
Non-ferrous, with Hold-Open feature.

Type 8.13.
Ferrous, with Hold-Open feature.

Type 8.14.
Non-ferrous, without Hold-Open feature.

Type 8.15.
Ferrous, without Hold-Open feature.

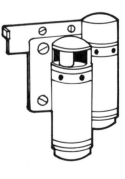

Closing Hinges for Metal and Dwarf Doors

NOTE: Spring hinges this page are for metal doors and frames. Those on page 1 are for wood.

Tension Spring Hinge. Half Surface, Single-Acting, Adjustable Tension. 4″, 6″, 7″.

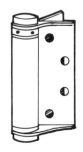

Type 8.16.
Non-ferrous.

Type 8.17.
Steel.

Type 8.18.
Same as 8.16 (Non-ferrous) but available only with 4½″ flange for standard butt hinge cutouts.

Type 8.19.
Same as 8.16 but Ferrous.

Tension Spring Hinge. Full Surface, Single-Acting, Adjustable Tension. 6″–7″.

Type 8.20.
Non-ferrous.

Type 8.21.
Steel.

Tension Spring Hinge. Full Mortise, Single-Acting, Adjustable Tension. 6″–7″.

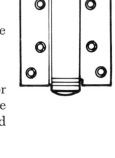

Type 8.22.
Non-ferrous. For use on Fire Doors when permissible.

Type 8.23.
Same as 8.22 but Steel, and for doors for which closers are specified. This hinge is equipped with a safety device.

Tension Spring for Metal-Covered Door. Full Mortise, Double-Acting, Adjustable Tension. Hanging Strip required.

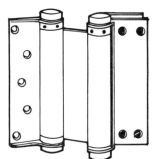

Type 8.24.
Non-ferrous.

Type 8.25.
Steel.

Tension Spring for Metal-Covered Door. Full Mortise, Double-Acting, Adjustable Tension. No Hanging Strip required.

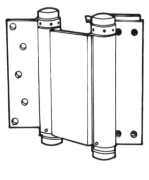

Type 8.26.
Non-ferrous.

Type 8.27.
Steel.

Gravity Pivot Hinge. No Springs. For Dwarf Door, ¾″ to 1¾″.
NOTE: Placing a stop on jamb makes gate single-acting when so desired.

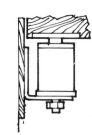

Type 8.28.
Non-ferrous. Surface-Applied as shown.

Type 8.29.
Same as 8.28 but Mortise Applied as shown below.

Spring Pivot Hinge. For Dwarf Door, 1⅛″ to 2½″.
NOTE: Placing a stop on jamb makes gate single-acting when so desired.

Type 8.30.
Non-ferrous, Mortise-Applied as shown.

Type 8.31.
Same as 8.30 but Surface-Applied as shown for Type 8.28.

Closing Pivots, Floor

Floor Spring Pivot. Heavy Duty, Double-Acting, 90° automatic Hold Open. For doors 1⅛″ to 2¾″.

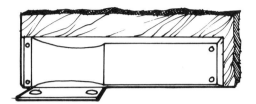

Type 8.32.
Non-ferrous.

Type 8.33.
Steel.

Floor Spring Pivot. Standard Duty, Double-Acting, 90° automatic Hold Open. For doors 1⅛″ to 1¾″.

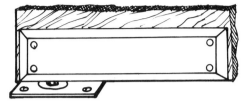

Type 8.34.
Non-ferrous.

Type 8.35.
Steel.

For light commercial work there is available a lower grade, similar in design and function and popular in economy jobs.

Type 8.36.

Spring and Springless Floor Pivots, illustrated below, serve a very useful purpose for certain conditions, such as where doors are extremely heavy or of unusual thickness as described below.

When pivot must be set in concrete, it is available with cement box, which it is the responsibility of the hardware supplier to furnish. On heavy doors it is also prudent to include at top, "Walking Beam Pivots."

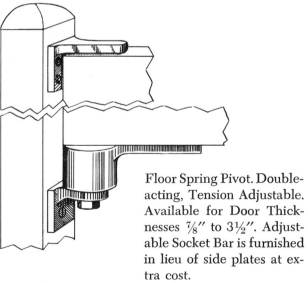

Floor Spring Pivot. Double-acting, Tension Adjustable. Available for Door Thicknesses ⅞″ to 3½″. Adjustable Socket Bar is furnished in lieu of side plates at extra cost.

Type 8.37.
Non-ferrous.

Type 8.38.
Steel.

Floor Springless Pivot. Available for Door Thicknesses ⅞″ to 1¾″.

Such a hinge can swing a door up to 2,000 lb. satisfactorily. While such extreme weight is rare, this capacity is important when needed. All sizes have ball bearings, reducing friction and giving easy and silent action.

In specifying, give only the type number below. As noted above, it is the responsibility of the hardware supplier to furnish proper size as recommended by the manufacturer.

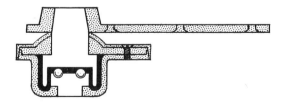

Type 8.39.

Industrial Trucking Door Hinges, Bumpers, and Bolts

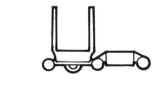

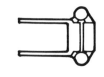

Double-Acting Heavy Spring Hinges for Industrial Trucking Doors.

Available for three maximum door thicknesses:

Dr 1¾″   Flange 15¾″
Dr 2¼″   Flange 20⁵⁄₁₆″
Dr 2¾″   Flange 23⅜″

Adjustable Tension, Protected Springs. Door, Frame Flange, and Door Channel all of Hvy Malleable Iron.

These hinges open 180° unless jamb detail prevents.

It is especially important that such hardware be used where doors are pushed open by hand trucks.

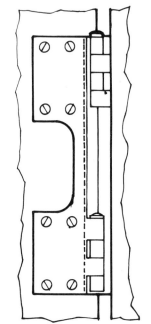

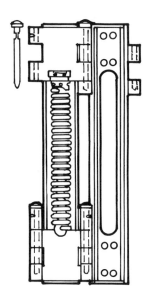

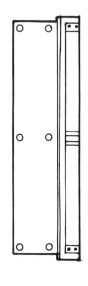

Type 8.40.

As described above.

Type 8.41.

Similar to 8.40, but this hinge uses 4 Springs, and Door Channel is Steel.

Spring Steel Bumper Springs. Used when hinges shown above are specified.

These come packed 4 to a set and serve to protect doors both sides of each leaf. Minimum length 19″; minimum width 8″.

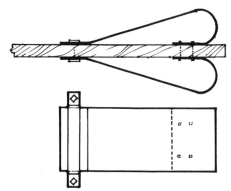

Type 8.42.
Spring Steel.

Type 8.43.
Stainless Steel.

Chain Bolt. Steel. Bolt length, 6″. Chain length 24″. For head of door.

Often used on both leaves when not necessary to lock from outside. If this is wanted, specify 2/8.44.

Type 8.44.
Steel.

Foot Bolt. Steel. Length, 6″. For bottom of door. Often used on both leaves as noted for Type 8.44. Can also be used as a door holder when extra strike is installed at hold-open position.

Type 8.45.
Steel.

CHAPTER 9

Door-Closing Hinges and Pivots, Checking

1. The hardware supplier is responsible for selection of type and size per his manufacturer's recommended sizes and conditions.

2. Hold-open feature with floor hinges (Option #1) is available with most checking floor hinges when necessary, but this option is not as satisfactory as a separate door-holding device, except when conditions or economy make the option advisable.

3. Check carefully for use of cement box or twin cement box. Some types listed do not include cement boxes. If needed, add Option #2.

4. Where U.L.-rated Doors are used in conjunction with floor hinges, malleable iron pivots are mandatory.

tion with floor hinges, malleable iron pivots are mandatory.

5. Especial care must be taken to specify the correct hinge in regard to whether it is (a) double- or single-acting and (b) pivoted at center or butt or offset pivoted.

Three Ways of Hanging Doors with Floor Hinges

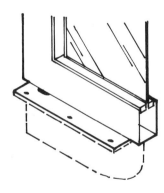

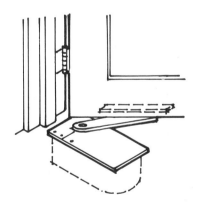

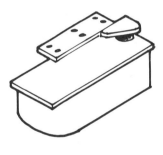

Mounting A
Double-Acting or Single-Acting.
If to be embedded in concrete, Cement Box is required, Option 2

Mounting B
Single-Acting,
   Hung on Butt Hinges.
   NOTE: Hinges must be specified separately; see Chapter 7.
   Add Option 2 if Cement Box is required.

Mounting C
Single-Acting, Offset Pivoted.
   If to be embedded in concrete, Cement Box required, Option 2

Floor Hinge Door Closers

Type No.	Kind of Use	Mounting See Page 1	Method of Hinging or Pivoting	Recommended Specification
9.1	Double-Acting	A	Center Pivoted	For Extra Heavy Dr, High Frequency Use
9.2	Double-Acting	A	Center Pivoted	For Heavy Dr, Medium Frequency Use
9.3	Double-Acting	A	Center Pivoted	For Standard Interior Dr Only
9.4	Double-Acting	A	Center Pivoted	For Light Interior Dr Only
9.5	Single-Acting	A	Center Pivoted	For Extra Heavy Dr up to 1,000 lb
9.6	Single-Acting	A	Center Pivoted	For Heavy Dr, High Frequency Use
9.7	Single-Acting	A	Center Pivoted	For Standard Interior Dr Only
9.8	Single-Acting	A	Center Pivoted	For Heavy Dr, High Frequency Use
9.9	Single-Acting	A	Center Pivoted	For Standard Interior Dr Only
9.10	Single-Acting	A	Center Pivoted	For Light Interior Dr Only
9.11	Single-Acting	B	Butt Hung	For Extra Heavy Dr, High Frequency Use
9.12	Single-Acting	B	Butt Hung	For Heavy Dr, High Frequency Use
9.13	Single-Acting	B	Butt Hung	For Standard Interior Dr Only
9.14	Single-Acting	C	Offset Pivoted	For Extra Heavy Dr, High Frequency Use
9.15	Single-Acting	C	Offset Pivoted	For Heavy Dr, High Frequency Use
9.16	Single-Acting	C	Offset Pivoted	For Standard Interior Dr Only
9.17	Single-Acting	C	Offset Pivoted	For Light Interior Dr Only
9.18	Single-Acting	C	Offset Pivoted	For Extra Heavy Dr, High Frequency Use
9.19	Single-Acting	C	Offset Pivoted	For Extra Heavy Dr up to 1,000 lb

Type 9.20.

Floor Pivot Closer. Single-Acting. Has Back Check and Automatic Hold-Open feature. Closes doors up to 4 ft wide. Available in 3 sizes.

Must specify as to whether Mortise Hinge, Center Pivot, or Offset Pivot.

NOTE: For all Offset Extra Heavy and Heavy Checking Floor Hinges, Intermediate Hinges should also be specified. See page 4, this chapter.

This is particularly important for Exterior or Lead-Lined Doors.

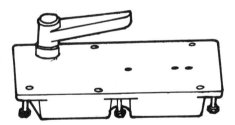

Thresholds for Checking-Type Floor Pivots

Recommended thresholds for use with respective floor hinges. Thresholds also for use with exit devices, Chapter 14. Other Thresholds shown in Chapter 16.

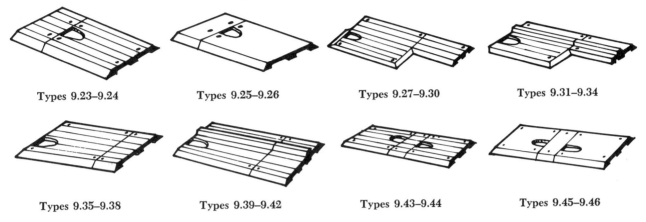

| Types 9.23–9.24 | Types 9.25–9.26 | Types 9.27–9.30 | Types 9.31–9.34 |

| Types 9.35–9.38 | Types 9.39–9.42 | Types 9.43–9.44 | Types 9.45–9.46 |

Type No.	Description
9.23	For center-pivoted doors. Available widths, 6¾″ to 8¼″. Grooved Surface. Unpolished Brass or Bronze.
9.24	Same as 9.23 but of Unpolished Aluminum.
9.25	Same as 9.23 but With Smooth Surface.
9.26	Same as 9.23 but With Smooth Surface and of Unpolished Aluminum.
9.27	For offset-pivoted doors with offset at end and mitered ends. Available widths, 3¾″ to 5¼″. Grooved Surface. Unpolished Brass or Bronze.
9.28	Same as 9.27 but of Unpolished Aluminum.
9.29	Same as 9.27 but With Smooth Surface.
9.30	Same as 9.27 but With Smooth Surface and of Unpolished Aluminum.
9.31	Same as 9.27 but With Stop Strip.
9.32	Same as 9.27 but With Stop Strip and of Unpolished Aluminum.
9.33	Same as 9.27 but With Stop Strip and Smooth Surface.
9.34	Same as 9.27 but With Stop Strip and Smooth Surface and of Unpolished Aluminum.
9.35	For offset-pivoted doors with mitered ends and no offset at end. Available widths, 3¾″ to 5¼″. Grooved Surface. Unpolished Brass or Bronze.
9.36	Same as 9.35 but of Unpolished Aluminum.
9.37	Same as 9.35 but With Smooth Surface.
9.38	Same as 9.35 but With Smooth Surface and of Unpolished Aluminum.
9.39	Same as 9.35 but With Stop Strip.
9.40	Same as 9.35 but With Stop Strip and of Unpolished Aluminum.
9.41	Same as 9.35 but With Stop Strip and Smooth Surface.
9.42	Same as 9.35 but With Stop Strip and Smooth Surface and of Unpolished Aluminum.
9.43	For offset-pivoted pair of doors with cement boxes back to back. Available widths, 3¾″ to 5¼″. Grooved Surface. Unpolished Brass or Bronze.
9.44	Same as 9.43 but of Unpolished Aluminum.
9.45	Same as 9.43 but With Smooth Surface.
9.46	Same as 9.43 but With Smooth Surface and of Unpolished Aluminum.

Pivots and Pivot Sets Not Shown in Chapter 8

Offset Pivots for Offset Floor Closers This Chapter, Page 2

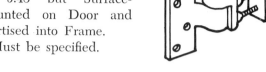

Type 9.47.
Top Pivot Offset. Also available: Full Surface, Half Mortise, Half Surface.

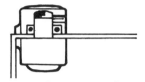

Not necessary to give type number in specification because this pivot is part of a set.

Type 9.49.
Half Surface Pivot. Same as 9.48 but Surface-Mounted on Door and Mortised into Frame.
Must be specified.

Type 9.48.
Intermediate Pivot. Mortised, Vertical Adjustment.
Must be specified. Can be used independently. 3 pivots required per door.

Type 9.50.
Extra Heavy Pivot. Full Mortise. For Lead-Lined or other Extra-Heavy Doors.
Must be specified.

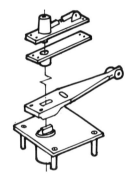

PIVOT SETS, ALL NON-SELF-CLOSING
Can be used in conjunction with door closers subject to proper detail.

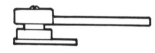

Type 9.51.
Offset Pivot Set. Floor Mounted. For doors to 125 lb.

Type 9.52.
Offset Pivot Set. Jamb Mounted. For doors to 125 lb.

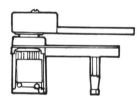

Type 9.53.
Offset Pivot Set. Floor Mounted. For heavy doors to 350 lb.

NOTE: All sets this page usually furnished with Top Pivot as 9.47, but can be supplied with any other offset Top or Intermediate Pivot as shown on this page when so specified.

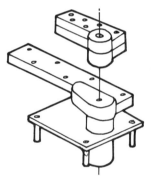

Type 9.54.
Offset Pivot Set. For extra heavy or lead-lined doors to 1,500 lb.

Type 9.55.
Same as 9.54 but for doors to 250 lb.

Type 9.56.
Same as 9.55 but jamb-mounted like 9.52.

Type 9.57.
Full Mortise. For doors to 150 lb.

Type 9.58.
Same as 9.57 but jamb mounted.

Type 9.59.
Same as 9.57 but ferrous, for use with fire doors.

Type 9.60.
Center Pivot Set. Full Mortise, Extra Heavy, bottom pivot embedded in floor. For extra heavy or lead-lined doors up to 1,000 lb.

Type 9.61.
Same as 9.60 but for doors to 250 lb.

Type 9.62.
Same as 9.60 but for doors to 150 lb.

NOTE: Conventional top walking beam pivot as illustrated above.

CHAPTER 10

Conventional Mortise Locks and Latches

On pages 2 through 5 are described 35 lock functions. Since all manufacturers do not make locks with all functions, their catalogues should be consulted.

The type numbers in this chapter give first the chapter, then the function, then the grade as described below.

Backset

The proper selection of backset is important. Where details permit, a minimum backset of 2¾″ should be provided to prevent the user from scraping his knuckles. Backsets are specified in manufacturers' catalogues.

Options

The 36 options on page 6 of this chapter serve to specify the finish, which is determined by the selection of metal, and the design. Both finish and design are usually chosen by the architect, working with the hardware consultant, and are carefully recorded, covering all details of the project, before the specifications are made. Steps 2(a) and 2(b) in Chapter 2 provide for this.

In order to specify a full lock set with a type number, option numbers representing specific trim must follow the type number. For example, the number for an Apartment Entrance Lock, Grade 1, with Cast Bronze Knobs would be 10.10.1-1. The same with Screwless Knobs and Roses would be the number 10.10.1-1-3-4, specifying Options 1, 3, and 4 on page 6.

The use of mortise locks and latches makes possible a wide choice of designs and other options.

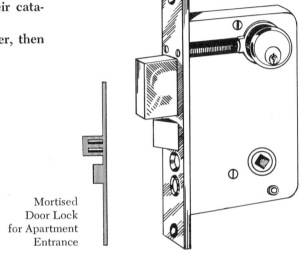

Mortised Door Lock for Apartment Entrance

Among these is the type of knob and spindle. The various types of lock fronts, hubs, and lock strikes are shown on page 7.

Grades

Grade 1 locks are standardized by all mortise lock manufacturers to have 8″ x 1¼″ fronts and strikes to conform to the criterions of the American Standards Association.

Grade 2 locks are standardized by some mortise lock manufacturers but vary from one manufacturer to another.

Grade 3 locks are not standardized and vary from one manufacturer to another. This grade is generally used for light commercial and residential work and for wood doors and frames.

Mortise Locks for Apartment and Store Door Sets

Minimum Door Thickness: For Heavy Duty Locks, 1¾″. For Standard Duty Locks, 1⅜″.

Function 1. Latch bolt operated by thumbpiece from outside and inside, except when outside thumbpiece is locked by key from inside. When outside thumbpiece is locked, latch bolt may be operated by outside key or inside thumbpiece. Auxiliary dead latch.

Type 10.1.1.
Recommended for Hvy Duty.

Function 2. Latch bolt operated by outside thumbpiece and inside knob, except when outside thumbpiece is locked by inside key. When outside thumbpiece is locked, latch bolt may be operated by outside key or inside knob. Auxiliary dead latch.

Type 10.2.1.
Recommended for Hvy Duty.

Function 3. Latch bolt operated by thumbpiece from either side except when outside thumbpiece is locked by outside key. When outside thumbpiece is locked, latch bolt can be retracted by outside key and by inside thumbpiece. Auxiliary dead latch.

Type 10.3.1.
Recommended for Hvy Duty.

Function 4. Latch bolt operated by outside thumbpiece and inside knob except when thumbpiece is locked by outside key. When thumbpiece is locked, latch bolt can be retracted by outside key and by inside knob. Auxiliary dead latch.

Type 10.4.1.
Recommended for Hvy Duty.

Function 5. Latch bolt operated by thumbpiece from either side except when outside thumbpiece is locked by stop in face. When outside thumbpiece is locked, latch bolt may be operated by outside key and inside thumbpiece. Dead bolt operated by key from either side.

Type 10.5.1.
Hvy Duty.

Type 10.5.2.
Std Duty.

Function 6. Latch bolt operated by thumbpiece from either side except when outside thumbpiece is locked by stop in face. Dead bolt operated by thumb turn inside. Key outside operates both bolts.

Type 10.6.1.
Hvy Duty.

Type 10.6.2.
Std Duty.

Function 7. Latch bolt operated by thumbpiece from either side. Dead bolt operated by key from either side.

Type 10.7.1.
Hvy Duty.

Type 10.7.2.
Std Duty.

Function 8. Latch bolt operated by thumbpiece from either side. Dead bolt operated by key outside and thumb turn inside.

Type 10.8.1.
Hvy Duty.

Type 10.8.2.
Std Duty.

Locks for Residence, Apartment, Dormitory, and Store

Minimum Door Thickness: For Heavy Duty Locks, 1¾″. For Standard Duty Locks, 1⅜″.

Function 9, Front Door Residential. Latch bolt operated by thumbpiece outside, knob inside, except when outside thumbpiece is locked by stop in face. Dead bolt operated by thumb turn inside. Key outside operates both bolts.

Type 10.9.1. Hvy Duty.

Type 10.9.2. Std Duty.

Type 10.9.3.
    Non-Std Front. Min. Dr Thickness, 1⅜″.

Function 10, Apartment Entrance. Latch bolt operated by knob from either side except when outside knob is locked by stop in face. Dead bolt operated thumb turn inside. Key outside operates both bolts. Dead bolt has 1″ throw with hardened steel pins in bolt to prevent sawing bolt off.

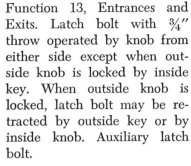

Type 10.10.1. Hvy Duty.

Type 10.10.2. Std Duty.

Function 11, Apartment Exit or Public Toilet. Latch bolt operated by knob from either side, except when outside knob is locked by inside key. When outside knob is locked, latch bolt can be retracted by outside key or inside knob. Auxiliary dead latch.

Type 10.11.1. Hvy Duty.

Type 10.11.2. Std Duty.

Function 12, Dormitory and Corridor Doors. Latch bolt operated by knob from either side except when outside knob is locked by stop in face. Dead bolt projected by key from either side. Dead bolt retracted by outside key. Both bolts retracted by inside knob.

Type 10.12.1. Hvy Duty.
Type 10.12.2. Std Duty.

Function 13, Entrances and Exits. Latch bolt with ¾″ throw operated by knob from either side except when outside knob is locked by inside key. When outside knob is locked, latch bolt may be retracted by outside key or by inside knob. Auxiliary latch bolt.

Type 10.13.1.
    Hvy Duty.

Type 10.13.2.
    Std Duty.

Function 14, Entrances and Exits. Deadlocking latch bolt with ¾″ throw operated by knob from either side except when outside knob is locked by outside key.

Type 10.14.1.
    Hvy Duty.

Type 10.14.2.
    Std Duty.

Function 15, Store and Utility Doors. Latch bolt operated by knob from either side. Dead bolt operated by key from either side.

Type 10.15.1.
    Hvy Duty.

Type 10.15.2.
    Std Duty.

Function 16, Store and Utility Doors. Latch bolt operated by knob from either side. Dead bolt operated by outside key and by inside knob.

Type 10.16.1.
    Hvy Duty.

Type 10.16.2.
    Std Duty.

Locks for Office, Classroom, Store, Darkroom, Conference Room, and Hotel Guestroom

Minimum Door Thickness: For Heavy Duty Locks, 1¾″. For Standard Duty Locks, 1⅜″.

Function 17, Front Doors. Latch bolt operated by knob from either side except when outside knob is locked by stop in face. Dead bolt operated by thumb turn inside. Key outside operates both bolts.

Type 10.17.1. Hvy Duty.

Type 10.17.2. Std Duty.

Type 10.17.3.
Non-Std Face. Min. Dr Thickness, 1⅜″.

Function 18, Office Doors. Latch bolt operated by knob from either side except when outside knob is locked by stop in face. Key outside operates latch bolt. Auxiliary dead latch.

Type 10.18.1. Hvy Duty.

Type 10.18.2. Std Duty.

Function 19, Classroom Doors. Deadlocking latch bolt operated by knob from either side except when outside knob is locked by key outside. Inside knob always operative.

Type 10.19.1. Hvy Duty.

Type 10.19.2. Std Duty.

Function 20, Classroom and Hospital Doors. Deadlocking latch bolt operated by knob from either side except when outside knob is locked by outside key. Latch bolt may be locked in retracted position by key. Inside knob always operative.

Type 10.20.1. Hvy Duty.

Type 10.20.2. Std Duty.

Function 21, Store and Utility Doors. Deadlocking latch bolt operated by outside key or by inside knob. Outside knob is always fixed.

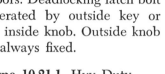

Type 10.21.1. Hvy Duty.

Type 10.21.2. Std Duty.

Function 22, Conference and Darkroom Doors. Latch bolt operated by knob from either side except when outside knob is locked by stop in face. Latch bolt operated by outside key. Dead bolt projected by thumb turn inside shuts out all keys.

Type 10.22.1. Hvy Duty.

Type 10.22.2. Std Duty.

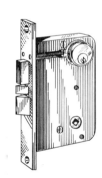

Function 23, Hotel Guestroom Doors. Latch bolt operated by inside knob and all corridor keys except when dead bolt thrown by inside key; then only emergency and display keys open. Inside key cannot be withdrawn when locked. Auxiliary latch bolt. Outside knob always fixed.

Type 10.23.1. Hvy Duty.

Type 10.23.2. Std Duty.

Function 24, Hotel Guestroom Doors. Latch bolt operated by both knobs all times. Dead bolt by all keys from corridor and guest key inside. When dead bolt thrown by guest key inside or from corridor by emergency or display keys, the guest, master, and grand master keys are inoperative. When locked from inside, guest key cannot be withdrawn. When dead bolt thrown from outside by guest key, inside knob retracts both bolts. Indicator button.

Type 10.24.1. Hvy Duty.

Mortise Cylinder Deadlocks and Standardized Faces

Minimum Door Thickness: For Heavy Duty Locks, 1¾″. For Standard Duty Locks, 1⅜″.

Function 25, Latch Only. Latch bolt operated by knob from either side at all times.

Type 10.25.1. Hvy Duty.

Type 10.25.2. Std Duty.

Type 10.25.3.
  Non-Std Face, Minimum Dr Thickness 1⅜″.

Function 26, ¾″ Throw Latch. Latch bolt operated by knob from either side at all times. Latch bolt has ¾″ throw.

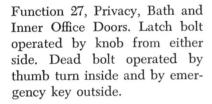

Type 10.26.1. Hvy Duty.

Type 10.26.2. Std Duty.

Function 27, Privacy, Bath and Inner Office Doors. Latch bolt operated by knob from either side. Dead bolt operated by thumb turn inside and by emergency key outside.

Type 10.27.1. Hvy Duty.

Type 10.27.2. Std Duty.

Type 10.27.3. Non-Std Face.

Function 28, Communicating Doors. Latch bolt operated by knob from either side. Two dead bolts or split dead bolt operated independently by thumb turns from both sides. Should not be used on doors in rooms that have no other entrance.

Type 10.28.1. Hvy Duty.

Type 10.28.2. Std Duty.

Function 29, 2-Cylinder Deadlock. Dead bolt operated by key from either side. 2 cylinders.

Type 10.29.1. Hvy Duty.

Type 10.29.2. Std Duty.

Function 30, 1-Cylinder Deadlock With Thumb Turn. Dead bolt operated by key outside and by thumb turn inside. 1 cylinder.

Type 10.30.1. Hvy Duty.

Type 10.30.2. Std Duty.

Function 31, 1-Cylinder Deadlock. Dead bolt operated by outside key only.

Type 10.31.1. Hvy Duty.

Type 10.31.2. Std Duty.

NOTE: Mortise latches and deadlocks are manufactured in a wide variety of non-standard types and with many brackets. Use catalogue numbers to specify items in this category, but for the numbering system of this handbook the following type numbers apply.

Type 10.32.1.
  Ex Hvy Deadlock w. 1″ Throw.

Type 10.33.2.
  Std Deadlock w. ¾″ Throw.

Type 10.34.1.
  Deadlock with Short Backset.

Type 10.35.1.
  Mortise Night Latch w. Cyls or Thumb Turns.

Trim for Mortise Locks Classified as Options

Mortise lock trim to complete a lock set is classified here as option numbers. For example, to specify the heavy duty office door lock, described on page 4, with the particular spindle of Option -6, use type number 10.18.1–6.

When design or finish is not specified by the option, it can be indicated on the specification according to the decisions reached according to Steps 2(a) and 2(b) in Chapter 2, page 6.

Option Key

Option -1
Escutcheon. Plain, Cast, Non-ferrous, Hdles and Plates both sides.

Option -2
Same as -1 but Plates only are Wrt, both sides.

Option -3
Handle Set. Ornamental, Cast, Non-ferrous, Hdles both sides.

Option -4
Same as -3 but Hdle Outside, Knob Inside with TP Trim.

Option -5
Knob and Rose. Cast, Non-ferrous, w. Threaded Spindle.

Option -6
Same as -5 but Wrt.

Option -7
Screwless Knob and Rose. Cast, Non-ferrous, w. Screwless Spindle.

Option -8
Same as -7 but Knob Wrt, Shank and Rose Cast.

Option -9
Pr of Escutcheons w. Lugs bolted through Dr. Check catalogues for availability. This type seldom used except for some government projects.

Option -10
Escutcheon. Contemporary (also available Plain), Cast, Non-ferrous.

Option -11
Same as -10 but Wrt.

Option -12
Escutcheon. Gothic (many other designs available), Cast, Non-ferrous.

Option -13
Cyl Collar. Cast, Non-ferrous. Several designs available.

NOTE: When sectional trim locks are selected, they are usually furnishd with a cylinder ring only if a design cylinder collar is wanted. Option -13 applies to such a case.

Option -14
Drop-Ring Hdles, Pr. Non-ferrous and other designs.

Option -15
Drop-Ring Hdle, Sgle. To be used with another option such as Knob, -5, for other side of door.

Option -16
Flush-Cup Hdles, Pr. Cast. Non-ferrous.

Option -17
Flush-Cup Hdle, Sgle.

Option -18
Drop Key Plate.

Option -19
Key Plate. Cast, Non-ferrous.

Option -20
Same as -19 but Wrt.

Option -21
Thumb Turn. Cast, Non-ferrous.

Option -22
Same as -21 but Wrt.

Option -23
Thumb Turn. Cast, Non-ferrous.

Option -24
Same as -23 but Wrt.

Option -25
Lever Hdles, Pr. Cast, Non-ferrous.

Option -26
Lever Hdle, Sgle. Cast, Non-ferrous.

NOTE: Lever handles should be used with spring-type roses or with a strong spring in the lock.

Bolts, Strikes, Faces, and Hubs for Mortise Locks

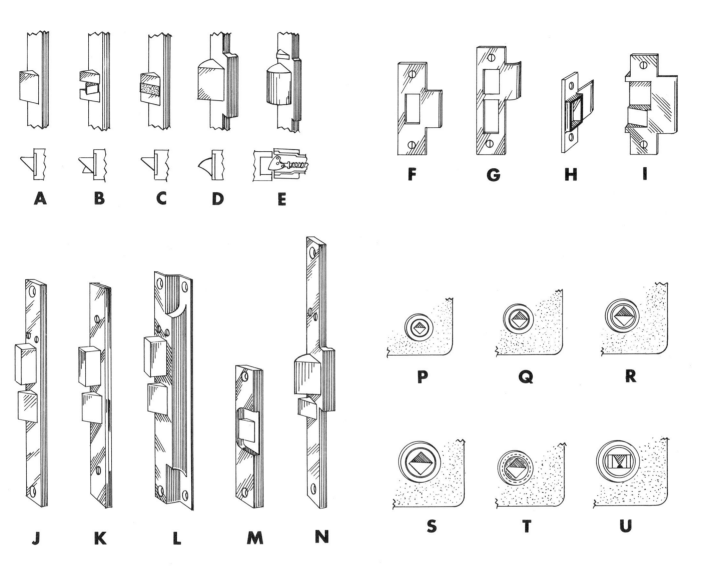

A. Plain latch bolt.
B. Anti-friction latch bolt.
C. Wood or nylon inserted in latch bolt.
D. Car-type latch bolt.
E. Roll-fold type latch bolt.

F. Plain strike—straight lip.
G. Plain strike—curved lip.
H. Cast-box strike.
I. Open-back strike for pair of doors.

J. Plain-type lock face.
K. Armored-type lock face.
L. Rabbeted-type lock face.
M. Recessed-type lock face.
N. Winged-type lock front.

P. ¼″ diamond-shaped lock hub.
Q. ⁵⁄₁₆″ diamond-shaped lock hub.
R. ⅜″ diamond-shaped lock hub.
S. ½″ diamond-shaped lock hub.
T. Diamond-shaped compensation lock hub.
U. Square compensation lock hub.

NOTE: One manufacturer makes many of his lock hubs square rather than diamond-shaped. Be sure that such items as lever handles are ordered either for square or for diamond-shaped hubs, as required.

CHAPTER 11

Unit and Integral Locks and Latches

Unit Locks and Latches

(Pages 1 through 4)

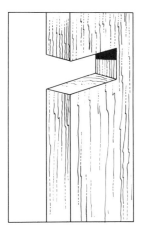

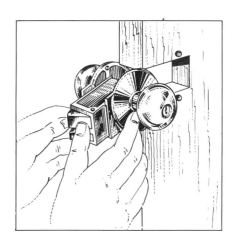

(Left) The Mortise for the Unit Lock. (Above) A Type of Unit Lock. (Right) Applying a Unit Lock.

No grades are given for the unit lock because they are all of a uniform high-quality grade except, as mentioned in Chapter 1, page 4, the original manufacturers can still supply an extra heavy grade for some functions in some designs.

Since all 24 functions described here are not all made by all manufacturers, catalogues should be consulted for numbers before specifying.

The unit lock over the years has been recognized as most rugged, easily installed and with key in the knob. Higher priced than many other locks, it still has gained wide acceptance because of its easy installation and durability.

Throw of Bolt

Latch bolts with a ¾″ throw are standard with some manufacturers.

Backsets

Backsets vary, but 2¾″ is standard. One manufacturer makes a 2½″ backset optional; another has a 3 ¾″ optional.

In more recent years, the idea has been modernized and streamlined. Many of the principles of this lock vary by manufacturer. Specifiers of this type lock should use care in selection. While it does not offer as wide a variety of functions as does the conventional mortise lock, the available functions are those most generally used.

For available finish and design and for special trim, consult the manufacturers' catalogues before specifying. Some manufacturers, for example, list unit locks with lever handles. This would be indicated by selecting the type number and adding to it the appropriate option number from Chapter 10, page 6.

Special Features

A great variety of special features, such as dummy trim, is available, so the specifier should check the catalogues carefully.

Unit Locks and Latches (Continued)

Function 36, Office and Store Entrances. Dead-locking latch bolt oper-ated by knob from either side except when out- 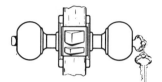 side knob is locked by turn button in inside knob. Key in outside knob retracts latch bolt. Turn button must be manually rotated to unlock outside knob.

Type 11.36.

Function 37, Office Doors. Deadlocking latch bolt operated by knob from either side except when outside 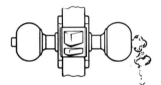 knob is locked by push button in inside knob. Key in outside knob retracts latch bolt and releases push button. Closing door does not release push button.

Type 11.37.

Function 38, Apartment and Store Entrances. Deadlocking latch bolt operated by outside key or inside knob. Outside knob is always fixed.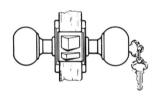

Type 11.38.

Function 39, Apartment and Toilet Entrances. Latch bolt operated by knob from either side except when outside 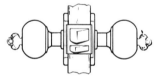 knob is locked by key inside. When outside knob is locked, latch bolt may be retracted by key out-side or by inside knob. Auxiliary dead latch.

Type 11.39.

Function 40, Store Doors and Others. Deadlock-ing latch bolt operated by knob from either side except when both knobs are locked by key from either side.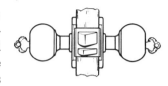

Type 11.40.

Function 41, Store Doors and Others. Latch bolt operated by knob from either side. Dead bolt op-erated by key from either side.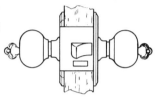

Type 11.41.

Function 42, Classroom Doors and Others. Dead-locking latch bolt oper-ated by knob from either side except when outside is locked by outside key. Inside knob is always op-erative.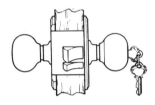

Type 11.42.

Function 43, Hotel and Motel Guestroom Doors. Deadlocking latch bolt operated by inside knob at all times. Outside knob 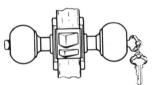 always fixed. Latch bolt operated by outside key except when push button inside is depressed, thus shutting out all keys except emergency key. De-pressing push button operates visual indicator in face of cylinder, showing room is occupied. Turn-ing inside knob or closing door releases indicator and shut-out feature except when push button is turned to shut-out position with special key, shut-ting out all keys except emergency key. Inside knob always operative.

Type 11.43.

Unit Locks and Latches (Continued)

Function 44, Utility and Patio Doors. Deadlocking latch bolt operated by key in inside knob or by rotating inside knob. Outside knob is always fixed.

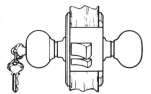

Type 11.44.

Function 45, Utility and Other Doors. Deadlocking latch bolt retracted by inside knob at all times. Outside knob is always fixed.

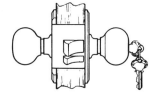

Type 11.45.

Function 46, Passage and Closet Doors (where no lock is required). Latch bolt operated by knob from either side at all times.

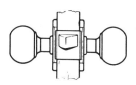

Type 11.46.

Function 47, Bath and Bedroom Doors. Latch bolt operated by knob from either side. Outside knob is locked by push button inside and unlocked by emergency key outside or by rotating inside knob or closing door.

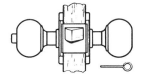

Type 11.47.

Function 48, Inner Office Doors. Latch bolt operated by knob from either side. Outside knob is locked by push button inside and unlocked by rotating inside knob or closing door.

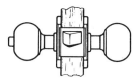

NOTE: Do not use on door when there is no other entrance to room.

Type 11.48.

Function 49, Communicating Doors. Deadlocking latch bolt operated by knob from either side. Turn button in either knob locks or unlocks opposite knob.

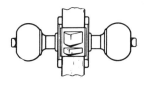

NOTE: Should not be used on doors in rooms that have no other entrance.

Type 11.49.

Function 50, Dormitory and Public Toilet Doors. Deadlocking latch bolt operated by knobs from either side except when outside knob is locked by push button or key. Turning inside knob or closing door automatically releases. This prevents any accidental lockout.

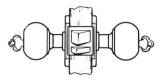

Type 11.50.

Function 51, Asylum and Other Institutional Doors. Deadlocking latch bolt operated by knobs from either side except when both knobs are locked by key in outside knob.

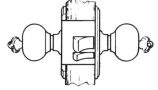

NOTE: Do not use this function unless occupants must be locked inside.

Type 11.51.

Unit Locks and Latches with Dead Bolt Functions

Function 52, Store Entrance and Communicating Doors. Latch operated by knob from either side. Dead bolt operated by key from either side. When dead bolt is thrown, it also deadlocks latch.

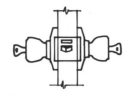

Type 11.52.

Function 53, Residence Front and Office Entrance Doors. Latch operated by knob from either side except when outside knob is locked by inside push button. Has auxiliary latch. Key outside or knob inside unlocks latch and dead bolt.

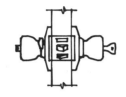

Type 11.53.

Function 54, Classroom Doors and Others. Latch operated by knob from either side except when outside knob and bolt are locked by outside key. Inside knob throws both latch and bolt automatically.

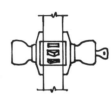

Type 11.54.

Function 55, Hotel and Motel Guestroom Entrance Doors. Outside knob always rigid. Auxiliary latch key outside. Thumb turn inside throws dead bolt. Has shutout and emergency key control and indicator button.

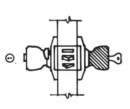

Type 11.55.

Function 56, Bath and Bedroom Doors and Other Privacy Uses. Latch operated by knob from either side. Thumb turn inside locks bolt and both knobs. Unlocked only by thumb turn or outside emergency key.

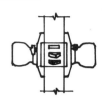

Type 11.56.

Function 57, Communicating Door Where Double Bolts Needed. Latch operated by knob from either side. Thumb turn either side throws separate dead bolts. Both must be unlocked by thumb turns.

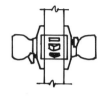

CAUTION: Never use unless another entrance is available.

Type 11.57.

Function 58, Patio and Similar Exterior Doors. Latch operated by knob from either side. Inside key throws bolt and locks both knobs and latch.

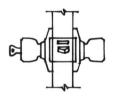

Type 11.58.

Function 59, Closet Doors and Similar Uses. Latch operated by knob from either side. Outside key throws bolt and locks both knobs and latch.

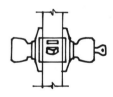

Type 11.59.

Integral Locks and Latches

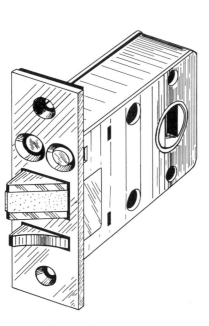
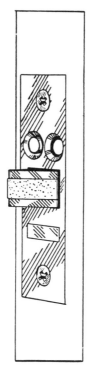
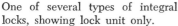

One of several types of integral locks, showing lock unit only.

An integral lock applied to door.

The integral lock, available from only one manufacturer, has the key-in-knob feature of the cylinder, tubular, and unit locks. Sixteen of its functions are described on the following pages. Some of them incorporate the stops in face and dead bolt of the mortise locks. Rabbetted faces are available when required.

All functions have a backset of 2¾" and a latch throw of ½". Particular attention is called to the fact that when other functions, backsets, or throws are required, this manufacturer can provide them.

Two grades are listed under functions simply to show that these functions are available for doors 1⅜" thick; there are six such functions. These are all Grade 1 for use with 1⅜" doors. All functions listed by this manufacturer are Grade 1 products identical to and interchangeable with locks for 1¾" doors.

Some designs are also available in stainless steel, fired copper, and Delrin. Specifying the design establishes the type of trim.

It is recommended that the hardware specifier consult this manufacturer's catalogue for further description and other options available when he elects to specify Integral Locks.

Integral Locks and Latches (Continued)

Function 60, Entrances and Public Toilet Doors. Deadlocking latch bolt operated by knob from either side except when outside knob is locked

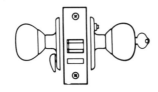

by turn button in inside knob. Key in outside knob retracts latch bolt. Turn button must be manually rotated to unlock outside knob.

Type 11.60.

Function 61, Store Doors and Others. Latch bolt operated by knob from either side. Dead bolt operated by key from either side.

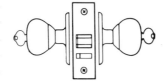

Type 11.61.

Function 62, Asylum and Utility Doors. Deadlocking latch bolt operated by key from either side. Both knobs always fixed.

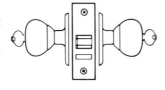

Type 11.62.

Function 63, Utility and Storeroom Doors. Deadlocking latch bolt operated by outside key or by inside knob. Outside knob is always fixed.

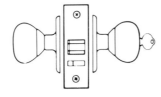

Type 11.63.

NOTE: This lock is also available for doors 1⅜″ thick.

Function 64, Utility and Emergency Doors. Latch bolt operated from outside by key and from inside by knob. Outside knob is rigid at all times. Guarded latch bolt.

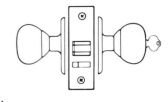

Type 11.64.

NOTE: This lock is also available for doors 1⅜″ thick.

Function 65, Entrance and Office Doors. Latch bolt operated by knob from either side except when outside knob is locked by stop in face.

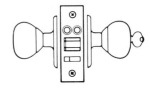

Outside key operates latch bolt. Auxiliary dead latch.

Type 11.65.

Function 66, Classroom and Other Doors. Deadlocking latch bolt operated by knob from either side except when outside knob is locked by

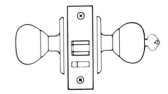

outside key. Inside knob always operative.

Type 11.66.

Function 67, Hotel and Motel Guestroom Door. Latch bolt operated by knob from inside. Dead bolt operated from outside by all keys unless

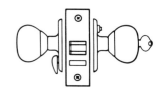

projected from inside by thumb turn; then all keys are shut out except display and emergency keys. Emergency key acts as shut-out key. Outside knob always fixed with indicator button.

Type 11.67.

Integral Locks and Latches (Continued)

Function 68, Front Entrances and Other Doors. Latch bolt operated by knob from either side except when outside knob is locked by stop in face. Dead bolt operated by thumb turn inside. Key outside operates both bolts.

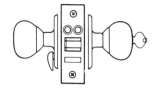

Type 11.68.

Function 69, Service Station and Exit Doors. Deadlocking latch bolt operated by knob from inside. Outside knob is always fixed. Latch bolt operated from outside by key and from inside by knob.

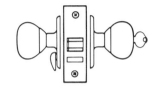

Type 11.69.

Function 70, Playroom and Patio Doors. Deadlocking latch bolt operated by knob from either side except when outside knob is locked by key inside.

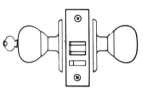

Type 11.70.

Function 71, Playroom and Patio Doors. Deadlocking latch bolt operated by knob from either side except when outside knob is locked by stop in face.

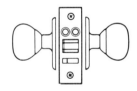

Type 11.71.

Function 72, Passage and Closet Doors. Latch bolt operated by knob from either side at all times.

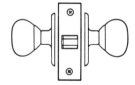

Type 11.72.

NOTE: This latch also available for doors 1⅜″ thick.

Function 73, Privacy and Inner Office Doors. Latch bolt operated by knob from either side. Dead bolt operated by thumb turn from inside.

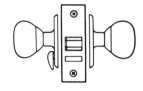

Type 11.73.

NOTE: This lock also available for doors 1⅜″ thick.

Function 74, Bath, Bedroom, and Other Doors. Latch bolt operated by knob from either side. Dead bolt operated by thumb turn inside and by emergency key outside.

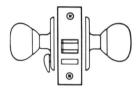

Type 11.74.

NOTE: This lock also available for doors 1⅜″ thick.

Function 75, Communicating Doors. Latch bolt operated by knob from either side. Two dead bolts or a split dead bolt operated independently by thumb turns from either side. Should not be used on doors in rooms that have no other entrance.

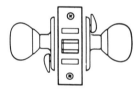

Type 11.75.

NOTE: This lock also available for doors 1⅜″ thick.

CHAPTER 12
Cylindrical and Tubular Locks and Latches (Bored Sets)

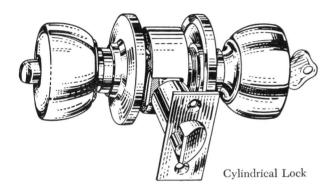

Cylindrical Lock

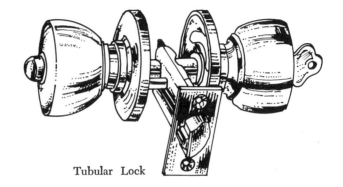

Tubular Lock

Cylindrical and tubular locks (or bored locks, as they both may be called) have won great popularity and wide acceptance. Incorporating the "key-in-knob" principle, and with it rapid installation features, it embodies a most acceptable product.

One lock manufacturer has recently introduced a lock combining cylinder and dead bolt functions that closely parallel the mortise lock dead bolt functions in Chapter 10. See pages 4 and 5 of this chapter.

They are available in a wide variety of backsets, 2⅜″, 2¾″, 3¾″, 5″, and longer by some manufacturers. Also available are ¾″ throw latches. The one drawback to this lock has been that it did not provide dead bolt functions. The alternative was to use an auxiliary dead bolt lock of tubular construction, so in this chapter such locks and latches are shown on page 6.

This type of lock comes in Grades 1, 2, and 3, except for some functions for which only Grade 1 locks should be used. For such functions, only Grade 1 is shown.

The type numbers for this chapter do not distinguish between cast and wrought trim, but such points can be established according to Step 2, Chapter 2, page 6.

Some manufacturers offer a lever handle option for some functions. Consult manufacturers' catalogues.

The 27 functions described here are those most often used in the trade. Still other functions can be found in catalogues.

All hollow metal doors should be reinforced for locks. The reinforcing unit is usually supplied by the door manufacturer, but in specifying a lock, one must know whether the H.M. door is so supplied or whether the unit must be supplied by the lock manufacturer and write the specification accordingly.

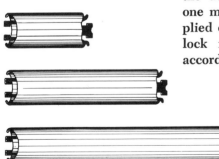

Connecting links provide a wide selection of backsets.

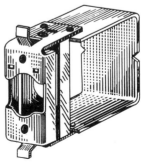

Reinforcing unit for hollow metal doors.

83

Cylindrical Locks and Latches

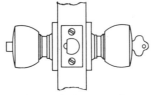

Function 76, Apartment Exits and Public Toilet Doors. Latch bolt operated by knob from either side except when outside knob is locked by inside key. When outside knob is locked, latch bolt may be retracted by outside key or by inside knob. Auxiliary dead latch.

Type 12.76.1.

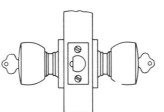

Function 77, Asylum and Utility Doors. Deadlocking latch bolt operated by key from either side. Both knobs always fixed.

Type 12.77.1.

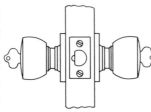

Function 78, Store and Other Doors. Deadlocking latch bolt operated by knob from either side except when both knobs are locked by key from either side.

Type 12.78.1.

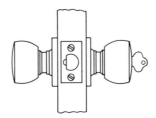

Function 79, Utility and Store Doors. Deadlocking latch bolt operated by outside key or by inside knob. Outside knob is always fixed.

Type 12.79.1.

Type 12.79.2.

Type 12.79.3.

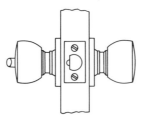

Function 80, Office and Other Entrances. Deadlocking latch bolt operated by knob from either side except when outside knob is locked by turn button in inside knob. Key in outside knob retracts latch bolt. Turn button must be manually rotated to unlock outside knob.

Type 12.80.1.

Type 12.80.2.

Type 12.80.3.

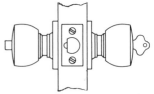

Function 81, Entrances and Corridor Doors. Deadlocking latch bolt operated by knob from either side except when outside knob is locked by push button in inside knob. Outside key or rotating inside knob releases push button except when slotted push button is turned to lock position. Closing door does not release push button. Inside knob always operates.

Type 12.81.1.

Type 12.81.2.

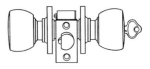

Function 82, Classroom and Other Doors. Deadlocking latch bolt operated by knob from either side except when outside knob is locked from outside by key. Inside knob always operative.

Type 12.82.1.

Type 12.82.2.

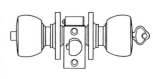

Function 83, Hotel and Motel Guestroom Doors. Deadlocking latch bolt operated by knob from inside at all times. Outside knob always fixed. Latch bolt operated by outside key except when inside push button is depressed, thus shutting out all keys except emergency key. Depressing push button operates visual indicator in face of cylinder, showing room is occupied. Turning inside knob or closing door releases indicator and shutout feature, except when push button is turned to shut-out position with special key, shutting out all keys except emergency key.

Type 12.83.1.

Type 12.83.2.

Type 12.83.3.

Cylindrical Locks and Latches (Continued)

Function 84, Office Doors. Deadlocking latch bolt operated by knob from either side except when outside knob is locked by push button in inside knob. Key outside retracts latch bolt and releases push button. Closing door does not release push button.

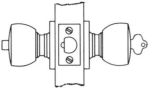

Type 12.84.1.

Type 12.84.2.

Type 12.84.3.

Function 85, Office Entrances and Exits. Deadlocking latch bolt operated by knob from either side except when outside knob is locked by turn button in inside knob. Turn button must be manually rotated to unlock outside knob.

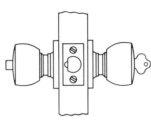

Type 12.85.1.

Type 12.85.2.

Type 12.85.3.

Function 86, Exits and Patio Doors. Deadlocking latch bolt retracted by inside knob at all times. Outside knob is always fixed.

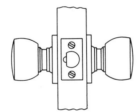

Type 12.86.1.

Type 12.86.2.

Type 12.86.3.

Function 87, Service Entrances and Exits. Deadlocking latch bolt operated by knob from either side except when outside knob is locked by inside push button. Outside key, inside knob, or closing door releases push button, unlocking outside knob, except when slotted push button is rotated to a locked position. Inside knob always operates.

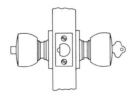

Type 12.87.1.

Type 12.87.2.

Function 88, Passage and Closet Doors. Latch bolt operated by knob from either side at all times. No lock.

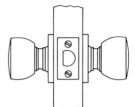

Type 12.88.1.

Type 12.88.2.

Type 12.88.3.

Function 89, Privacy and Inner Office Doors. Deadlocking latch bolt operated by knob from either side. Outside knob is locked by push button inside and unlocked by rotating inside knob or closing door.

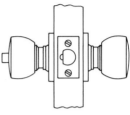

NOTE: Do not use on door when there is no other entrance to room.

Type 12.89.1.

Type 12.89.2.

Type 12.89.3.

Function 90, Bedroom Doors. Latch bolt operated by knob from either side. Outside knob is locked by push button inside and unlocked by emergency key outside and by rotating inside knob.

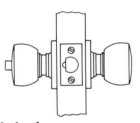

Type 12.90.1.

Type 12.90.2.

Type 12.90.3.

Function 91, Communicating Doors. Deadlocking latch bolt operated by knob from either side. Turn button in either knob locks or unlocks opposite knob. Should not be used on doors in rooms that have no other entrance.

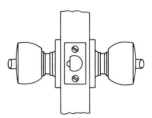

Type 12.91.1.

Type 12.91.2.

Cylindrical Lock Sets with Dead Bolt Functions

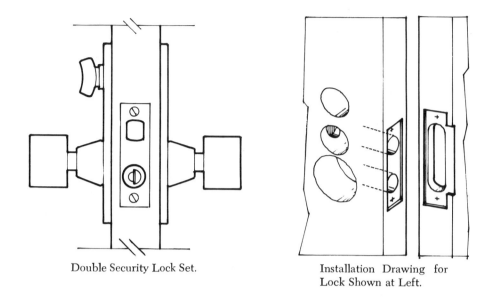

Double Security Lock Set.

Installation Drawing for
Lock Shown at Left.

This page and the next describe the cylinder lock sets that include the dead bolt function. Five functions are shown on the next page, but others will probably be made available. The locks are available in many designs and finishes. Consult manufacturers' catalogues.

Security Features

Cylinder lock sets with dead bolts have the following security features, according to the present manufacturer's catalogue:

1. Recessed cylinder discourages forceful removal.
2. Steel armor plate concealed under outside rose resists drilling.
3. When button of inside knob is positioned, outside key spins free, which prevents forced entry by application of a wrench to knob.
4. Latch unit gives combined protection of a dead bolt and deadlocking latch bolt.
5. Dead bolt projects 1″. It is made of solid brass with a concealed, hardened steel roller to resist sawing.

These recognized safety factors compare favorably with the long-proven 1″ throw bolts available in mortise locks shown in Chapter 10. With the increasing need for lock security, it is expected that other manufacturers will increasingly supply reinforced bolts with a 1″ throw.

Cylindrical Lock Sets with Dead Bolt Functions (Continued)

Function 92, Entrance and Office Doors. Deadlocking latch bolt is operated by knobs from either side except when outside knob is locked by inside push button. Dead bolt is operated by key outside and thumb turn inside. Inside knob or thumb turn retracts both bolts. Closing door does not release button.

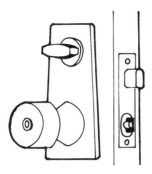

Type 12.92.1.

Function 93, Entrances and Office Doors. This is similar to Function 92 at left except that it uses a turn button in knob in place of a push button. Turning button on inside knob to a horizontal position locks outside knob. This button does not release until it is manually turned to vertical position.

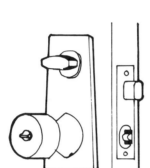

Type 12.93.1.

Function 94, Entrances and Office Doors. This is similar to Function 92 except that turning inside button to a horizontal position fixes outside knob.

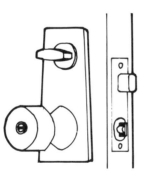

Type 12.94.1.

Function 95, Entrances and Office Doors. This function is similar to Function 94 at left except that closing the door automatically releases the button, which in effect then makes the outside knob operative until reset by the inside button.

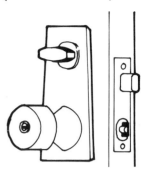

Type 12.95.1.

Function 96, Hotel and Motel Guestroom Doors. Turning inside knob will retract latch bolt. Outside knob is always fixed. Pushing button in thumb turn in horizontal position shuts out all keys except emergency key and extends an indicator button which provides a key stop inside the keyway that prevents guest or master key operation. Rotating inside knob or thumb turn releases button and shut-out feature automatically. Rotating thumb turn inside or key outside will throw the dead bolt to a locked position. Latch bolt automatically deadlocks when door is closed. With thumb turn in horizontal position, its button may be fixed in shut-out position by using a spanner key and turning to the right.

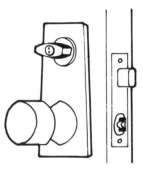

Keys for guest, maid, housekeeper, display, and emergency are similar to those for hotel-motel locks, Chapters 10 and 11, as required.

Type 12.96.1.

Auxiliary (Tubular) Locks and Latches

The auxiliary tubular locks shown below are often used in addition to a cylinder lock when the deadlock feature is required. In such cases, the hardware specifier may choose to have both locks keyed alike for double security, although more often a simple latch set such as that shown in Function 12.88 is used with the auxiliary.

These auxiliary locks are frequently used alone with no lock or latch below.

It is important that the backset of the auxiliary lock match that of the lock or latch below. The standard backset for years has been 2⅜″, but most manufacturers also provide locks with backsets of 2¾″ and 1¾″, the latter for doors with a narrow stile. The third part of the type number denotes the backset, not the grade. The quality is the same for all.

Function 97, 2-Cyl Dead Bolt. Dead bolt operated by key from either side. Bolt automatically deadlocks when fully thrown.

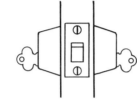

Type 12.97.1. 2¾″ BS.

Type 12.97.2. 2⅜″ BS.

Type 12.97.3. 1¾″ BS.

Function 98, 1-Cyl w. Thumb Turn and Dead Bolt. Dead bolt operated by outside key and by thumb turn inside. Bolt automatically deadlocks when fully thrown.

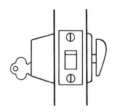

Type 12.98.1. 2¾″ BS.

Type 12.98.2. 2⅜″ BS.

Type 12.98.3. 1¾″ BS.

Function 99, Cyl One Side Only w. Dead Bolt. Dead bolt operated by key outside. Blank plate inside. Bolt automatically deadlocks when fully thrown.

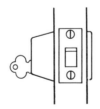

Type 12.99.1. 2¾″ BS.

Type 12.99.2. 2⅜″ BS.

Type 12.99.3. 1¾″ BS.

Function 100, 2-Cyl Spring Latch. Deadlocking latch bolt operated by key from either side.

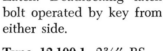

Type 12.100.1. 2¾″ BS.

Type 12.100.2. 2⅜″ BS.

Type 12.100.3. 1¾″ BS.

Function 101, Cyl w. Thumb Turn and Spring Latch. Deadlocking latch bolt operated by outside key and thumb turn inside. Latch bolt may be held retracted by slide on thumb turn plate.

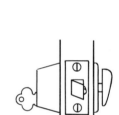

Type 12.101.1. 2¾″ BS.

Type 12.101.2. 2⅜″ BS.

Type 12.101.3. 1¾″ BS.

Function 102, Classroom Deadlock. Deadlocking latch bolt operated by outside key. Thumb turn inside will retract latch bolt but will not lock it.

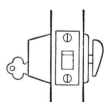
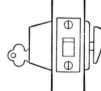

Type 12.102.1. 2¾″ BS.

Type 12.102.2. 2⅜″ BS.

Type 12.102.3. 1¾″ BS.

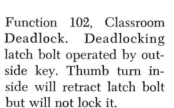
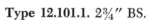

CHAPTER 13

Special Purpose and Non-Standardized Locks and Latches

While the majority of lock requirements for any building is covered in Chapters 10, 11, and 12, there remains a category of special purpose locks for which there is a continuing demand. Such locks are described in this chapter. Special purpose and non-standardized locks and latches of every kind continue to be listed in the catalogues, but it is neither feasible nor desirable to include them in this handbook.

Design and finish may be specified by the addition of option numbers as given in Chapter 10, page 6. The only exceptions to this are instances such as Type 13.13.1, where the 1 specifies the finish.

Page 2

Non-Standardized Locks (mortise and rim) for Residential Use. Other mortise locks are described in Chapter 10.

Page 3

Classroom Deadlock, Night Latch, Sliding Door Lock, Jimmy-Proof Lock, and Padlock. These are less frequently used but are still specified in many instances.

Page 4

Locks for Narrow-Stile Glass Doors, Hinged and Sliding. The increased use of glass doors in aluminum frames has challenged door manufacturers to supply locks that are secure despite the narrow stile; backsets may be as short as $\frac{7}{8}''$.

Page 5

Emergency Exit Locks and Alarms. Strength and reliability are prime requisites for these items. Still more sophisticated locks and alarm systems than those shown are continually being developed and made available.

Page 6

Drawer and Cupboard Locks with Pin Tumbler. Shown is just a small sample of the great variety of this type of lock available. The specifier should consult manufacturers' catalogues in order to provide a specification that is exact and complete. Drawer and cupboard locks can be keyed into a building's Master Key System.

Non-Standardized Locks for Residential Use

Function 1, Latch Only. Latch operated by knob from either side at all times.

Type 13.1.1.
Dble Sprg, Ex Hvy.

Type 13.1.2.
Sgle Sprg, Hvy.

Type 13.1.3.
Sgle Sprg, Lt Steel Face.

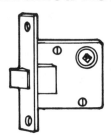

Function 2, Bit Key. Latch operated by knob from either side. Bolt operated by bit key from either side.

Type 13.2.1.
3 Tumblers, Dble Compression Sprg.

Type 13.2.2.
1 Tumbler, Easy Compression Sprg.

Type 13.2.3.
1 Tumbler, Steel Face.

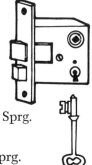

Type 3, Bath or Privacy Door. Latch operated by knob from either side. Dead bolt operated by turn knob inside and by emergency key outside.

Type 13.3.1.
Dble Compression Sprg.

Type 13.3.2.
Easy Compression Sprg.

Type 13.3.3
Steel Face.

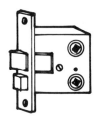

Function 4, Communicating Door. Latch operated by knob from either side. The split bolt is operated independently by thumb turns one side—two turns with each lock.

Type 13.4.1.
Dble Compression Sprg.

Type 13.4.2.
Easy Compression Sprg.

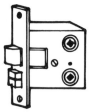

Function 5, French Doors. Latch operated by lever one side and by knob other side. Button in face locks out side trim. Dead bolt operated by key outside and by thumb turn inside. Other functions available. Consult manufacturers' catalogues.

Type 13.5.1.
1½" or 1¾" BS.

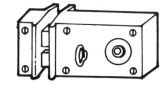

Function 6, Ornamental Brass Rimlock. Latch operated by knob either side except when outside knob is locked by stop in face, then latch operated by key outside and by knob inside. Dead bolt operated by key outside and by thumb turn inside. Also available with dummy trim for pairs of doors.

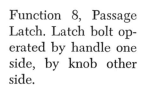

Function 7, Passage Latch. Latch bolt operated by handle from either side.

Type 13.7.1.

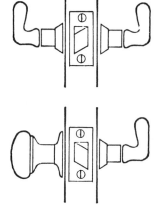

Function 8, Passage Latch. Latch bolt operated by handle one side, by knob other side.

Type 13.8.1.

Classroom Deadlock, Night Latch, Sliding Door Lock, Jimmy-Proof Lock, and Padlock

To specify grade, follow type number with Option -1 for Ex Hvy (hardened steel pins embedded in bolt), -2 for Hvy, or -3 for Std.

Function 9, Mortise Deadlock.

Type 13.9.1.
  2 Cyl.

Type 13.9.2.
  1 Cyl, 1 Thumb Turn.

Type 13.9.3.
  1 Cyl Only.

Function 10, Mortise Classroom Deadlock. Cylinder outside, thumb turn inside. To prevent accidental lock-in, thumb turn operates only when door is locked by key outside.

Type 13.10.1.

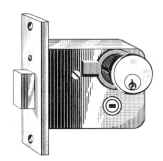

Function 11, Mortise Cylinder Night Latch. Latch bolt operated by outside key and inside thumb turn. Auxiliary latch deadlocks main latch. When not locked, stop in face holds latches retracted.

Type 13.11.1.

Function 12, Mortise Cylinder Sliding Door Lock.

Type 13.12.1.
  Split hook bolt operated by keys from either side.

Type 13.12.2.
  Same as 13.12.1. but bolt operated by key from one side only.

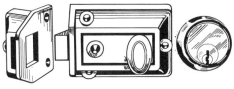

Function 13, Rim Night Latch w. Cylinder. Latch bolt operated by key outside and thumb turn inside. Sliding button on case holds latch retracted. Available also with reverse bevel for doors that open out. Hardware supplier must furnish proper strike.

Type 13.13.1. All Bronze Case.

Type 13.13.2. Cast Iron Case.

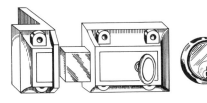

Function 14, Rim Deadlock w. Cylinder. Same operation as Function 13 except deadlock instead of latch bolt, and must be manually locked.

Type 13.14.1. Cast Iron Case.

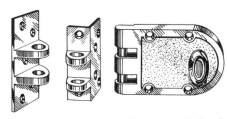

Function 15, Jimmy-Proof Rim Lock. Vertical dead bolts made of hardened steel.

Type 13.15.1. Cyl Both Sides.

Type 13.15.2. Cyl Outside, Thumb Turn Inside.

Function 16, Padlock. Type number indicates Padlock. Type, size, and material must be specified. Type shown is cylinder, with pin tumblers. Available in larger sizes for keying into Master Key System. Usual case sizes are 1½″, 1¾″, and 2″. Materials may be solid or reinforced brass, laminated case, steel, or stainless steel. Shackle may be of hardened steel. To include a chain, add -C to type number.

Type 13.16.1.

Locks for Narrow-Stile Glass Doors, Hinged and Sliding

Function 17, 3-Point Lock, for Pairs of Hinged Doors. Key on either side, or key on one side and thumb turn on the other, operates (1) a deadlocking bolt horizontally into opposite door, (2) a vertical drop bolt into threshold or floor, and (3) a positioner bolt upward into the header. Inactive leaf has positioner bolt.

Type 13.17.1.
  2 Cylinders.

Type 13.17.2.
  1 Cylinder, 1 Thumb Turn.

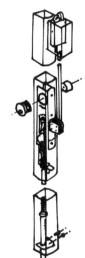

Function 18, 2-Point Lock, for Pairs of Hinged Doors. Key on either side, or key on one side and thumb turn on the other, operates (1) a deadlocking bolt horizontally into opposite door and (2) a vertical drop bolt into threshold or floor. Inactive leaf has positioner bolt into header.

Type 13.18.1.
  2 Cylinders.

Type 13.18.2.
  1 Cylinder, 1 Thumb Turn.

Function 19, 1-Point Deadlock, for Single Hinged Door. Key on either side, or key on one side and thumb turn on the other, operates pivoted or conventional deadlocking bolt into jamb. Backsets from ⅞″ to 1½″. Consult manufacturer's catalogue.

Type 13.19.1.
  2 Cylinders.

Type 13.19.2.
  1 Cylinder, 1 Thumb Turn.

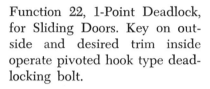

Function 20, 1-Point Dead Latch, for Single Hinged Door. Outside key and inside lever operate latch bolt. Auxiliary dead latch. Latch bolts may be held retracted. Available with electric strike.

Type 13.20.1.

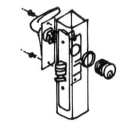

Function 21, 1-Point Deadlock, for Sliding Doors. Key on either side operates pivoted hook type deadlocking bolt.

Type 13.21.1.

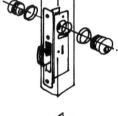

Function 22, 1-Point Deadlock, for Sliding Doors. Key on outside and desired trim inside operate pivoted hook type deadlocking bolt.

Type 13.22.1.

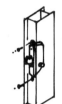

Emergency Exit Locks and Alarms

This hardware performs the functions of sounding an alarm upon door opening in an emergency and upon unauthorized opening at other times. All types shown except the Exit Alarm also keep the door locked from the outside. With the power to the alarm turned off, the door-opening "panic bar" serves only as a means of exit.

The alarm horns for all the devices can be located remotely or directly on the door, and all devices can be wired to show operation and location on a remote indicating panel. The power is supplied by batteries for a door-located alarm horn or from a low-voltage system off the main power supply.

In order to be assured of doors with a high degree of security from breaking in and reliable operation in emergencies, the specifier should consider only those approved by a nationally recognized independent testing laboratory and by Underwriters Laboratories, Inc.

Exit Alarm. This alarm can be used with or without outside door key control. The alarm can be silenced for authorized exit or entry by means of an on-off key or by electronic delay circuitry. For doors that open out, the alarm is mounted on the door. For doors that open in, it can be mounted on door or frame. Size: approximately 11″ long, 2″ deep, 3″ wide.

Type 13.23.

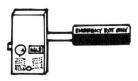

Exit Control or Exit, Single Door, Short Bar. Has "short" (less than door width) panic bar with push plate or paddle, and can be mounted directly on latch side. The dead bolt enters a keeper which can be either mortised or surface mounted, and which can be furnished with a microswitch for providing a signal. For doors opening out or in. Size: minimum 9″ high, 3″ deep, 18″ wide.

Type 13.24.

Exit Control or Exit, Single Door, Long Bar. Has panic bar that extends across the door, and is mounted on door at both sides. Size depends on door width. Otherwise same as 13.24.

Type 13.25.

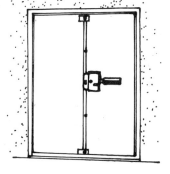

Exit Control or Exit, Double Door, Short Bar on One Door. Has vetrical rod assembly on active door and overlap plates on inactive door. Both doors open when lock is released. Otherwise same as 13.24.

Type 13.26.

Exit Control or Exit, Double Door, Long Bar on One Door. Has vertical rod assembly on active door and overlap plates on inactive door. Both doors open when lock is released. Otherwise same as 13.25.

Type 13.27.

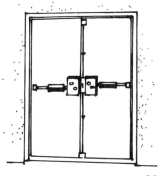

Exit Control or Exit, Double Door, Short Bar on Both Doors. Has vertical rod assembly on active door with double-door keeper plate. Inactive door also has exit device 13.24 without vertical rod assembly. Otherwise same as 13.24.

Type 13.28.

Exit Control or Exit, Double Door, Long Bar on Both Doors. Has vertical rod assembly on active door with double-door keeper plate. Inactive door also has exit device 13.25 with vertical rod assembly. Otherwise same as 13.25.

Type 13.29.

Drawer and Cupboard Locks with Pin Tumbler

Function 30, Drawer Lock, Large. Key projects and retracts dead bolt. 4 pins for $\frac{7}{8}$″ cylinder. 5 pins for $1\frac{1}{8}$″ cylinder. 5 pins (minimum) for $1\frac{3}{8}$″ cylinder.

Type 13.30.

Function 31, Drawer Lock. Key Projects and Retracts Dead Bolt. 5 pins (minimum).

Type 13.31.

Function 32, Cupboard Door Lock. Key projects and retracts dead bolt. 4 pins for $\frac{3}{4}$″ cylinder. 5 pins for $\frac{7}{8}$″ cylinder. 5 pins (minimum) for $1\frac{1}{8}$″ cylinder.

Type 13.32.

Function 33, Cupboard Door Lock. Key projects and retracts dead bolt. 5 pins (minimum).

Type 13.33.

Function 34, Lock for Bypassing Cupboard Doors. Bolt pushes in to engage and interlock with strike, which is furnished. Key is removable in locked and unlocked positions. 5 pins (minimum).

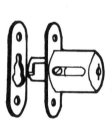

Type 13.34.

Function 35, Cam Lock. Key rotates cam 90° or 180° (specify). Key removable in locked or unlocked position. Cam fastened by screw or hex nut. 4 pins for $\frac{5}{8}$″ cylinder. 5 pins (minimum) for cylinders over $\frac{5}{8}$″.

Type 13.35.

Function 36, Cam Lock. Key rotates cam 90° or 180° (specify). Key removable only in locked position. Cam fastened with nut. 4 pins for $\frac{5}{8}$″ cylinder. 5 pins for 1″ cylinder. 5 pins for $1\frac{3}{16}$″ cylinder.

Type 13.36.

Function 37, Cam Lock. Key rotates cam 90°. Key removable in locked position only. Specify as to whether for right or left-hand door. 4 pins (minimum).

Type 13.37.

CHAPTER 14
Exit Devices

No item of door hardware is more important, from a standpoint of safety, than exit devices, discussed in this chapter, and exit locks with alarms, described in Chapter 13, page 5. We are therefore considering only such hardware as is rated Class A by the National Bureau of Fire Underwriters, products that fully meet safety standards. Other items with lower class ratings, such as paddle openers (as opposed to cross-bar openers), may be found listed in manufacturers' catalogues.

When exit devices are used on labeled fire doors, such devices cannot incorporate any dogging feature to lock the cross-bar down, although this fea-ture is usually found on unlabeled doors. Rather than list the presence of a latch dogger as separate functions, we will just suggest that the specifier make certain that the supplier omit any dogging device when outfitting labeled fire doors.

Four categories of exit devices are shown below —rim, mortise, vertical, and concealed—and the functions available in each are described on pages 2 and 3. The category is shown in the third part of the type number, so that Function 4 in the rim category would appear as 14.4.1, with options following, as described on page 5.

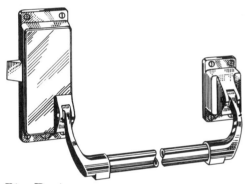

Rim Device

Types 14.1.1 through 14.8.1

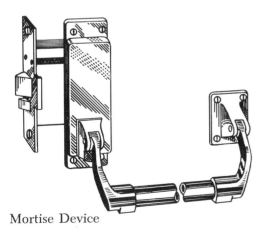

Mortise Device

Types 14.1.2 through 14.8.2

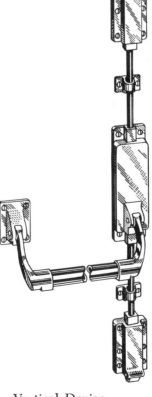

Vertical Device

Types 14.1.3, 14.3.3, 14.7.3, and 14.8.3

Concealed Device

Types 14.1.4, 14.7.4, and 14.8.4

Exit Device Type Numbers,
Showing Functions and Available Options

Type Number	Options Available	Description	Type Number	Options Available	Description
14.1.1	-1-5-6	Rim Device, No Outside Trim	14.3.3	-1-4-5 -6	Vertical Device, Outside Cyl and Knob w. Esc
14.2.1	-1-2-3 -5-6	Rim Device, Cyl Outside Only	14.5.3	-1-4-5 -6	Vertical Device, Cyl and Hdle w. TP Outside
14.3.1	-1-2-3 -4-5-6	Rim Device, Outside Cyl and Knob w. Escutcheon (Esc)	14.8.3	-1-4-5 -6	Vertical Device, Hdle Outside (No Cyl or TP)
14.4.1	-1-2-3 -4-5-6	Rim Device, Cyl and Knob w. Esc Outside, Cyl Inside	14.1.4	-1-5	Concealed Device, No Outside Trim
14.5.1	-1-2-3 -4-5-6	Rim Device, Cyl and Hdle w. Thumbpiece (TP) Outside	14.7.4	-1-5-4	Concealed Device, Outside Cyl and Hdle (No TP)
14.6.1	-1-2-3 -4-5-6	Rim Device, Cyl and Hdle w. TP Outside, Cyl Inside	14.8.4	-1-4-5	Concealed Device, Hdle Outside (No Cyl or TP)
14.7.1	-1-2-3 -4-5-6	Rim Device, Cyl and Hdle Outside (No TP)	14.9		Removable Mullion, Steel
14.8.1	-1-2-3 -4-5-6	Rim Device, Hdle Outside (No Cyl or TP)	14.10		Removable Mullion, Stainless Steel
14.1.2	-1-5-6	Mortise Device, No Outside Trim	14.11		Removable Mullion, Aluminum
14.2.2	-1-2-3 -5-6	Mortise Device, Cyl Outside Only	14.12		Compensating Astragal, for Wood Doors
14.3.2	-1-2-3 -4-5-6	Mortise Device, Outside Cyl and Knob w. Esc	14.13		Compensating Astragal, of Extruded Bronze, for Metal or Wood Doors
14.4.2	-1-2-3 -4-5-6	Mortise Device, Cyl and Knob w. Esc Outside, Cyl Inside	14.14		Compensating Astragal, of Extruded Aluminum, for Metal or Wood Doors
14.5.2	-1-2-3 -4-5-6	Mortise Device, Cyl and Hdle w. TP Outside	14.15		Astragal Coordinator for Pair of Doors
14.6.2	-1-2-3 -4-5-6	Mortise Device, Cyl and Hdle w. TP Outside, Cyl Inside	14.16		Threshold for Pair of Concealed Doors
14.7.2	-1-2-3 -4-5-6	Mortise Device, Cyl and Hdle Outside (No TP)	14.17		Threshold for Latching Type Door
14.8.2	-1-2-3 -4-5-6	Mortise Device, Hdle Outside (No Cyl or Tp)	14.18		Exit Device for 1 Dr of a Pr of 2-Way drs w. Smoke Control Releases
14.1.3	-1-5-6	Vertical Device, No Outside Trim			

Exit Device Functions

Rim Functions

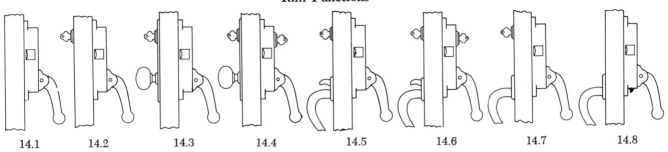

14.1   14.2   14.3   14.4   14.5   14.6   14.7   14.8

Mortise Functions

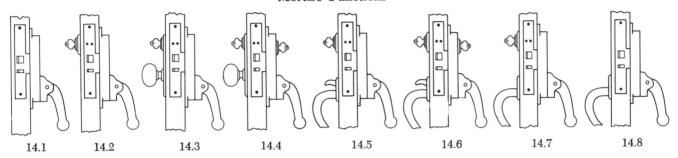

14.1   14.2   14.3   14.4   14.5   14.6   14.7   14.8

Vertical Functions

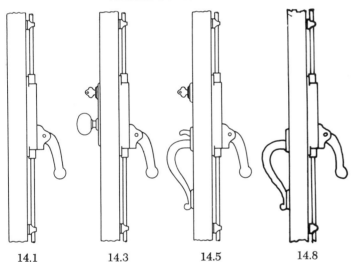

14.1   14.3   14.5   14.8

Concealed Functions

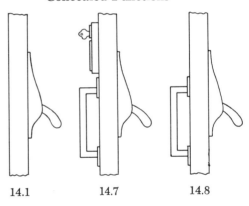

14.1   14.7   14.8

Description of Lock Functions

1. No outside trim.
2. Cylinder outside only. Key operates latch.
3. Cylinder and knob with escutcheon outside. Key operates latch. Knob retracts latch, except when locked by key.
4. Two cylinders and knob with escutcheon outside. Knob retracts latch, except when locked from inside; then key outside retracts latch, but knob remains locked.
5. Cylinder and handle outside. Handle thumbpiece retracts latch, except when locked by key.

6. Two cylinders and handle outside. Handle thumbpiece retracts latch, except when latch is deadlocked by key inside; then key outside retracts latch, but thumbpiece remains locked.
7. Cylinder and handle pull outside (no thumbpiece). Latch is retracted by key outside. Handle pull is used only when latch is held retracted by dogging mechanism.
8. Handle pull outside (no thumbpiece). Inoperative from outside except when latch is held retracted by dogging device.

97

Exit Device Accessories and Options

Thresholds for exit devices are described in Chapter 9, page 3.

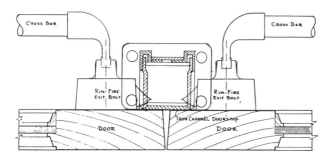

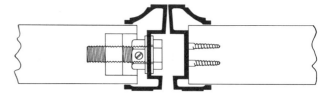

Removable Pipe Mullion. Channel-bar door stop takes the place of the standard split astragal. The channel bar, or pipe, mullion is easily and quickly removed from its fastenings at head and sill when a full double-door opening is wanted. This mullion uses standard rim fire-exit bolts, eliminating the use of double-door fire exit bolts. It does not require dead-locking or vertical top and bottom bolts, since each door can be opened independently.

Channel-bar Mullion, Removable. For use w. Pr of Drs. Rim exit devices recommended for use w. mullion. The view above is from the top. The view at the right is from inside, with doors open.

Type 14.9. Steel Mullion.

Type 14.10. Stainless Steel Mullion.

Type 14.11. Aluminum Mullion.

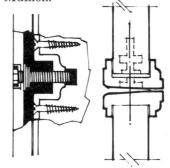

Compensating Astragal for Wood Doors, Rim Functions.

Type 14.12.

Compensating Astragal for Metal or Wood Doors. Astragal of Extruded Bronze.

Type 14.13.

Compensating Astragal for Wood or Metal Doors. Astragal of Extruded Aluminum.

Type 14.14.

▲ NOTE: Compensating astragals are intended for use only with rim type devices.

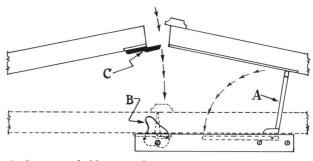

A. Stop arm—holds active door.
B. Releasing lever—permits inactive door to close first, then releases A.
C. Bolt protector—required only when latch bolt projects beyond astragal.

Coordinator for Pr of Drs when Astragal is used.

Type 14.15.

NOTE: Use of a coordinator should be avoided, if possible. One combination that does not require a coordinator is the mortise device 14.2.2 with the vertical device 14.3.3.

Two vertical devices should not be used when one door has an astragal, because the astragal prevents exit through the inactive door until the active door is opened.

Option Key

-1 Reinforcement for tubular crossbars. Should always be used for bars over 3′ wide.
-2 Hold-open back strike. Occasionally required.
-3 Electric strike.
-4 Special design. Should be described.
-5 Non-standard crossbar height. Example: low bars for kindergartens, grade schools.

-6 Sex bolts through-mounted for rim exit devices.
-7 No latch-dogging device. For use with exit devices for Class A and B labeled fire doors when dogging device regularly would be present.

Exit Devices for Two-Way Double Doors

There is an increasing need for double-door exit devices that provide escape in either direction. Such a need may exist, especially in schools, hotels, hospitals, and wherever both sides must be accessible from the other.

At least one manufacturer has received UL approval of his B and C labeled doors.

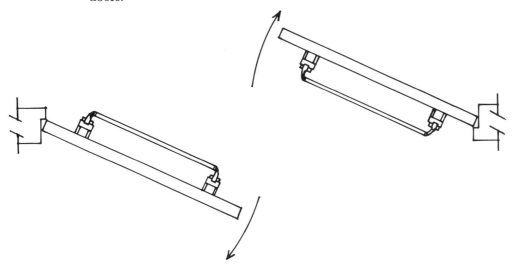

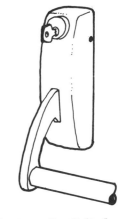

Exit Device for 1 Dr of a Pr of Two-Way Drs w. Smoke Control Release (one release for each door).

Type 14.18.

Option -8. Cylinder and Bar Lockdown. Turn of key holds down bar and keeps latch retracted. Available from some mfrs. w. several functions.

A hinged crossbar, illustrated below, is available in several of the functions shown on page 3.

To specify the hinged crossbar, select the type number, which indicates the function and category of opener, add -HCB, and then add also the manufacturer's catalogue number.

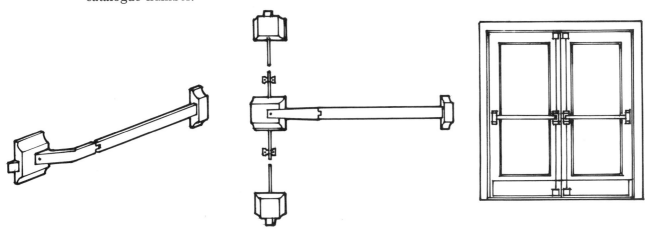

Hinged crossbar used as a rim device (left) and a vertical device (center), and on a pair of doors with vertical latches (right).

CHAPTER 15

Door Closers

All door closers, as the term is used here, close the door at a controlled speed and have no hinge or pivot function. Checking (door-closing) hinges and pivots are discussed in Chapter 9 (and on page 4 of Chapter 15). When door closers are specified, regular hinges (Chapter 7) must be specified separately.

The recommended closer sizes in the table below are for operation under normal conditions. For special conditions—involving, say, drafts, wind, lead-lined doors, or parallel-arm operation—use the closer manufacturer's recommended size.

The descriptions in this chapter are for single acting closers unless double acting is specified.

Closers are usually spray painted to match the color of the other door hardware. Matching plated finishes are available, but they cost more. Solid bronze closers are occasionally specified, particularly for government projects and when the atmosphere is damp or corrosive, as in marine use.

Information and items to be specified include:

1. Type of closer
2. Method of attachment (e.g., sex bolts)
3. Type of bracket
4. Parallel arm or regular arm
5. Mortised or surface mounted
6. Adjustable checking action or not
7. For left-hand or right-hand door
8. Hold-open feature or not
9. Single acting or double acting

Recommended Closer Size

Closer Size	Amount of Use	Maximum Dimensions Exterior	Maximum Dimensions Interior
II	Light. Only for storm or screen doors	3'0" x 7'0" x 1⅜"	2'8" x 7'0" x 1¾"
III	Standard duty	2'6" x 7'0" x 1¾"	3'4" x 7'0" x 1¾"
IV	Standard duty	3'0" x 7'0" x 1¾"	4'0" x 7'0" x 1¾"
V	Heavy duty	3'6" x 7'0" x 1¾"	4'0" x 7'0" x 1¾"
VI	Extra heavy duty	4'0" x 7'0" x 2¼"	4'0" x 8'0" x 2¼"

The construction, design, and appearance of the door closer and the limit of its closing speed control are important. Another feature provided by many manufacturers is back-check control, which cushions the force of the opening door. This control may be adjustable. Consult manufacturers' catalogues to determine whether this feature is provided.

Types of Door Closers and Available Options

Type No.	Description	Options Available
15.1	Standard Design, Surface Mounted, Arm Regular	-1-2-4-5-6-7-8-9-11-12-13-14-15-17
15.2	Standard Design, Surface Mounted, Arm Parallel	-1-3-4-5-6-7-8-10
15.3	Modern Design, Surface Mounted, Arm Regular, With Cover	-1-2-4-9-11-12-16-18
15.4	Modern Design, Surface Mounted, Arm Regular, No Cover	-1-2-4-8-11-12-16-18
15.5	Modern Design, Surface Mounted, Arm Parallel, With Cover	-1-3-4-10
15.6	Modern Design, Surface Mounted, Arm Parallel, No Cover	-1-3-4-10
15.7	Modern Design, Mounted on Head of Frame, With Cover	-1-2-4-9
15.8	Concealed in Door, Interior Doors Only, Surface Shoe	-1-2-4-9
15.9	Concealed in Door, Interior Doors Only, Mortise Soffit Plate	-1-2-4-9
15.10	Overhead Concealed, Exposed Arm, for Butt-Hung Doors	-1-2-4-9
15.11	Overhead Concealed, Exposed Arm, for Offset-Pivot-Hung Doors	-1-2-4-9
15.12	Overhead Concealed, Concealed Arm, for Butt-Hung Doors	-1-2-4-9
15.13	Overhead Concealed, Concealed Arm, for Offset-Pivot-Hung Doors	-1-2-4-9
15.14	Overhead Concealed, Concealed Arm, for Center-Pivoted Doors	-1-2
15.15	Overhead Concealed, Concealed Arm, for Center-Pivoted Doors, Double Acting	
15.16	For Screen and Storm Doors, Hydraulic Control Adjustable, Needs 3⅝″ Clearance From Main Door, Standard Design	-1-2-4
15.17	For Screen and Storm Doors, Hydraulic Control Adjustable, Needs 3⅝″ Clearance From Main Door, Modern Design	-1-2-4
15.18	Closing Pivot for Gate or Dwarf Doors, Hydraulic Control Adjustable, Single or Double Acting, Surface Mounted	
15.19	Closing Pivot for Gate or Dwarf Doors, Hydraulic Control Adjustable, Single or Double Acting, Mortised	
15.20	Closing Hinge for Light, Interior Doors, Hydraulic Control Adjustable, Single Acting, Mortised	
15.21	Covered Helical Spring Closer for Screen or Storm Doors, Pneumatic Checking Action Adjustable, Outside Diameter of Tube 1¼″ Minimum	

Types of Door Closers—Illustrated

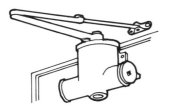

Standard Design, Surface Mounted, Arm Regular

Type 15.1.

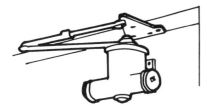

Standard Design, Surface Mounted, Arm Parallel

Type 15.2.

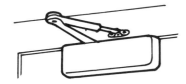

Modern Design, Surface Mounted, Arm Regular

Type 15.3. With Cover.

Type 15.4. No Cover.

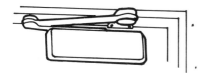

Modern Design, Surface Mounted, Arm Parallel

Type 15.5. With Cover.

Type 15.6. No Cover.

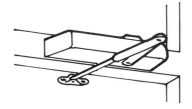

Modern Design, Mounted on Head of Frame, With Cover

Type 15.7.

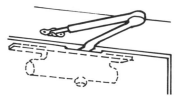

Concealed in Door, Interior Doors Only

Type 15.8. Surface Shoe.

Type 15.9. Mortise Soffit Plate.

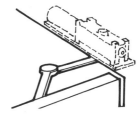

Overhead Concealed, Exposed Arm

Type 15.10. For Butt-Hung Doors.

Type 15.11. For Offset-Pivot-Hung Doors.

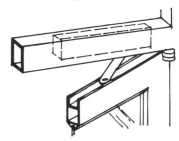

Overhead Concealed, Concealed Arm

Type 15.12. For Butt-Hung Doors.

Type 15.13. For Offset-Pivot-Hung Doors.

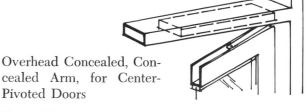

Overhead Concealed, Concealed Arm, for Center-Pivoted Doors

Type 15.14.

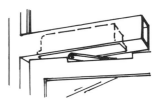

Overhead Concealed, Concealed Arm, for Center-Pivoted Doors, Double Acting

Type 15.15.

Closers for Light Doors—Options -1 to -4

For Screen and Storm Doors, Hydraulic Action Adjustable, Standard Design. Needs 3⅝" Clearance from Main Door

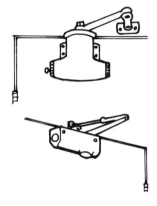

Type 15.16.
Standard Design.

Type 15.17.
Modern Design.

Options

Available as Noted on Page 2

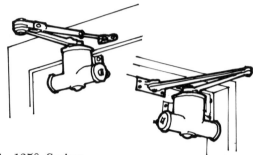

Closing Pivot for Gate or Dwarf Doors, Hydraulic Control Adjustable, Single or Double Acting, Surface Mounted

Type 15.18.

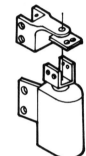

Option -1. 135° Swing.

Option -2. 180° Swing.
Holder Arm Optional With Regulating Adjustment, Arm Regular

Closing Pivot for Gate or Dwarf Doors, Hydraulic Control Adjustable, Single or Double Acting, Mortised

Type 15.19

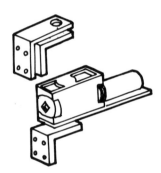

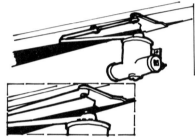

Option -3
Extension Foot, Holder Arm Optional With Regulating Adjustment, Arm Parallel

Closing Hinge for Light, Interior Doors, Hydraulic Control Adjustable, Single Acting, Mortised

Type 15.20.

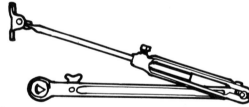

Option -4
180° Swing, Arm Regular, Corner Bracket Required in Many Instances, see manufacturers' catalogues

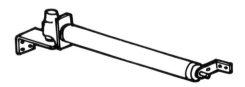

Covered Helical Spring Closer for Screen or Storm Doors, Pneumatic Checking Action Adjustable, Outside Diameter of Tube 1¼" Minimum

Type 15.21.

Options -5 to -18 for Door Closers

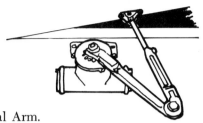

Option -5. Hospital Arm.
Two-Point Hold at Approx. 10° and 45°

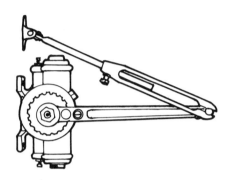

Option -6. Coupon Booth Arm.
One-Point Ventilation Hold When Set by Attendant

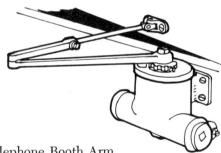

Option -7. Telephone Booth Arm.
One-Point Automatic Hold Open

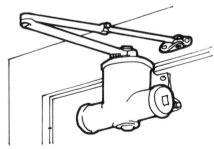

Option -8. Delayed Action.
Momentary Hold-Open Before Checked Closing
Action. For any Regular Type Closer

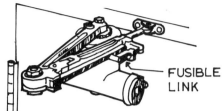

Option -9.
Fusible Link, Arm Regular.
When temperature rises to 160°, link fuses, releasing holder. Must have UL listing.

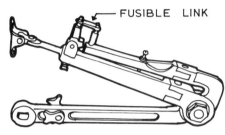

Option -10. Fusible Link, Arm Parallel.
When temperature rises to 160°, link fuses, releasing holder. Must have UL listing.

Option -11.
Corner Bracket With 135° Opening.

Option -12.
Corner Bracket for 180° Opening.

Option -13.
Soffit Bracket for 135° Opening.

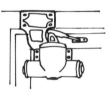

Option -14.
Flush Bracket.

Option -15.
Drop Plate Affixed to Door for
Standard Closer.

Option -16.
Drop Plate Affixed to Door for Modern Closer.

Option -17.
Drop Plate Affixed to Door for
Standard Closer.

Option -18.
Drop Plate Affixed to Door for Modern Closer.

Specifying Closers and Other Hardware for Arched Doors

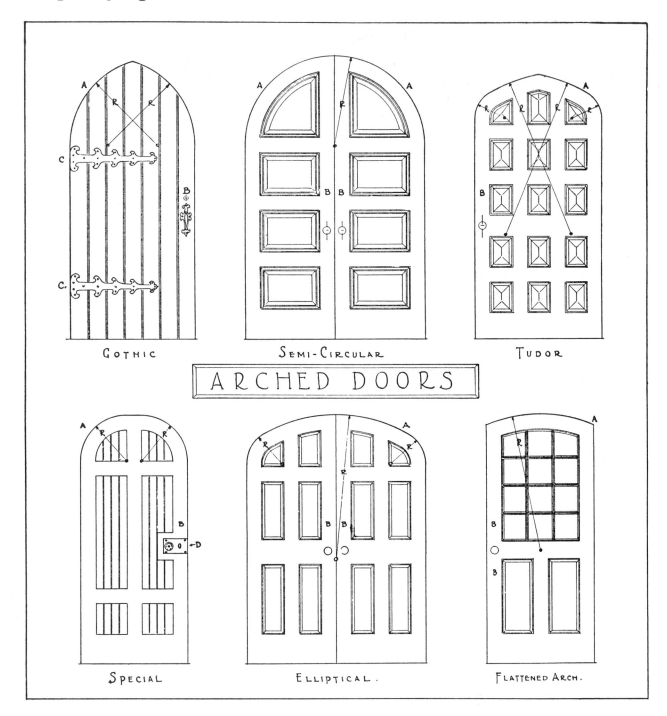

A. To specify door closers and brackets for arched doors, send to hardware manufacturer details of door and jamb sizes including radii (mark R).

B. Specify width and thickness of stile.

C. When hinge plates (top left) are required, specify door width. Plate length is usually two-thirds of door width.

D. Locks with deep backset (bottom left) may be used with box-type doors, flush-panel doors, or on cross rails.

CHAPTER 16

Architectural Trim

Pull Bars, Push Bars, Kick Plates, Mop Plates

Extended Pull Bar with Pull Grip extending to bottom rail of door. The Pull Grip is attached to the Cross Bars. Non-ferrous. Available in other designs.

Type 16.1.

Pull Bars and Push Bars in Matching Set. Used back to back. Double Bars both sides. Pull Grip attached to Cross Bars on one side only. Non-ferrous. Available in other designs.

Type 16.2.

Pull Bars and Push Bars in Matching Set, Contemporary Design. Used back to back. Double Bars both sides. Pull Grip, for one side only, may be omitted. Non-ferrous. Other designs available.

Type 16.3.

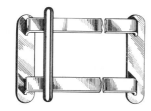

Name and Number Plates

Type 16.27.1. Horizontal Name Plate.

Type 16.27.2. Vertical Name Plate.

Type 16.28. Horizontal Number Plate.

Type 16.29.1. Individual Digits, Plain.

Type 16.29.2. Individual Digits, Ornamental.

Name and number plates are available and can be specially made in a variety of dimensions, materials and weights, including cast bronze, with lettering in contrasting color. Aluminum and plastic plates also available. Consult manufacturers' catalogues.

Double Bars for Double Acting Doors. Used back to back. Non-ferrous.

Type 16.4.

Same as 16.4 but Single Bars. Other designs available.

Type 16.5.

Armor Plate, Beveled 3 sides. Specify height. Width is of Sgle Dr less 2″ (for Stops), of Pr of Drs less 1″.

Type 16.6. Non-ferrous, 16 Ga.

Type 16.7. Non-ferrous, 14 Ga.

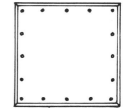

Type 16.8. Stainless Steel, 16 Ga.
Type 16.9. Stainless Steel, 14 Ga.
Type 16.10. Aluminum, 16 Ga.
Type 16.11. ⅛″ Plastic (choice of color).
Type 16.12. Same as 16.6 but ⅛″ Plain Steel Finish 671.

Kick Plate. Specify height, usually 8″, 10″, or 12″.

Type 16.13. Non-ferrous, 16 Ga.
Type 16.14. Non-ferrous, 14 Ga.
Type 16.15. Stainless Steel, 16 Ga.
Type 16.16. Stainless Steel, 14 Ga.
Type 16.17. Aluminum, 16 Ga.
Type 16.18. ⅛″ Plastic (choice of color).
Type 16.19. Same as 16.13 but ⅛″ Plain Steel Finish 671.

Mop Plate. Specify height, usually 4″.

Type 16.20. Non-ferrous, 16 Ga.
Type 16.21. Non-ferrous, 14 Ga.
Type 16.22. Stainless Steel, 16 Ga.
Type 16.23. Stainless Steel, 14 Ga.
Type 16.24. Aluminum, 16 Ga.
Type 16.25. ⅛″ Plastic (choice of Color).
Type 16.26. Same as 16.13 but ⅛″ Plain Steel Finish 671.

Door Pulls and Push Plates

The type numbers below represent the most frequently required designs of pulls and push plates. Following the appropriate type number should be the catalogue number of the manufacturer. The specification should make clear the material—e.g., type of metal, or wood, or ceramic. All sizes here are approximate.

Door Pull and Plate, Squared Ends on Plate.

Type 16.30.

Door Pull and Plate, Rounded Ends on Plate.

Type 16.31.

Door Pull With No Plate.

Type 16.32.

Push Plate With Squared Ends.

Type 16.33.

Push Plate With Rounded Ends.

Type 16.34.

Push Plate. Special Dimensions. A dimension frequently required is that of a kick plate (almost width of door) to protect surface of door.

Type 16.35.

Arm Pull, for hospital use. Typical dimensions: Base 1½″ x 2⅛″. Projection, 3½″. Clearance, 3″.

Type 16.36.

Arm or Hand Pull, for hospital use. Typical dimensions: Distance between base centers, 6″. Base diameter, 1½″. Projection, 2⅜″. Clearance, 1⅛″.

Type 16.37.

Push-and-Pull Plate chiefly for hospital use. Typical dimensions: 3½″ x 16″. Clearance under lip, ⅞″.

Type 16.38.

Door Pull, Solid Face. Typical dimensions: Face, 6″ x 12″. Base, 1⅜″ x 12″. Centers, 10½″. Projection, 2¼″. Clearance, 1⅞″.

Type 16.39.

Door Pull, Cutout Face. Typical Handle dimensions, 3″ x 12″.

Type 16.40.

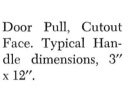

Pair of Door Pulls, Cutout Faces. Fastened back to back with studs and cap nuts.

Type 16.41.

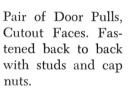

Door Pull, Special Design or Imprint.

Type 16.42.

Thresholds for Non-Checking Hinges

Grooved Surface, Bronze, With Center Supports. Available in widths from 5″ to over 7″. Height ½″.

Type 16.43.

Type 16.44. Same as 16.43 but Aluminum.

Grooved Surface, Bronze, No Center Supports. Available in widths up to 4″. Height, ½″.

Type 16.45.

Type 16.46. Same as 16.45 but Aluminum.

Smooth Surface (Unpolished), Bronze. Widths from 2½″ to 3″.

Type 16.47.

Type 16.48. Same as 16.47 but Aluminum.

Rough Surface, Bronze, Widths from 4″ to 7″. Minimum height, ³⁄₁₆″.

Type 16.49.

Type 16.50. Same as 16.49 but Aluminum.

Double Lip, Bronze. Width, 3½″.

Type 16.51.

Type 16.52. Same as 16.51 but Aluminum.

Single Lip, Bronze. Widths from 3½″ to 4½″.

Type 16.53

Type 16.54. Same as 16.53 but Aluminum.

Single Lip, Grooved Surface, Bronze. Widths from 1⅛″ to 1½″.

Type 16.55.

Type 16.56. Same as 16.55 but Aluminum.

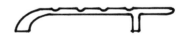

Vinyl Strip Sealer, Aluminum, Grooved Top. Widths from 3½″ to 4″.

Type 16.57.

Type 16.58. Same as 16.57 but Smooth Surface.

Miscellaneous Door Pulls

Edge Door Pull, Non-ferrous. For pocket sliding doors.

Type 16.59.

Door Pull, Flush, Non-ferrous. For light sliding doors. Available in other shapes and sizes.

Type 16.60.

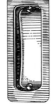

Round Pull, Flush, Non-ferrous. For light sliding doors. Available in many diameters, 1″ through 3″.

Type 16.61.

Round Pull, Swing-Out Type, Non-ferrous. Has many uses.

Type 16.62.

Steel Pull for Heavy Hinged Doors, such as warehouse doors. Available in several sizes and designs.

Type 16.63.

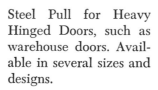

Pull for Heavy Sliding Doors, such as warehouse doors, Non-Ferrous, Flush.

Type 16.64.

Pull for Heavy Sliding Doors, such as institutional doors, Non-ferrous, Flush. 3¾″ x 4½″. Opening 1½″ x 3″ x ⅞″.

Type 16.65.

Door Edges and Caps

Door edges and caps are available in several materials. For a door thickness of 1¾″, the material is commonly 0.050″ thick. Other thicknesses can be ordered specially.

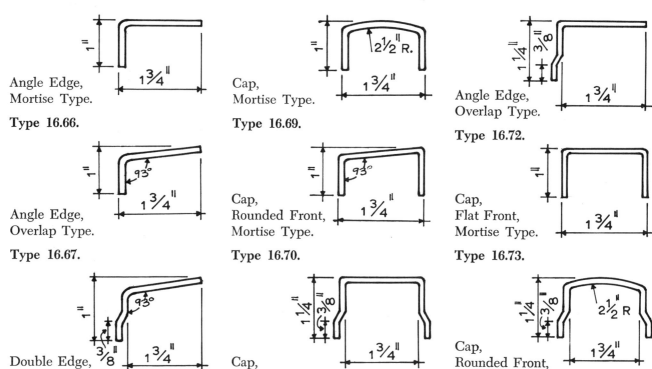

Angle Edge, Mortise Type.

Type 16.66.

Angle Edge, Overlap Type.

Type 16.67.

Double Edge, Mortise Type.

Type 16.68.

Cap, Mortise Type.

Type 16.69.

Cap, Rounded Front, Mortise Type.

Type 16.70.

Cap, Overlap Type.

Type 16.71.

Angle Edge, Overlap Type.

Type 16.72.

Cap, Flat Front, Mortise Type.

Type 16.73.

Cap, Rounded Front, Overlap Type.

Type 16.74.

CHAPTER 17

Lavatory Stall Hardware

Lavatory door hardware was formerly supplied as a specialty line by hardware manufacturers. When steel began to replace slate and marble as a construction material for booths, the steel booth manufacturers generally provided the hardware, since the conventional type was not readily adaptable to steel doors and partitions.

Although steel booths are now specified frequently, there is still, where quality is important, a constant demand for the conventional type of stall hardware. The items described in this chapter will be found in the finish hardware section of specifications for some of the better projects.

The spring hinges described here are generally closing hinges, but most of them are available with a Reverse Spring, so that the stall door stands open when not bolted shut. This reverse feature is specified by adding -R.S. to the type number.

For light duty or low-frequency use, one spring hinge with one springless hinge is adequate. Examples of these are included on the next two pages. Another type of springless hinge is a closing hinge that works by gravity. These are described on page 3.

Lavatory hardware should have high resistance to rust or corrosion. Ferrous springs may be used, but they must be protected from the atmosphere by the hinge barrel. It is generally left to the manufacturer's judgment as to whether a part should be cast, wrought, or extruded.

Once the hardware supplier has been notified of the door thickness, it is his responsibility to furnish hinges and keepers with the correct width of flange. It is his responsibility also to furnish the proper attachments (bolts and screws), and the most frequently used kinds are shown on page 5.

For the less frequently specified items not shown in this chapter, consult manufacturers' catalogues.

Spring Hinges

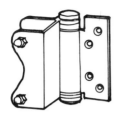

Single acting. Adjustable Tension and Flange.

Type 17.1. 4″ Flange.

Type 17.2. 3″ Flange.

Type 17.3. 4″ Flange, for use w. Springless Hinge shown above at center.

Type 17.4. 3″ Flange, for use w. Springless Hinge shown below.

Springless Hinge.
For use with Types 17.3 or 17.4.

Springless Hinge.
For use with Type 17.10.

Type 17.5.

Dble Acting. Non-adjustable Tension, Adjustable Flange.

Type 17.6. 4″ Flange.

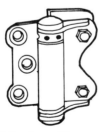

Sgle Acting. Half Surface Clamp Flange for Stile.

Type 17.7. 3″ Flange.

112

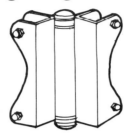

Sgle Acting. Adjustable Tension and Two Adjustable Flanges.

Type 17.8. 4″ Flange.

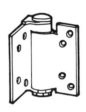

Sgle Acting. Adjustable Tension, Jamb Flange for Flat Wall.

Type 17.9. 4″ Flange.

Type 17.10. 4″ Flange for use w. Springless Hinge shown at left.

Sgle Acting. Adjustable Tension, for Pipe Standards.

Type 17.11. 4″ Flange.

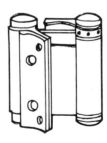

Dble Acting. Adjustable Tension, for Pipe Standards.

Type 17.12. 4″ Flange.

Sgle Acting. Adjustable Tension, Clamp for Partition Without Stile, for Door Opening In.

Type 17.13. 4″ Flange.

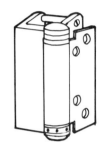

Sgle Acting. Adjustable Tension, Clamp for Partition Without Stile, for Door Opening Out.

Type 17.14. 4″ Flange.

Sgle Acting. Adjustable Tension, for Two Doors, one left-hand and one right-hand. Clamp for Partition Without Stile, for Doors Opening In.

Type 17.15. 4″ Flange.

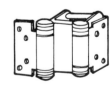

Sgle Acting. Adjustable Tension, for Two Doors, one left-hand and one right-hand. Clamp for Partition Without Stile, for Doors Opening Out.

Type 17.16. 4″ Flange.

Spring and Gravity Hinges

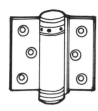

Hinge mounted inside stall cannot be seen from outside. Sgle Acting, Full Surface, Adj Tension, Heavy Cast Metal.

Type 17.17. 3″ Flange.

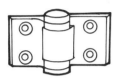

Sgle Acting, Full Surface, Adj Tension, Heavy Cast Metal.

Type 17.18. 3″ Flange.

Sgle Acting, Full Surface, Adj Tension, Heavy Cast Metal.

Type 17.19. 4″ Flange.

Springless Hinge, for use with one Spring Hinge.

Type 17.20. Use w. 17.18, 3″ Flange.

Type 17.21. Use w. 17.19, 4″ Flange.

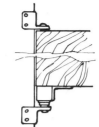

Mounted With Flanges Turned Out.

Type 17.23. Adj Tension.

Type 17.24. Fixed Tension.

Type 17.25. Gravity Hinge.

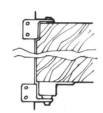

Mounted With Flanges Turned In.

Type 17.26. Adj Tension.

Type 17.27. Fixed Tension.

Type 17.28. Gravity Hinge.

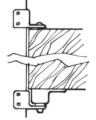

Mounted With 1 Flange Turned Out, 1 Turned In.

Type 17.29. Adj Tension.

Type 17.30. Fixed Tension.

Type 17.31. Gravity Hinge.

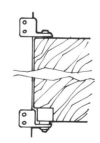

Mounted with Bottom Pivot Casing Mortised Into Door.

Type 17.32. Adj Tension.

Type 17.33. Fixed Tension.

Type 17.34. Gravity Hinge.

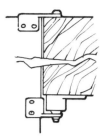

Top Pivot Mounted on Top of Jamb.

Type 17.35. Adj Tension.

Type 17.36. Fixed Tension.

Type 17.37. Gravity Hinge.

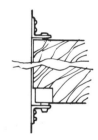

Mounted on Face of Jamb, Casing Mortised, Flanges Turned Out.

Type 17.38. Adj Tension.

Type 17.39. Fixed Tension.

Type 17.40. Gravity Hinge.

Mounted on Pipe Stile, Flanges Turned Out.

Type 17.41. Adj Tension.

Type 17.42. Fixed Tension.

Type 17.43. Gravity Hinge.

Stops, Keepers, and Bolts

Stop, Mounted on Door or Jamb.

17.44.

Stop and Keeper for Swing Latch. Open In.

17.45.

Stop and Keeper for Rim or Slide Bolt. Open In.

17.46.

Stop, Mounted on Door Surface Flush w. Jamb.

17.47.

Stop and Keeper for Rim or Slide Bolt. For Pipe Standards, Open In.

17.48.

Stop (no keeper). For Pipe Standards.

17.49.

Stop and Keeper for Swing Latch. For Pipe Standards. Open In.

17.50.

Stop and Keeper for Rim or Slide Bolt. Angle Flange. Open In.

17.51.

Stop and Keeper for Rim or Slide Bolt. Clamp for Jamb. Open In.

17.52.

Stop and Keeper for Rim or Slide Bolt. Clamp for Jamb. Open Out.

17.53.

Stop and Clamp for Jamb. Open In or Out.

17.54.

Stop and Keeper for Mortise Bolt. Clamp for Jamb. Open In or Out.

17.55.

Stop and Keeper for Round Mortise Bolt. Clamp for Jamb. Open In or Out.

17.56.

Stop and Keeper for Swing Latch. Clamp for Jamb. Open In.

17.57.

Stop and Keeper for Swing Latch. Clamp for Jamb. Open Out.

17.58.

Keeper for Dble Acting Doors. Clamp for Jamb.

17.59.

Stop and Keeper. Cut Optional for Two Doors. Clamp for Partition (no jamb). Open In.

17.60.

Stop and Keeper Cut Optional, for Two Doors. Clamp for Partition (no jamb). Open In.

17.61.

Stop and Keeper Cut Optional, for One Door. Clamp for Partition (no jamb). Open Out.

17.62.

Stops and Keeper Cuts Optional, for Two Doors. Clamp for Partition (no jamb). Open Out.

17.63.

Rim slide Bolt. Case, 2½″ x 2¾″. Bolt, ⅞″ x ¼″ Min.

17.64.

Mortise Slide Bolt. Case, 1⅝″ x ⅞″. Face Plate, 3″ x ⅝″ Min. Bolt, ⅞″ x ½″ Min.

17.65.

Indicator, Use Optional, for Rim or Mortise Bolts.

17.66. For use w. 17.64

17.67. For use w. 17.65

Slide Bolts, Hooks, and Bumpers

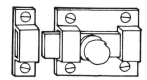

Slide Bolt, Keeper Optional. Plate, 2⅜″ x 2¾″. Bar, ⅞″ x ¼″. Sizes Minimum.

17.68.

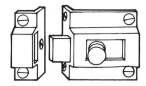

Slide Bolt, Keeper Optional. Plate, 2″ x 2½″. Bar, ¾″ x ³⁄₁₆″. Sizes Minimum.

17.69.

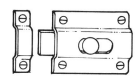

Slide Bolt, Keeper Optional. Plate, 2″ x 2¾″. Bar, ¾″ x ¼″. Sizes Minimum.

17.70.

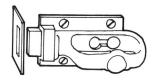

Slide Bolt and Bumper, Keeper Optional.

17.71.

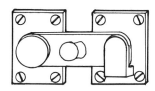

Swing Latch, Keeper Optional. Large Plate, 2″ x 2″, Large Bar, 1⅛″ x 4¼″. Small Plate, 2″ x 1⅝″, Small Bar, ⅞″ x 3¼″ x ³⁄₁₆″.

17.72. Large

17.73. Small

Lavatory Dr Pull. Length 4½″, Bases 1⅛″ x ⅝″. Sizes Minimum.

17.74.

Door Hook and Bumper, Spindle and Dowel Attachment. Base, 2″ x 1½″, or 1⅞″ O.D. Projection, 3¾″. Sizes Minimum.

17.75.

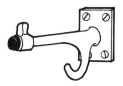

Door Hook and Bumper. Base 2″ x 1½″, or 1⅞″ O.D. Projection 3¾″. Sizes Minimum.

17.76.

Lavatory Hardware Attachments

These are some of the more commonly used attachments usually packed with lavatory hardware. Lavatory stall standards and fittings are occasionally in the hardware specifications. Consult manufacturers' catalogues for the wide variety available.

Cap and Nut

Flat Head and Nut

Sleeve Bolt

Sleeve With Oval Head

Closed-Cap Nut

Metal Anchor, for Wood Scrs

Expansion Anchor for Machine Scrs

Toggle Bolt, for Machine Scrs

Flat and Countersunk Washers

Open-Cap Nut

CHAPTER 18

Cabinet Hardware

Hinges and Pivots

The cabinet hinges and pivots shown here are the most representative types of the large number available. Specification writers should consult the manufacturers' catalogues closely and include all details, such as size and door details. Shown immediately below are just a few of the methods of cabinet door hanging. The hardware supplier must know all such details in order to be responsible for supplying the appropriate hardware. The type numbers here emphasize the importance of specifying either ferrous or non-ferrous.

Overlay Square Edge

Overlay Inset Lip

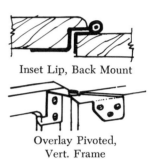

Inset Lip, Edge Mount

Inset Lip, Back Mount

Full Surface Flush

Full Surface Offset

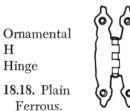

Overlay Pivoted, Horiz. Frame

Overlay Pivoted, Vert. Frame

Full Mortise Hinge

18.1. Non-ferrous.

18.2. Ferrous.

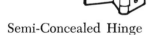

Semi-Concealed Hinge

18.3. Non-ferrous.

18.4. Ferrous.

Full Surface Hinge

18.5. Non-ferrous.

18.6. Ferrous.

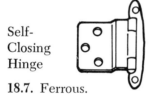

Self-Closing Hinge

18.7. Ferrous.

Institutional Hinge

18.8. Non-ferrous.

18.9. Ferrous.

Pivot Hinge

18.10. Non-ferrous.

18.11. Ferrous.

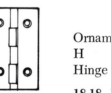

Continuous Hinge

18.12. Non-ferrous.

18.13. Ferrous.

Invisible Hinge

18.14. Non-ferrous.

18.15. Ferrous.

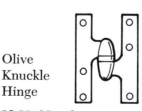

Olive Knuckle Hinge

18.16. Non-ferrous.

18.17. Ferrous.

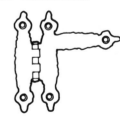

Ornamental H Hinge

18.18. Plain Ferrous.

18.19. Ornamental.

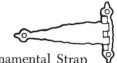

Ornamental L Hinge

18.20. Plain Ferrous.

18.21. Ornamental.

Ornamental Strap Hinge

18.22. Plain Ferrous.

18.23. Ornamental.

18.24. Strap (No Hge.).

Pulls and Knobs

Cabinet door pulls, like hinges, are available in a wide variety of styles, mounting methods, sizes, and materials. Type numbers here represent the broadest categories of pulls and knobs and again should be supplemented with exact catalogue number and details.

Extruded Surface Pull. Brass, Brze, or Alum. Fasten from back.

Type 18.25.

Wrought Surface Pull. Brass, Brze, or Steel. Fasten from back.

Type 18.26.

Cast Surface Pull. Brass, Brze, or Die Cast Zinc. Fasten from back.

Type 18.27.

Ornamental Drop Pull. Die Cast Zinc only. Fastened from back.

Type 18.28.

Ornamental Pull. Plain or Pattern, in Wrt Brass, Brze, Steel or Die Cast Zinc. Surface mounted.

Type 18.29.

Ornamental Pull. Cast Brass, Brze, or Die Cast Zinc. Fasten from back.

Type 18.30.

Ornamental Knob Pull. Brass, Brze, Alum, or Die Cast Zinc. Fastened from back.

Type 18.31.

Plain Knob Pull. Brass, Brze, Alum, or Die Cast Zinc. Fastened from back.

Type 18.32.

Machined Knob Pull. Brass, Brze, Alum, or Steel. Fastened from back.

Type 18.33.

Flush Pull for Sliding Door. Wrought Brass, Brze, Alum, or Steel in various sizes and depths.

Type 18.34.

Flush Pull for Sliding Door. Wrought Brass, Brze, Alum, or Steel in various sizes and depths.

Type 18.35.

Flush Pull for Sliding Door. Wrought Brass, Brze, Alum, or Steel in various sizes and depths.

Type 18.36.

Cabinet Door Catches and Latches

The most widely used principles for holding cabinet doors shut are shown here. Magnetic catches should have an operating life of 50,000 cycles minimum. Cabinet locks are shown in Chapter 13, page 6.

Elbow Catch. For inactive Dr of a Pr of Drs.

Type 18.37. Brass

Type 18.38. Iron or Steel.

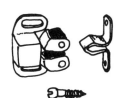

Roller Catch. Wrt Steel. Rollers of Plastic or Rubber.

Type 18.39. Dble Roller.

Type 18.40. Sgle Roller.

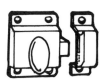

Thumb Turn Latch. Oval or Round Knob.

Type 18.41. Brass or Cast Brze.

Type 18.42. Steel.

Magnetic Catch, Light Duty. 4-lb. Pull. For Under Shelf and Narrow Jamb. Plastic or Aluminum Case.

Type 18.43.

Magnetic Catch for Dbl Drs. 4-lb. Pull, Each Leaf. Plastic or Aluminum Case.

Type 18.44.

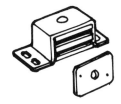

Magnetic Catch, Hvy Duty. 11-lb Pull. Aluminum Case

Type 18.45.

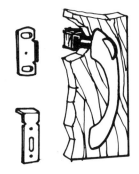

Thumb Latch. Reversible. Brass, Brze, Steel or Die Cast Zinc.

Type 18.46.

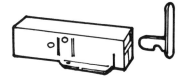

Touch Latch. Mount Surface Inside, Push to Open.

Type 18.47.

Secret Panel Latch w. Pusher. Mount Surface Inside, Push to Open. Brass.

Type 18.48.

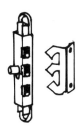

Safety Latch. Triple Latches. Steel.

Type 18.49.

Bar Latch. Plain or Ornamental Steel.

Type 18.50. Full Surface Flush

Type 18.51. Full Surface ⅜″ Offset.

Ball Bearing Latch. Surface or Mortise Mounted, Adjustable Tension. Extruded Brze.

Type 18.52.

Shelf Rests, Standards, and Brackets

Shelf Rest for Wood Frame

Type 18.53. Steel.

Shelf Rest for Standard. For Standards 18.58–18.61. Projection, ¾″ Min. Closed.

Type 18.54. Wrt Brass.

Type 18.55. Wrt Steel.

Shelf Rest for Standard. For Standards 18.58–18.61. Projection, ¾″ Min. Open.

Type 18.56. Wrt Brass.

Type 18.57. Wrt Steel.

Adjustable Shelf Standard. Slots spaced ½″. Surface Mounted.

Type 18.58. Wrt Brass.

Type 18.59. Wrt Steel.

Adjustable Shelf Standard. Slots spaced ½″. Surface or Mortise Mounted.

Type 18.60. Wrt Brass.

Type 18.61. Wrt Steel.

Adjustable Shelf Standard. Vertical Slot. In lengths from 12″ to 144″.

Type 18.62. Aluminum.

Type 18.63. Wrt Steel.

Shelf Bracket. In sizes from 3″ x 4″ to 16″ x 18″.

Type 18.64. Wrt Steel.

Shelf and Rod Bracket. 9¾″ High x 11″ Wide.

Type 18.65. Wrt Steel.

Adjustable Shelf Bracket. For Standards 18.62 and 18.63. For Shelf Widths 4″ to 20″.

Type 18.66. Aluminum.

Type 18.67. Wrt Steel.

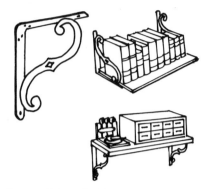

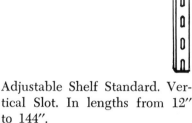

Reversible Shelf Bracket. Sizes Available: 3½″ x 4½″, 5½″ x 7½″, 9½″ x 11¼″.

Type 18.68. Wrt Steel.

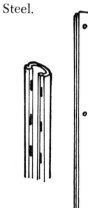

Standard
For Bracket 18.69.

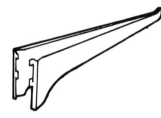

Double Arm Shelf Bracket. For Shelf Widths 6″, 8″, 10″.

Type 18.69. Wrt Steel.

Drawer Rollers, Glides, and Rotating Shelves

Flanged Drawer Rollers. Plastic Roller. Steel Bracket. Flange prevents drawer from rubbing.

Type 18.70.

Drawer Glide. Plastic to replace front rollers.

Type 18.71.

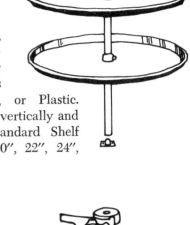

Drawer Glide, Center Bottom Mount. Roller bracket attached to back of drawer. Plastic glides may replace roller at front.

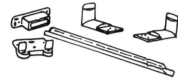

Type 18.72.

Rotating Shelves, Full Round. Center Post Metal or Tubular. Shelves of Metal, Wood, or Plastic. Shelves adjustable vertically and lock in place. Standard Shelf Diameters: 18″, 20″, 22″, 24″, 28″.

Type 18.79.

Drawer Slide, Bottom Mount. Slide of Wrt Steel, Plastic Rollers. Guides both sides under drawer. Roller brackets to front of drawer, rollers on rear bracket.

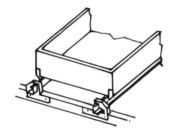

Type 18.73. Rotating Bearing.

Type 18.74. Non-rotating Bearing.

Drawer Slide, Side Mount. Mounted on sides of drawer, rollers front and rear.

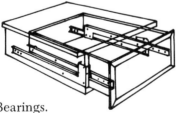

Type 18.75.
    Steel Rollers, Ball Bearings.

Type 18.76. Plastic Rollers, Ball Bearings.

Type 18.77. Plastic Rollers, Plain Bearings.

Rotating Shelves, Notched. Specifications and sizes same as for 18.79 at left. This type may be supported with or without a post. Mechanism will hold unit in a closed position.

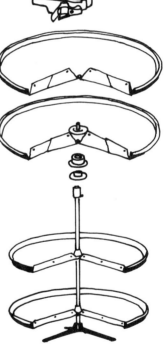

Type 18.80.

Drawer Slide, Center Bottom Mount. Slide of Wrt Steel, Plastic Rollers. Two rollers each side, front rollers adjustable. Drawer removable.

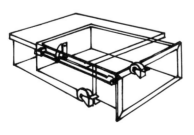

Type 18.78.

Sliding Door Sheaves, Tracks, and Guides

Sheave for Sliding Door. Steel Ball Bearings Available. Heavy Duty Flange, 4″. Standard Duty Flange, 2¾″.

Type 18.81. Heavy Duty.

Type 18.82. Standard Duty.

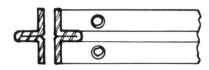

Track for Sheaves.

Type 18.83.
   Heavy Duty Track for 18.81.

Type 18.84.
   Standard Duty Track for 18.82.

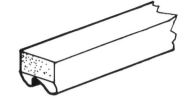

Mortised Track

Type 18.85.

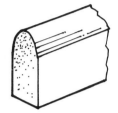

Fiber Guide for 18.85.

Type 18.86.

NOTE: Now available is "Cabinet Hardware Standards" together with Performance Test Requirements, published by the Builders Hardware Manufacturers Association in cooperation with the Kitchen Cabinet Manufacturers Association.

Because of the wide variety of cabinet hardware available, the specification writer should use the type numbers for functions but amplify as to design, finish, or special conditions. At the top of this page, for example, tracks and sheaves are available for single or bypassing sliding doors. Channel types are also available, including those for glass sliding doors. Usually these items are covered under Cabinet Work and do not need to be specified under Finish Hardware.

CHAPTER 19

Hardware for Sliding and Folding Doors

Sliding doors, as designed earlier in this century and the preceding one, achieved considerable acceptance in residences, particularly between rooms for general use and as room dividers. Certain inherent disadvantages in their design, however—expense of installation, noise of operation, and even the fact that they were not draft-proof—led to a decline in their use.

Hardware manufacturers, recognizing the potential market for sliding and folding doors as space savers with living space at an increasing premium, were able to make some remarkable design improvements that to a great extent eliminated the disadvantages. During the 1950's, both sliding and folding doors were specified for and installed in new homes and apartments, not only between rooms but also as closet doors.

This chapter describes sliding and folding doors in a general way in order to include the largest variety of applications, both residential and light commercial. The hardware for the heavier sliding doors, weighing from several hundred pounds to over a ton, has special installation requirements, frequently including specific engineering advice that the manufacturer will readily provide.

Both the hardware specifier and the supplier should be alert to the manufacturer's recommendations as to grade of hardware for a particular door and its capacity to do a satisfactory job. The hardware supplier should see that all required hardware is included.

For many of the functions and types of doors described here the hardware is supplied in complete sets. But often, too, especially in light commercial work, the set will not include a door pull or a lock when these may be required for the installation. For sliding doors of heavy construction, the hardware is seldom sold as sets, and track, hangers, brackets, guides, pulls, locks, and stops must be specified individually.

The type and spacing of brackets are particularly important. The manufacturer's recommendation should always be followed in this regard, for no matter how heavy the track may be, it cannot function properly if it is not amply supported by the proper type and number of brackets. The manufacturer's recommendation should also be followed as to bracket fastening, whether by lag, toggle, or other bolts, with or without expansion shields.

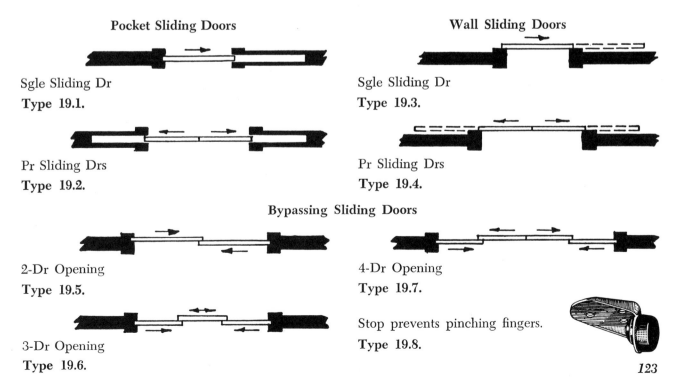

Pocket Sliding Doors

Sgle Sliding Dr

Type 19.1.

Pr Sliding Drs

Type 19.2.

Wall Sliding Doors

Sgle Sliding Dr

Type 19.3.

Pr Sliding Drs

Type 19.4.

Bypassing Sliding Doors

2-Dr Opening

Type 19.5.

3-Dr Opening

Type 19.6.

4-Dr Opening

Type 19.7.

Stop prevents pinching fingers.

Type 19.8.

Folding Doors

Bi-Fold and Multi-Fold Doors, Center-Hung and Heel-Hung.
Diagrams show general types. Specify number of doors separately.

Bi-Fold Dr, example
of Type 19.12. Shown:
2 Dr + 2 Dr.

Center-Hung, ½ Right, ½ Left, w. ½ Drs at
Jamb. Shown: 4½ Dr + 4½ Dr.
Type 19.9.

Center-Hung, all folding 1 way, w. ½ Dr at
Jamb. Shown: 6½ Dr Right.
Type 19.10.

Heel-Hung, all folding 1 way, Hinge Dr at
other end.
Type 19.11.

Heel-Hung, ½ Right, ½ Left. Shown: 4 Dr
+ 4 Dr.
Type 19.12.

Heel-Hung, all folding 1 way. Shown: 8 Dr
Right.
Type 19.13.

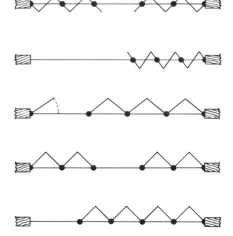

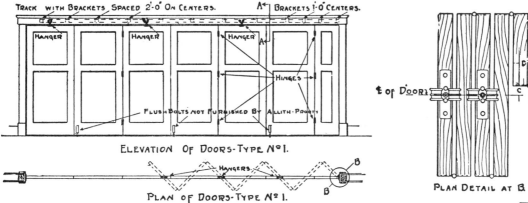

Installation of Center-Hung (Accordion) Folding Doors

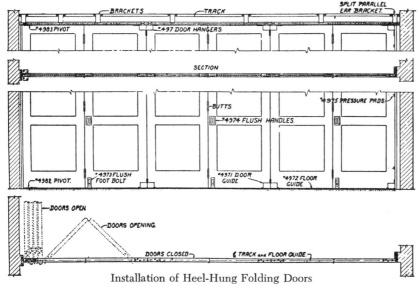

Installation of Heel-Hung Folding Doors

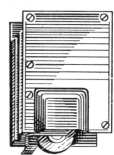

Floor Roller
A type of floor roller for
heel-hung folding doors

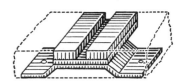

Floor Track
A type of floor track for
heel-hung folding doors

Sliding Door Hardware, Heavy Commercial

Track and Hangers for Sliding Door

Hardware shown on this page will roll doors from 100 lb. to 3,000 lb. depending on type of duty specified.

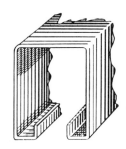

Overhead Track for Sliding Door(s). Follow type number with mfr catalogue number to denote specific type, size, and duty. For use w. hangers 19.15, 16, 17, 18.

Type 19.14.

Bracket Option Key

-1 No Ears
-2 Parallel Ears
-3 Cross Ears
-4 Double Track
-5 Triple Track
-6 Applied to Side Wall
-7 Applied Overhead.

Example: For an Intermediate Brkt, Dble Track, w. Parallel Ears and Applied Overhead, specify Type 19.21-2-4-7.

Hanger w. Sgle Plate Apron, vertical and horizontal adjustments. Sizes available for doors up to 800 lb.

Type 19.15.

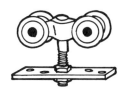

Hanger, fastens to top of door, for doors 200 lb. and less.

Type 19.16.

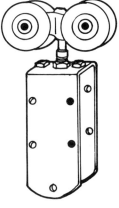

Hanger w. Dble Plate Apron, vertical and horizontal adjustments. For doors 800 to 2,000 lb.

Type 19.17.

Same as 19.17 but w. 4 wheels instead of 2 and for doors up to 3,000 lb. For door thicknesses from $1\frac{3}{4}''$ to $4\frac{1}{4}''$.

Type 19.18.

Brackets for Track Type 19.14.

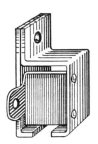

End Brkt (Shown as Side Wall Applied).

Type 19.19.

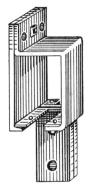

Center Stop Brkt (Shown as Side Wall Applied).

Type 19.20.

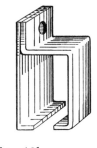

Intermediate Brkt (Shown as Side Wall Applied).

Type 19.21.

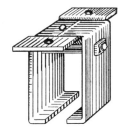

Intermediate Brkt (Shown as Overhead Applied).

Type 19.21.

Sliding Door Hardware Accessories

Floor Guides and Stops

Floor Guide for Bypassing Doors, Light Commercial.

Type 19.22.

Floor Guide for Single Sliding Doors, Light Commercial.

Type 19.23.

Floor Guide Strips, Light Commercial.

Type 19.24.

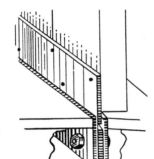

Floor Guide w. Engaging Slot in Floor. Heavy Duty.

Type 19.25.

Floor Center Stop, Surface Applied, Heavy Duty.

Type 19.26.

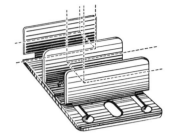

Floor Guide for Bypassing Doors, Heavy Duty.

Type 19.27.

Floor End Stop and Guide. Heavy Duty.

Type 19.28.

Center Floor Guide, for Heavy Doors. Heavy Duty.

Type 19.29.

Stay Roller, 2″ Diameter Min., Heavy Duty.

Type 19.30.

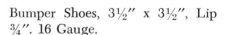

Door Stop. Made for required door thickness. Heavy Duty.

Type 19.31.

Bumper Shoes, 3½″ x 3½″, Lip ¾″. 16 Gauge.

Type 19.32.

Other Miscellaneous Hardware

Sliding Door Bolt, for use w. Padlock, which must be specified separately.

Type 19.33.

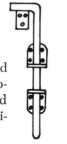

Vertical Bolt and Keeper for closed position. Will also hold door at other positions.

Type 19.34.

NOTE: Many other kinds of sliding door hardware are available. They include—

> Fire Door Hardware
> Slide-Up Door Hardware
> Jack Knife Vertical Fold
> Garage Hardware
> Light Flat Hardware
> Round Track Hardware

For these special types consult manufacturers' catalogues and/or their engineers.

CHAPTER 20

Window Hardware

Metal sashes and frames and their specialized hardware for years were displacing their wood counterparts. Now this trend is reversing, and the demand for hardware for wood windows is increasing.

The most basic hardware for wood sashes, transoms, shutters, and screens are illustrated in this chapter. All items are non-ferrous unless otherwise noted in the descriptions.

Sash Hardware for Double-Hung Windows

Crescent Sash Lock

Type 20.1. 1″ x 3″.

Type 20.2. 1″ x 2¾″.

Type 20.3. ⅞″ x 2½″.

Cam Sash Lock

Type 20.4. Spring.

Type 20.5. No Spring.

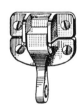

Signal Sash Lock. For High Sash; operated by pole hook.

Type 20.6.

Vent Sash Lock. Permits limited opening for ventilation.

Type 20.7.

Hook Sash Lift

Type 20.8. Cast.

Type 20.9. Wrt.

Flush Sash Lift

Type 20.10. Cast.

Type 20.11. Wrt.

Bar Sash Lift

Type 20.12. Cast, 5″.

Type 20.13. Cast, 4″.

Type 20.14. Offset, Cast, 4″.

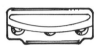

Hood Lip Sash Lift. Wrt, Lip ⅞″, Approx. Length 4″.

Type 20.15.

Sash Pull Plate, Cast.

Type 20.16.

Sash Pole Hanger, Cast.

Type 20.17.

Sash Pole Hook (w. 20.19).

Type 20.18.

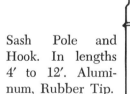

Wood Sash Pole (w. 20.18).

Type 20.19.

Sash Pole and Hook. In lengths 4′ to 12′. Aluminum, Rubber Tip.

Type 20.20.

Bead Screw and Washer, Adj.

Type 20.21.

Bead Screw and Washer, Flush, Not Adj.

Type 20.22.

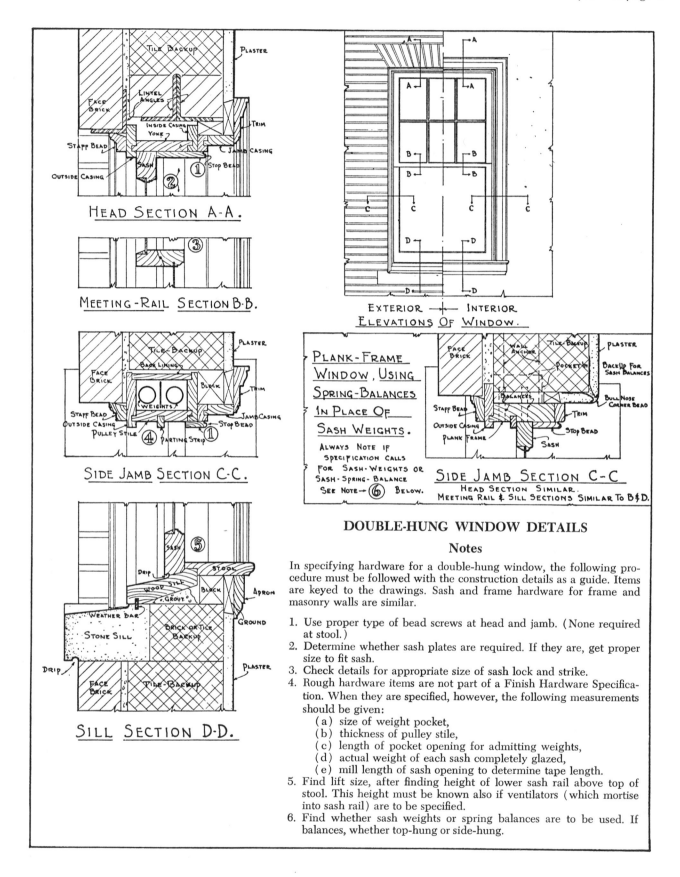

HEAD SECTION A-A.

MEETING-RAIL SECTION B·B.

SIDE JAMB SECTION C-C.

SILL SECTION D·D.

EXTERIOR ⟶ ⟵ INTERIOR
ELEVATIONS OF WINDOW.

PLANK-FRAME WINDOW, USING SPRING-BALANCES IN PLACE OF SASH WEIGHTS.

ALWAYS NOTE IF SPECIFICATION CALLS FOR SASH-WEIGHTS OR SASH-SPRING-BALANCE SEE NOTE ⑥ BELOW.

SIDE JAMB SECTION C-C
HEAD SECTION SIMILAR.
MEETING RAIL & SILL SECTIONS SIMILAR TO B & D.

DOUBLE-HUNG WINDOW DETAILS

Notes

In specifying hardware for a double-hung window, the following procedure must be followed with the construction details as a guide. Items are keyed to the drawings. Sash and frame hardware for frame and masonry walls are similar.

1. Use proper type of bead screws at head and jamb. (None required at stool.)
2. Determine whether sash plates are required. If they are, get proper size to fit sash.
3. Check details for appropriate size of sash lock and strike.
4. Rough hardware items are not part of a Finish Hardware Specification. When they are specified, however, the following measurements should be given:
   (a) size of weight pocket,
   (b) thickness of pulley stile,
   (c) length of pocket opening for admitting weights,
   (d) actual weight of each sash completely glazed,
   (e) mill length of sash opening to determine tape length.
5. Find lift size, after finding height of lower sash rail above top of stool. This height must be known also if ventilators (which mortise into sash rail) are to be specified.
6. Find whether sash weights or spring balances are to be used. If balances, whether top-hung or side-hung.

Sash Hardware for Casement Windows

Offset Casement Hinge, Opens Out Only. Permits cleaning outside glass from inside. (For standard hinges, see Chapter 7.)

Type 20.23.

Espagnolette Bolt, Surface-Applied. Locks top, bottom, and center. Operated from inside only.

Type 20.24.

Cremone Bolt, Surface Applied. Operated from inside only.

Type 20.25.

Same as 20.25 but opens both sides.

Type 20.26.

Same as 20.25 but has lever, no knob.

Type 20.27.

Same as 20.25 but opens both sides and has lever, no knob.

Type 20.28.

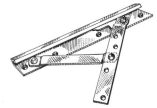

Combined Casement Hinge and Holder. Holds by friction.

Type 20.29.

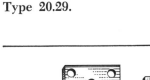

Rim
Strike

Lipped
Strike

Angle
Strike

Flat
Strike

Casement Fastener, made in various designs. Hardware supplier must include strike to fit, whether rim or mortise.

Type 20.30.

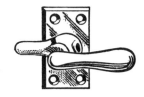

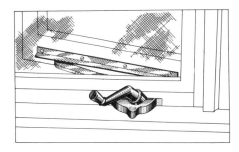

Casement Operator works by gears through screen. Made in various designs and sizes.

Type 20.31.

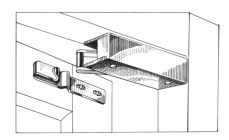

Top Snugger, for high casements. Prevents warpage, keeps window air-tight. Also for closet and cupboard doors.

Type 20.32.

Casement Holder. Holds by friction. Available in many designs to suit many special conditions.

Type 20.33.

Casement Operator and Holder. Holds by knob bolt. For out-swing casements. Surface applied.

Type 20.34.

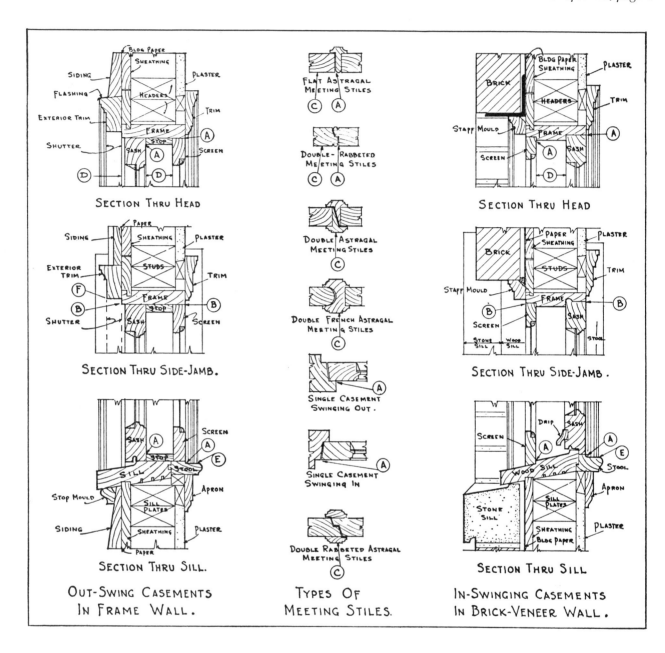

SECTION THRU HEAD

SECTION THRU SIDE-JAMB.

SECTION THRU SILL.

OUT-SWING CASEMENTS
IN FRAME WALL.

FLAT ASTRAGAL
MEETING STILES

DOUBLE-RABBETED
MEETING STILES

DOUBLE ASTRAGAL
MEETING STILES

DOUBLE FRENCH ASTRAGAL
MEETING STILES

SINGLE CASEMENT
SWINGING OUT.

SINGLE CASEMENT
SWINGING IN

DOUBLE RABBETED ASTRAGAL
MEETING STILES

TYPES OF
MEETING STILES.

SECTION THRU HEAD

SECTION THRU SIDE-JAMB.

SECTION THRU SILL

IN-SWINGING CASEMENTS
IN BRICK-VENEER WALL.

WOOD CASEMENT DETAILS

Notes

Hardware specifications for casement windows should take into account the following notes, which are keyed to the drawings. A copy of the details, furnished with the specifications, makes for better comprehension.

A. Note type of sash stop and dimensions in regard to hardware.
B. Give throw and size of hinges, whether butt or surface type.
C. Check width for bolts.
D. Find distance available for hardware between sash and screen.
E. Note width of stool, if adjusters are to be applied to it.
F. Check distances and dimensions for casement operators.

Transom and Shutter (Blind) Hardware

Transom Hardware
Friction Sash Center. Available for sashes 1⅜″ and 1¾″ thick.

Type 20.35.

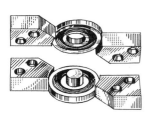

Mortise Sash Center. Available for sashes 1⅜″ to 2¼″ thick.

Type 20.36.

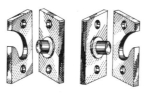

Plain Sash Center.

Type 20.37.

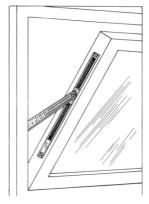

Friction Transom Stay. Type 20.29 is also used.

Type 20.38.

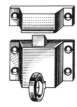

Transom Catch and Strike. Rim (shown) or flush. Latch available reversed for out-swinging transom.

Type 20.39.

Transom Ring. Engaged by hook on pole.

Type 20.40.

Transom Chain. Available in various lengths.

Type 20.41.

Transom Chain w. Snap.

Type 20.42.

Shutter Hardware

Compare Details in Chapter 24, Problem 9

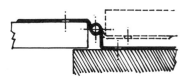

Reversible Shutter Hinge. Applied flush or offset.

Type 20.43.

Offset Shutter Hinge. Leaves bent so that screens can be hung without interference.

Type 20.44.

Straight Shutter Hinge. Applied flush w. casing.

Type 20.45.

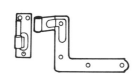

Offset Shutter Hinge. Applied flush w. casing.

Type 20.46.

Shutter Dog, or Turnbuckle. Holds shutter open.

Type 20.47.

Shutter Bolt. Holds shutters closed.

Type 20.48.

Shutter Hinge Strap, Straight. Available in various lengths and designs.

Type 20.49.

Shutter Hinge Strap, Offset. Available in various lengths and designs.

Type 20.50.

Screen Hardware

Hangers, Hinges, and Accessories for Screen and Storm Windows and Doors

See also hinges in Chapter 7. Mortise hinges with brass pins used also.
Hydraulic and pneumatic closers for storm and screen doors shown in Chapter 15.

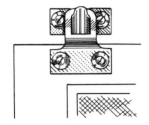

Surface Screen Hanger.

Type 20.51.

Full surface screen door hinge w. spring closer.

Type 20.52. Adjustable.

Type 20.53. Non-adjustable.

Half surface screen door hinge w. spring closer.

Type 20.54. Adjustable.

Type 20.55. Non-adjustable.

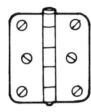

Full surface screen door hinge (no spring). Measures 3″ x 2¾″ when open.

Type 20.56.

Screen fastener.

Type 20.57.

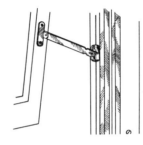

Storm Sash adjuster. Holds window open.

Type 20.58.

Screen door chain stop w. spring cushioner.

Type 20.59.

Screen door spring. Available in several sizes.

Type 20.60.

Screen Door Catches

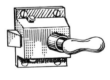

Screen door latch set, rim.

Type 20.61.

Screen door latch set, tubular.

Type 20.62.

Screen door latch set, mortise.

Type 20.63.

Screen door push-pull latch.

Type 20.64.

CHAPTER **21**

Door Bolts, Holders, and Stops

Careful attention in specifying the items shown in this chapter will avoid many difficulties that can arise in door operation.

No attachment methods are described, since it is the hardware supplier's responsibility to furnish the appropriate screws and bolts to anchor the product firmly.

Concealed Automatic Door Bolts

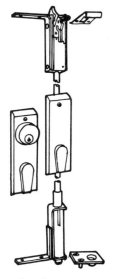

Operated by lever either side except when outside lever is locked by key outside. Inside lever always free. Top and bottom bolts can be locked open by key.

Type 21.1.

Same as 21.1 but cyl both sides.

Type 21.2.

Same as 21.1 but no outside operation and no inside key. Inside lever operates bolt at all times. Bolts cannot be locked open.

Type 21.3.

Automatic flush top bolt. U.L. listed. Standard for doors 1¾″ thick, but available also for doors 1⅜″ to 2½″. Also for rounded corners.

Type 21.4.

Automatic flush bottom bolt. Otherwise same as 21.4 and same options available.

Type 21.5.

Automatic flush bolt w. lever finger which extends only when door is open, thus preventing operation of active door of a pair until inactive door has closed. Use top and bottom of inactive door.

Type 21.6.

Strike furnished w. Types 21.6 and 21.7.

NOTE: Automatic bolts—instead of the manual, flush mounted types—are recommended for any door that must be depended upon as an exit, possibly in an emergency.

Automatic flush bolt. This is a simple roller bolt that releases under pressure. Use both top and bottom of inactive door.

Type 21.7.

133

Manual Door Bolts

Floor Strike, Dust-Proof, Flush. For use with bolts 21.8, 21.9, and 21.10 (must specify which).

Type 21.13.

Heavy Mortise Extension Bolt. Heavy 1″ throw, non-ferrous, 6″ long, ¾″ wide.

Type 21.17.

Flush Extension Bolt, Flat Face. Use 2 bolts on inactive door of pair of doors. Available in various lengths. When used as a bottom bolt, dust-proof strike 21.13 is recommended.

Type 21.8.

Flush Extension Bolt, Rabbeted Face. For use in pair of rabbeted doors, ½″ rabbet standard. Otherwise same as 21.8.

Type 21.10.

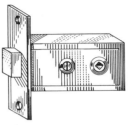

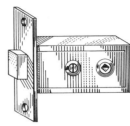

Heavy Mortise Bolt. Comes complete w. thumb turn.

Type 21.14.

Light Mortise Extension Bolt. Non-ferrous, 4″ long, ¾″ wide.

Type 21.18.

Dutch Door Bolt. Surface applied. Strike is surface applied or mortise. Rod lengths start at 4″, diameters at ⅝″.

Type 21.11.

Tubular Mortise Bolt, Light. Comes complete w. thumb turn.

Type 21.15.

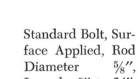

Standard Bolt, Surface Applied, Rod Diameter ⅝″, Lengths 6″ to 24″. Non-ferrous. Knob design optional.

Type 21.19.

Same as 21.19 but Rod Diameter ½″.

Type 21.20.

Flush Extension Bolt, Rounded Face. For use in pair of double-acting doors. Otherwise same as 21.8.

Type 21.9.

Dutch Dr Quadrant.

Type 21.12.

Mortise Jamb Bolt. For locking sliding door and other uses.

Type 21.16.

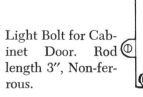

Light Bolt for Cabinet Door. Rod length 3″, Non-ferrous.

Type 21.21.

Door Holders and Stops

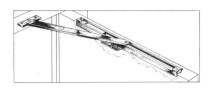

Holder Concealed in Head for Ext or Hvy Int Drs

21.22. Dr. w. Hinges.

21.23. Dr w. Offset Pivots.

21.24. Dr w. Center Pivots.

21.25. For D.A. Dr.

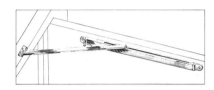

Stop, Surface Applied, for Ext or Hvy Int Drs

21.26. Dr w. Hinges.

21.27. Dr w. Offset Pivots.

21.28. Dr w. Center Pivots.

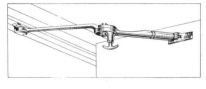

Holder, Surface Applied, for Ext or Hvy Int Drs

21.29. Manual Release.

Door Stop and Semi-automatic Holder, Floor Mounted.

21.30.

Door Stop and Manual Holder, Floor Mounted.

21.31.

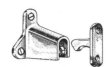

Door Stop and Automatic Holder, Wall Mounted.

21.32.

Door Holder, Overhead Surface Applied.

21.33. Hvy Duty.

21.34. Std Duty.

Overhead Concealed.

21.35. Stop and Friction Holder.

21.36. Stop only.

Overhead Surface Applied.

21.37. Stop and Friction Holder.

21.38. Stop only.

Overhead Concealed, for Light Interior Doors Only.

21.39. Stop and Friction Holder.

21.40. Stop only.

Rod Door Stop, Overhead Surface Applied, Heavy Duty.

21.41.

Heavy Duty, Floor Mounted.

21.42. Stop and Hook Holder.

21.43. Stop only.

Heavy Duty, Wall Mounted.

21.44. Stop and Hook Holder.

21.45. Stop only.

Plunger Holder, Door Surface Applied.

21.46.

Lever Holder, Door Surface Mounted.

21.47.

Door Stops

Floor-Mounted Stops

Dome Stop, 1″ High.

Type 21.50.

Hvy Duty Stop.

Type 21.48.

Dome Stop, 1⅜″ High.

Type 21.49.

Hook Stop.

Type 21.51. Hvy Duty.

Type 21.52. Light Duty.

Wall-Mounted Stops

Hvy Duty Stop.

Type 21.53.

Convex Bumper.

Type 21.54. Hvy Duty.

Type 21.55. Light Duty.

Concave Bumper.

Type 21.56. Hvy Duty.

Type 21.57. Light Duty.

Stop.

Type 21.58. Hvy Duty.

Type 21.59. Light Duty.

Door-Mounted Roller Stops

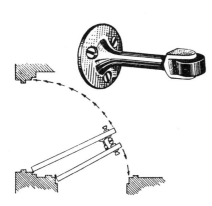

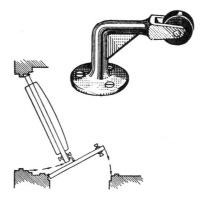

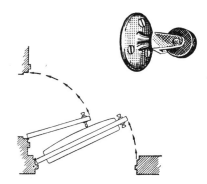

Straight Roller Stop.

Type 21.60. 4″ Long.

Type 21.61. 6″ Long.

Hook Roller Stop.

Type 21.62.

Short Roller Stop.

Type 21.63.

Door Silencers and Chain Stops

Door Silencer, for Metal Frame.

Type 21.64.

Door Silencer, for Wood Frame.

Type 21.65.

Chain Stop w. Spring Cushion. Length as required. No Cover.

Type 21.66.

Type 21.67.
    Same as 21.66 but Rubber Covered.

CHAPTER 22

Miscellaneous Hardware

Brought together in this chapter are all the hardware items that do not clearly belong in any of the categories covered by the preceding chapters. Although their functions and their degree of complexity vary greatly, from those of a hand rail bracket to those of an automatic door opener, each item is important in its own application. The products operated by electricity will require close cooperation between the hardware supplier and electrical contractor to ensure proper operation and service.

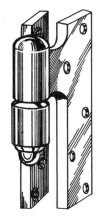

Ball Hinge, Adj. Many sizes available.

Type 22.1.

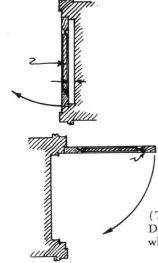

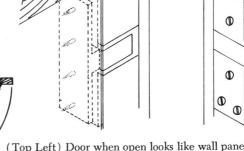

(Top Left) Door when open looks like wall panel. (Lower Left) Door closed. (Above Left) The hinge is concealed in a pocket when door is open. (Above Right) Hinge with door closed.

Harmon Hinge.

Type 22.2.

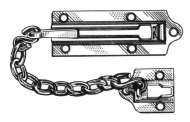

Chain Door Fastener, Surface Applied.

Type 22.3.

Closet Rod. Rods over 72″ long need intermediate support.

Type 22.4. Hvy.

Type 22.5. Med.

Coat and Hat Hook. Recommend at least four for each closet w. rod.

Type 22.6.

Robe Hook

Type 22.7. 2 Prongs.

Type 22.8. 1 Prong.

Electric Strike. Must match lock. Hardware supplier should correlate strike for specified lock.

Type 23.4.

Smoke Detector

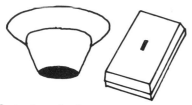

Photoelectric detector

Type 22.10.

Electromagnetic Door Holders

Single unit.

Type 22.11. Wall Mounted.

Type 22.12. Floor Mounted.

Floor Mounted. For back-to-back doors.

Type 22.13.

Electromagnetic Door Holder

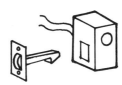

For heavy doors, incl. sliding and overhead doors.

Type 22.14.

Automatic Door Opener

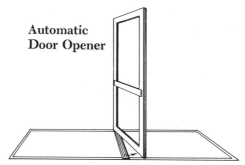

Type 22.15.
This type number is for operating mechanism only. Doors and trim must be specified separately. Locks should be deadlocks. Usually three extra-heavy duty hinges required, 5″ x 4″.

NOTE: For all electricity-operated products, the type numbers given here represent only the broadest categories. Manufacturers' catalogues and their engineer consultants' advice should be noted carefully in specifying such hardware.

Hand Rail Brackets

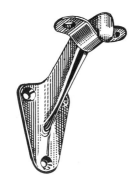

For wood hand rail.

Type 22.16.

For wood hand rail. Round base.

Type 22.17.

For heavy duty. With expansion shield.

Type 22.18.

For wood or metal rail. Reversible. Can be mounted in masonry or concrete wall.

Type 22.19.

Mailbox Plates

Determine minimum slot width, if any, required by Post Office.

   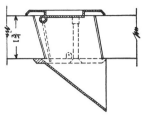

Inside cover, residential, in-swing lid.

Type 22.20.

Type 22.21.
  Same as 22.20 but out-swing lid.

Inside hood, residential, out-swing lid.

Type 22.22.

Type 22.23.
  Same as 22.22 but in-swing lid.

Out-swing lid, inside plate.

Type 22.24.

Type 22.25.
  Out-swing lid, inside hood.

Metal Liner (Chute). For use w. Types 22.24 or 22.25. Especially required for metal doors.

Type 22.26. Vertical.

Type 22.27. Horizontal.

NOTE: Architect should specify location on door, as Hinge Rail, Lock Rail, Bottom Rail, etc.

Surface-Mounted Mailboxes

 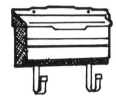

Vertical Box about 14″ high, 6″ wide. Gravity flap.

Type 22.28.
  W. Magazine Holder.

Type 22.29.
  No Holder.

Horizontal Box about 13″ wide, 7″ high. Gravity flap.

Type 22.30.
  W. Magazine Holder.

Type 22.31.
  No Holder.

Apartment Mail Boxes Installed in Wall

 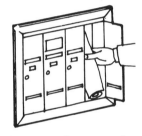

Ganged boxes. Delivery from top, retrieval at face.

Type 22.32.

Delivery and retrieval at face.

Type 22.33.

NOTE: Consult Post Office for regulations. Illustration shows only four bins, but a wide range of bin numbers and sizes is available. Resident's key may also operate his apartment front door if so specified.

Signs and Door Numbers

Sign Plates and Door Numbers are described in Chapter 16, page 1, under Architectural Trim. For the reader's convenience, the type numbers are repeated here.

  Type 16.27. Horizontal Name Plate.
  Type 16.28. Vertical Name Plate.
  Type 16.29. Horizontal Number Plate.
  Type 16.30. Individual Digits, Plain.
  Type 16.31. Individual Digits, Ornamental.

Knocker. Specify size and design.

Type 22.34. House front door.

Type 22.35. Guestroom door.

Miscellaneous Items

Door Viewer (sleeve type shown). Fits a ½″ hole. Length adjustable to door thickness. One-way wide-angle lens. Can be installed separately or in conjunction w. knockers at left.

Type 22.36.

CHAPTER 23
Keying, Security, Safety

Keying System for Office Buildings and Hotels

1. **Change Key**
   A key adapted to open only one of a set of locks.

2. **Master Key**
   Operates a given number of Change Key locks.

3. **Grand Master Key**
   Operates a given number of Change Key locks which also are Master Keyed or under two more Master Key systems.

4. **Great Grand Master Key**
   Operates a given number of Change Keys, a given number of Master Key systems, and/or other Grand Master Key systems.

5. **Construction Key**
   Often used on major buildings. **Must be specified.** Purpose: Temporarily, during construction, to have all locks keyed alike. This gives the various trades access and keeps keys Nos. 1, 2, 3, and 4 undistributed and protected from possible illegitimate use.

6. **Knock-Out Key**
   This is used (methods vary) to remove a pin or pins, voiding completely the operation of the Construction Key, No. 5.

7. **Key-Plug-Removing Key** (a type of Knock-Out Key)
   Used when a removable core cylinder system is specified. This system provides a method of removing only the cylinder plug for rekeying without removing the cylinder itself and permits a change of keys in seconds when another plug is ready to be inserted as a substitute for the old plug being removed.
   This system is available using all the first six keys enumerated.

8. **Emergency Key** (for Hotels and Motels)
   Operates all guestroom locks in a given project to lock out all other keys or gain entrance even though the door is locked inside.

9. **Display Key** (for Hotels and Motels)
   Operates only the lock on one door exactly as Key No. 8 does on all guestroom locks on the project. It is usually used on a display room door so that a guest with a valued display can lock out all maids and any other key except No. 8.
   A Maid's Key is really a Master Key, No. 2, and a Housekeeper's Key is really a Grand Master Key, No. 3, so no key numbers are recorded here.
   In Chapter 6, page 6, is a complete hotel hardware specification which includes keys in detail.

Important Note in Planning a Master Key System

Establish the possible maximum number of keys that may ever be needed. Be liberal in estimating present and future demands upon the Grand and Master Key Systems and the need for Change Keys.

It costs no more to provide for the future when the keying code is being established. Failure to do so greatly limits availability and leads to key duplication.

Cylinder Keying

The seven steps involved in rekeying a pin tumbler cylinder are shown and described on the next page. The cross-sectional views demonstrate the principle of cylinder lock construction. Although no lock with a keyway is pickproof, a well-designed and carefully assembled pin tumbler cylinder provides the utmost security and is more difficult to pick than any other lock type with a keyway.

Breaking and entering is an offense usually committed by the young and inexperienced, by those who have had little or no experience in lock picking. Burglars who are experienced lock pickers are probably accountable for less than five percent of the national robberies in any given period, and in these instances they expect a good haul.

Architects are not expected to be lock experts, but if they know the following principle, they can tell the degree of security provided by the locks specified for their structures. Briefly the principle is this: the greatest security is provided when no master keying is used, and conversely, the Great Grand Master Key System provides the least security.

When cylinders are Master Keyed, split pins are used, reducing the security from racking and picking and also reducing the number of possible change keys. Grand and Great Grand Master Keying progressively reduce the security and number of change keys. Further, the more the pins are split to accommodate the various Master Keys, the thinner they become and the sooner they wear out.

To overcome in some degree these limitations in keying systems, many manufacturers have locks with six or seven pins instead of the five shown on page 3. (Increasing the number of tumblers increases a lock's security and makes possible a greater number of change keys.) And they usually offer from five to a dozen or more keyways, which makes possible securer key changes.

Keying with Wing Bits

Master and Grand Master Keying is possible with lever tumbler locks operated by wing bit keys, but this old type of lock and key gives less protection than a cylinder lock with only four pins.

When specifying a Master Key system with lever tumbler locks, it is very important to check the manufacturer's catalogue to see that the functions specified are of the same "Key Class."

Rekeying a Pin Tumbler Cylinder

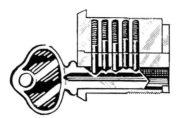

Cross-sectional view of five-pin
cylinder lock.

Step 1

Step 2
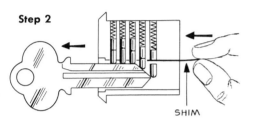

SHIM

Step 3
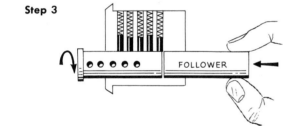

FOLLOWER

Step 4

Step 5

FILE FLUSH

Step 6
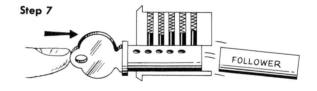

Step 7
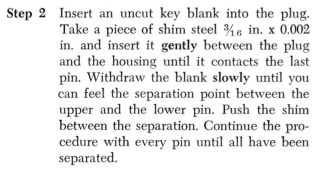

FOLLOWER

Step 1 Remove tailpiece. (Illustration shows screws, but some tailpieces are held on by expansion washers which can be pried off.)

Step 2 Insert an uncut key blank into the plug. Take a piece of shim steel $\frac{3}{16}$ in. x 0.002 in. and insert it **gently** between the plug and the housing until it contacts the last pin. Withdraw the blank **slowly** until you can feel the separation point between the upper and the lower pin. Push the shim between the separation. Continue the procedure with every pin until all have been separated.

Step 3 Turn plug 90° with tip of blank. Push out plug slowly with follower that is same diameter as plug. Avoid dropping the pins by holding cylinder so that the pin holes face up as the plug is pushed out.

Step 4 Remove pins carefully from plug.

Step 5 Insert new change key into plug, and reload plug with pins that are long enough to extend above the surface of the plug. Discard pins that are too short and replace with longer ones.

Step 6 Using a broad-mill file, take down all pins to the surface of the plug. Important: Do not file into body of plug!

Step 7 With new key in plug, insert in cylinder housing, thereby ejecting follower.

Door Security

There is much more to making a door burglar proof than just having a good cyinder lock. It is amazing how many homes, offices, and hotel guestrooms can be entered with only a stiff plastic credit card or a flexible piece of steel, and this can often be done faster than with a key. These same homes, offices, and rooms that are so easy to break into are very likely to have expensive architectural trim that does not contribute to door security.

The characteristic common to all doors that can be opened with a piece of flexible steel is lack of a dead bolt, or a dead bolt not thrown. To provide security, every spring latch, no matter what type of lock, should be supplemented with a deadlocking latch bolt or a dead bolt. The additional cost per door is measured in cents, not dollars.

Door security for hotels and office buildings depends not only on provision for a dead bolt but also on a reliable key control system. Visible indexed key control systems are described on page 7. This is an important part of the hardware specification, for control of both Master Keys and Change Keys.

The strongest door completely equipped with the best hardware can be made useless by poor key control, whether in the form of a resident "hiding" a key near his front door or a hotel clerk who gives out a room key without knowing a guest or asking for identification. If a clerk so obliges you, then your room in that hotel is open to anyone else who asks the clerk for your key by room number.

To prevent a firmly locked door from being opened to someone unknown, the door viewer shown in Chapter 22, page 3, is an asset.

Firm locks are a necessity for glass and aluminum doors with narrow stiles, and particularly for sliding doors of this type. Such locks are described in Chapter 13 page 4.

Jalousie doors are usually locked with only a button or a thumb turn. These are accessible to an intruder by just the turning of a slat. Such doors should have a dead bolt cylinder lock with cylinders inside and out.

Interior doors to closets and rooms that may contain valuables should be equipped with dead bolt cylinder locks, as should drawers and cupboards. All doors and drawers can be set up under a master key system so that the owner can open all of them with one key.

Hinges with pins that might be accessible to an intruder should be specified for non-removable pins (NRP).

Safety

The most important items of architectural hardware in regard to safety are exit devices (Chapter 14, pages 1 through 5) and smoke detectors (Chapter 22, page 2), both designed for larger buildings where people congregate. Other items, whether for large buildings or residences, can help prevent accidents, ranging from trivial to fatal, and law suits.

For example, a closet door should be equipped with knobs or levers on both sides. A child who finds himself shut inside can operate a knob or lever but may be too weak to turn a small spindle.

Bypassing sliding doors should be equipped with a stop as shown below to prevent pinched or broken fingers when using the flush pull.

A door stop for a hinged door should never be fastened to the floor if it could be a tripping hazard. Dome stops are appropriate behind doors in rooms but not in hallways, where wall bumpers or overhead stops are best. Where the swings of two doors

overlap, roller stops can prevent injured hands and damage to the doors.

Door closers when hung on brackets are dangerous, especially for tall persons, unless the doors are over seven feet high. The door closers described in Chapter 15 should be used on doors at least seven feet high.

The non-checking spring hinges described in Chapter 8 should be specified and selected with care, because in many locations a fast-closing door can lead to an accident.

Grooved thresholds offer better traction than those with a plain surface. The grooves are most useful if water is ever tracked onto the threshold, as would happen at an outside door in wet weather.

Specifying adequate screws, bolts, and brackets and proper installation are safety factors that can apply to all hardware.

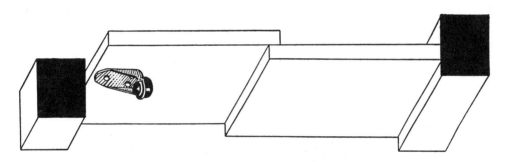

Special Locks; Electric Strikes

Locks for Twin Communicating Doors

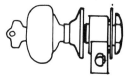

If doors are to be key locked, use this lock on one door and Type 23.2 on the other. See Chapter 6, page 10, door 5.

Deadlocking latch bolt. Rotating knob or thumb turn will retract latch bolt when unlocked. When locked by key, neither knob nor thumb turn will rotate.

Type 23.1.

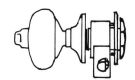

For use where space between doors does not permit use of knob inside. See Chapter 6, page 10, door 5. Deadlocking latch bolt. Rotating knob or thumb turn will retract latch bolt when unlocked. Turning button in knob (manually) to horizontal locks both knob and thumb turn.

Type 23.2.

Asylum or Institutional Lock

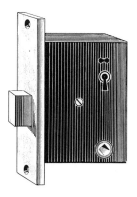

Mortise deadlock. Dead bolt operated by key from either side by bit key.

Type 23.3.

Electric Strike, Standard

Illustration is general in character. Many kinds are available to match specific locks. Supplier must furnish strike to suit conditions.

Type 23.4.

Electric Strike with Signal Switch

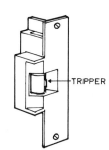

Strike will indicate remotely whether door is open or closed, locked or unlocked. Very useful for remote door surveillance to control alarms, indication lights, and inter-locks. Switch operated by trigger. Consult manufacturers' catalogues for other features.

Type 23.5.

Key Switch

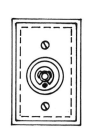

Key operates switch to perform various functions, with time delay when appropriate. Uses standard electrical outlets. One function is door opener. Person returning with arms full simply turns key and door springs open. Tamper resistant.

Type 23.6.

Key Control Systems, Visible Index

Multiple Drawer System

6-Drawer File. Hook Capacity, in even multiples of 100: 600, min. 1,600 max.

8-Drawer File. Hook Capacity, in even multiples of 100: 1,700 min. 2,200 max.

Type 23.7.

Wall-Mounted System

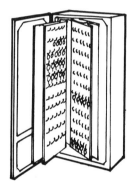

Hook Capacity: 25 to 100 in multiples of 25. 150 to 450 in multiples of 50. 500 to 1200 in multiples of 100.

Type 23.8.

Portable System

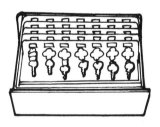

In tray, for mounting in cabinet or desk drawer. Hook Capacity: 21 to 49.

Type 23.9.

All systems should be equipped with a cylinder lock to lock all drawers unless otherwise specified.

Hook curves should be at least ⅝″ long. Hooks should be spaced horizontally with not less than 1⅜″ centers and vertically with not less than 3½″ centers.

When specifying, be sure to call for components as noted below.

Option Key

-1 **Labels.** Unless otherwise specified, labels should be provided numbered from 1 up to the capacity of the system and should fit the hook and label pockets in cabinet panels so as to be adequately protected.

-2 **Key Tags and Holders.** Provide two sets key tags with metal holders. One of these sets should be marked "File Key, Must Not Be Loaned." The other should be marked "Duplicate."

-3 **Envelopes.** One envelope for each key-holding hook, printed for recording all pertinent data. 24-lb. kraft stock minimum weight.

-4 **Receipts, Receipt Holders, and Key Records.** Receipt holder and 4 or more receipt blanks for each hook. Each system should have forms to list names of those holding keys in a quantity equal to three times the hook capacity.

-5 **Visible Indexing.** With visible cross index card folder. Cover of binders rigid, of 25-point minimum genuine pressboard. Card and sheet record forms of full capacity of system plus 25%.

-6 **Instruction Manual.** Printed and illustrated.

-7 **Complete installation** to be performed by manufacturer's trained personnel.

NOTE: In specifying key control systems add option numbers to type number. If all options are wanted, state, for example, Type 23.7, Options 1 through 7.

Key control is very important

CHAPTER 24
Unusual Hardware Problems Solved

So many architects and hardware consultants have shown such interest in the situations and solutions included in the author's previous publications that it was decided to keep such a feature in this book. On the following pages are 16 problems with illustrations showing how they were solved.

It is surprising how often such problems as these can be solved by using a hardware product currently in stock or by adapting a generally used item, making it heavier or lighter to handle a given situation, without changing a proven principle long in use. The examples which follow illustrate this.

Chapter Index

Problem 1

Shortly before the Denver Hilton was to be opened, the hotel management instructed the architects to have four huge doors installed in a row to serve as screens (see photograph). Each door was to be 6 ft. wide, 20 ft. high, and 4 in. thick and was to be pivoted.

There was no way to use a center swivel hanger in the ceiling since there was nothing that could carry the weight. The flooring contractor assured us that any pivot installed on the finished floor would splinter it when the door was hung.

The solution was to drill a hole in the floor for each bottom pivot and embed it on the structural slab so that the floor supported none of the doors' weight. This bottom pivot contained a large hardened steel ball bearing. The doors were center-pivoted, a long-established principle for swinging heavy doors.

When hung, the doors could be swung easily with one finger. The doors were locked open or closed with a flush extension bolt, Type 21.8, and an extra strike.

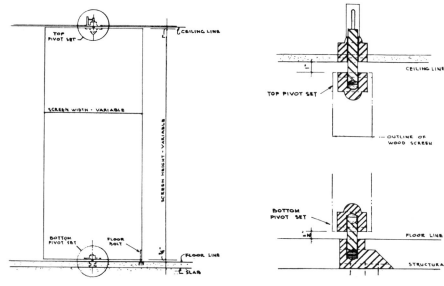

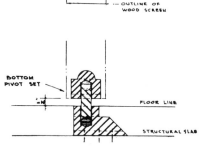

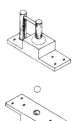

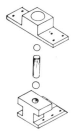

TOP PIVOT SET

BOTTOM PIVOT SET

Elevation   Section   Isometric

Problem 2

For a beautiful Palm Beach mansion overlooking the Atlantic ocean an architect designed the pair of main entrance doors shown below. The doors were rabbeted at the meeting rail and at the top. The lock, operated by drop rings outside and lever handles inside, required a special 8 in. backset.

The doors swung on pivots and had a special threshold. The hardware finish was antique brass and included dummy trim of studs inside and out. The architect wanted drop rings with a twisted rope effect.

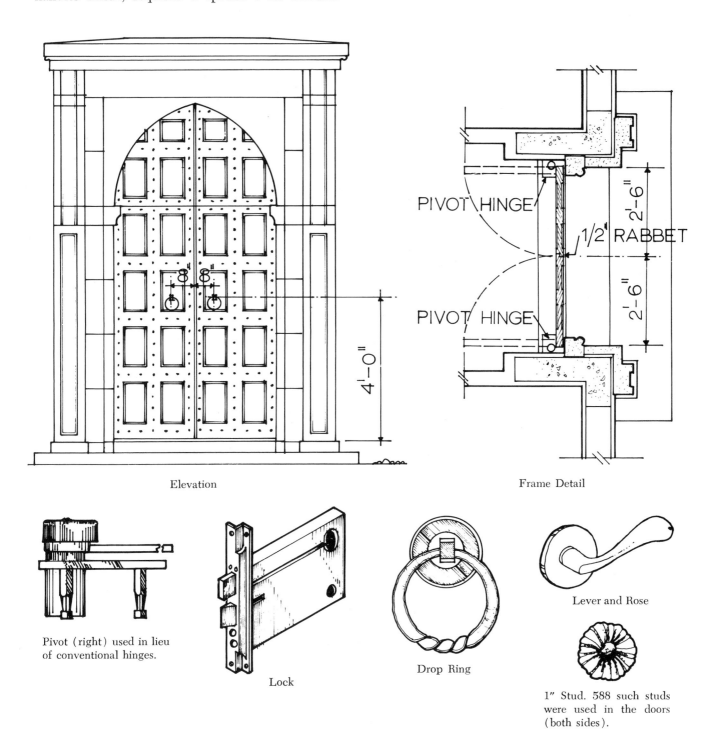

Elevation

Frame Detail

Pivot (right) used in lieu of conventional hinges.

Lock

Drop Ring

Lever and Rose

1" Stud. 588 such studs were used in the doors (both sides).

151

Problem 3

The proprietor of a Chinese restaurant in Pittsburgh wanted the versatility of booths to seat four persons, or eight persons, or no booths at all for occasional parties.

The requirement was met by hanging panels with heavy blank pivots in such a way that each panel could be swung flat against the wall in either direction. A heavy strip of steel was riveted to the top pivot, bent, and countersunk (concealed) into the top of the panel to prevent sagging. To hold each partition firmly open or closed a plunger (Type 21.46) and three floor sockets were used for each panel. The plunger rods were long enough to cover the few inches the panel was raised off the floor.

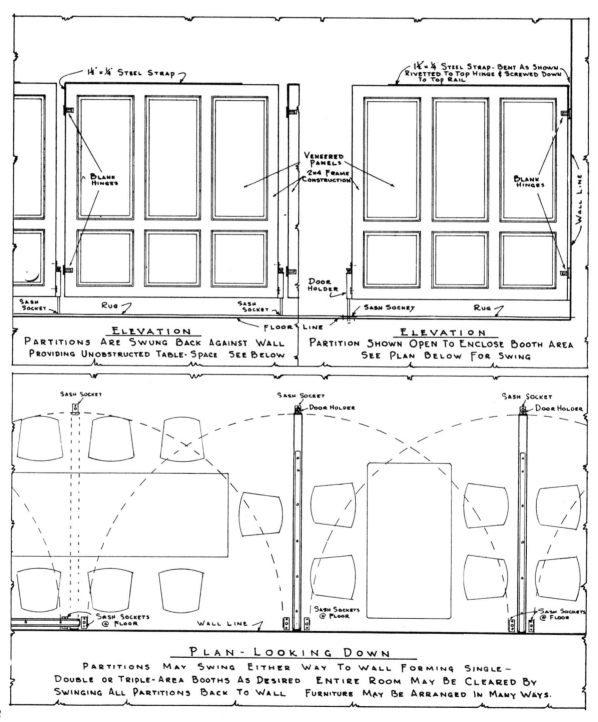

Problem 4

In finishing the interior construction at the Pittsburgh Hilton Hotel, it was necessary in each guestroom to hang a pair of doors for the closet, which had an opening 8 ft. high and of varying wide widths. The problem lay in the fact that the opening had no frame and the heavy doors would have to swing between two plaster walls and shut flush.

The situation was met by asking a manufacturer specially to design and manufacture a set of pivots that could stand the load, using a hanging principle successful in cabinet work. The pivots had nylon bushings and specially angled leaves to suit the detail. Wood stops were provided top and bottom, and magnetic catches held the doors shut.

NOTE: For large doors such as these, the door manufacturer should be consulted so that door specifications ensure that the doors will not warp. This was done for this job. A warped door puts extra strain on the hinges or pivots and brings the closing latch out of alignment.

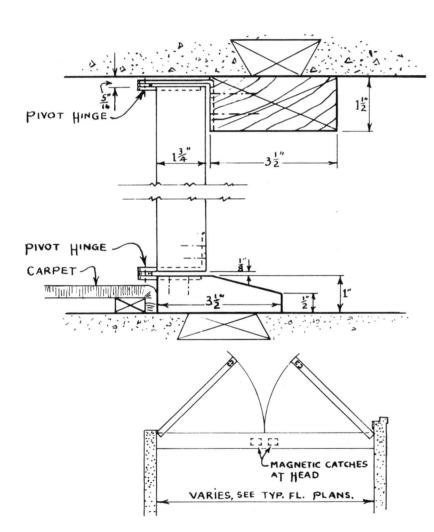

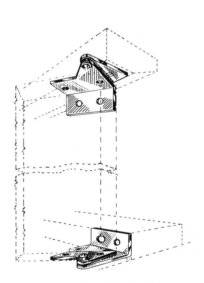

Pivots (above) with nylon bearings used for heavy doors. Architect's detail (left) for hotel closets in Problem 4.

Problem 5

A home owner in Bridgeport, Connecticut, wanted a bar installed in a paneled room in such a way that, when the bar was not in use, it could not be seen. This was accomplished by recessing the bar into the wall, as permitted by the structure of the house, and hiding it with a sliding door. The door, when closed, could not be distinguished from the room's paneling.

The door slid up to open and was held open by spring balances. A bar counter shelf, stored vertically, was lifted up and out into service position. This was held tight by two levers, one on each side. Mortised into the panel was a brass casting 5 in. long and ¾ in. wide with reinforcing angles at the side, a steel pin through it, and an angle-slotted top ¼ in. wide and 2 in. long. A special flat hook with a hole ⁵⁄₁₆ in. square fitted tightly on the steel spindle and was mortised into the door.

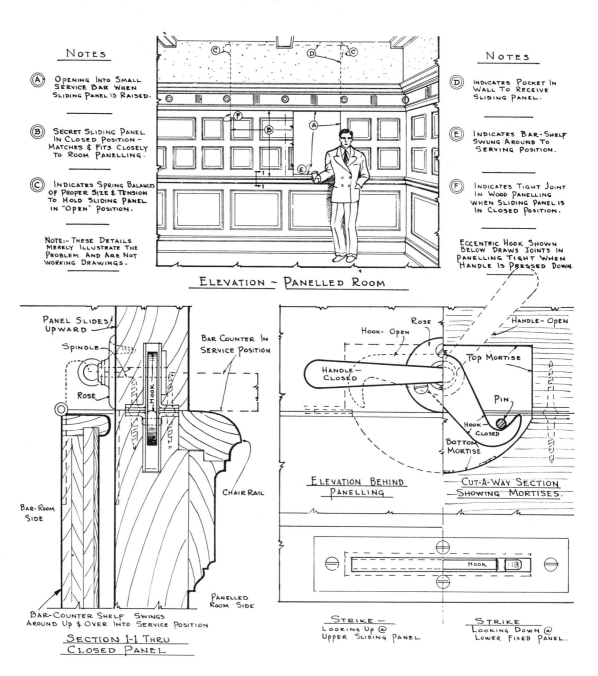

Problem 6

In a residence in Dallas, the owner wanted his den so concealed that no one would know about it or how to get into the room even if they knew of its existence. The sketch left below illustrates the layout. No hardware of any kind could appear on the foyer side.

The door was hung on invisible hinges, and on the den side the lock and trim were standard. To release the bolt on the foyer side, however, there was a secret release (Type 18.48) which withdrew the bolt when a button under the carpet was stepped on. The pusher that comes with this release opened the door a few inches.

Button actuator for secret bolt release can be installed on either floor or wall.

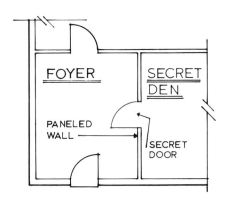

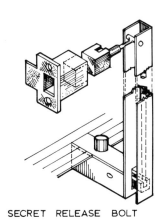

SECRET RELEASE BOLT

Problem 7

A pair of doors, as in a hotel corridor, can be made to disappear literally into the woodwork. This is done with the Harmon hinge (Type 22.2), named after the English inventor. When the door is open, it is flush with the corridor wall and forms part of the paneling or other surface.

Such doors can also be equipped with fusible arm closers. When these reach a certain temperature, as in the case of fire, they release the doors, which swing shut on closing hinges, thereby closing the corridor.

More sensitive to fire conditions than the fusible holders are smoke detectors (Type 22.10), which similarly can be adapted to doors hung on Harmon hinges. When smoke is detected, photoelectrically or by some other method, the doors swing shut.

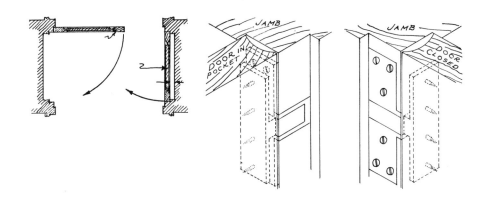

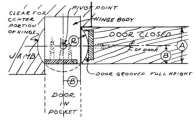

Radius (R) of Jamb Clearing

A	$1\frac{3}{4}''$	$2''$	$2\frac{1}{4}''$
R	$1\frac{7}{32}''$	$1\frac{15}{32}''$	$1\frac{21}{32}''$

Problem 8

An elegant mansion in New Britain, Connecticut, had several pairs of wood entrance doors opening out. The security of these doors was to be increased by the addition, outside, of a pair of wrought iron grille gates.

A T-bolt was anchored to the outside of the doors so as to engage a slot in the gates at one point of the swing. After closing from this point, the T-bolt was held in the slot, effectively holding and locking the gates when the doors were locked.

With the gates wide open, the doors could swing freely. Note the difference in swing centers.

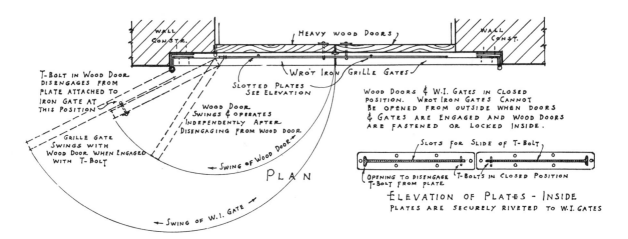

Problem 9

Late workers in a certain office building in Pittsburgh could not leave the building without finding the watchman and having him open one of a pair of main entrance doors with his key. This inconvenience was overcome by placing a jamb bolt (left) in the head of the door frame over one door. Thus during the day the doors were free swinging and double acting. After closing time one door was locked from both sides and the other door was locked from the outside only. When pushed open, it shut itself with its closing checking hinge and locked itself.

This was accomplished by removing the original deadlock and installing in its place a mortise night latch with an auxiliary latch bolt (right). This lock has two cylinders and a turn knob.

The watchman's key operates the inside cylinder only. In the morning he retracts the latch bolt and closes the jamb bolt, thereby making the doors double acting. At night he reverses the procedure, opening the jamb bolt and releasing the held-back lock, so that only one door operates and is single acting.

Problem 10

PLAN

1/4" x 1/4"

1/2"

DETAIL

A Florida architect wanted to be able to express his hospitality at the main entrance to his home on certain occasions by flinging both doors of a pair open at the same time. The proper hardware to satisfy this requirement was furnished as follows.

The doors were rabbeted as shown in the detail at left. In the illustration at the right, the active door is the one at the left, with locks at three points—top, bottom and in a strike mounted on the inactive door. It is operated by a cylinder lock. Both doors are opened from within by lever handles. The normally inactive door has locks top and bottom.

To ensure that the bottom locks would not mar the floor, devices were included to hold the latches open automatically until the doors are closed.

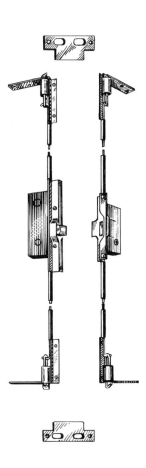

NOTE: This is also an excellent arrangement for French doors. A wide variety of backsets is available.

Problem 11

The same Florida residence mentioned in Problem 10 had shutters (blinds) for its windows. Except in the hurricane season they were held open against the exterior wall by shutter dogs (Type 20.47). During hurricane season they are closed and locked by shutter bars.

The only problem here was that in a high wind the shutter bars permitted the shutters to rattle. The illustration shows how an inventive Florida distributor solved the problem.

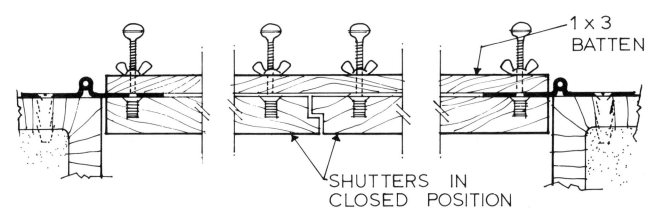

1 x 3 BATTEN

SHUTTERS IN CLOSED POSITION

Problem 12

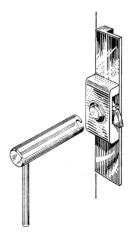

Hardware men do not usually furnish fixtures for metal windows, but an exception was made in this case. Strong winds were causing windows to rattle at the United Nations Secretariat Building in New York. The problem was solved with the special surface fastener and key shown at left. Windows are opened only for cleaning.

Problem 14

To avoid an inconvenient lock in the bottom rail of a glass door, the unique device shown provides a cylinder lock plus a push-pull plate. This also offers more lock functions than the bottom deadlock. Two through-bolts fasten it to the narrow stile.

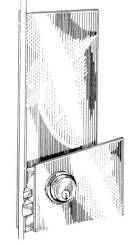

Problem 13

A Hospital in Detroit had some 400 wood veneer doors that would be repeatedly subjected to very strong cleaning solutions. To protect the wood finish and the trim the hardware man came up with a U-shaped sheath of black plastic that protected both sides and the bottom of the door perfectly.

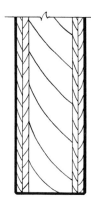

Problem 15

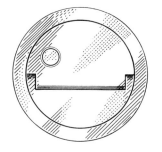
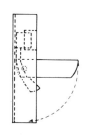

On a hinged door in a basketball court, it was necessary to operate a latch, but no hardware could protrude. The above flush ring solved this problem. A small button opens the pull which turns to operate.

Problem 16

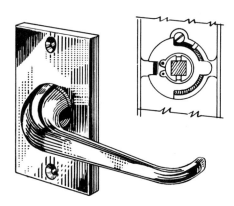

The architect occasionally specifies lever handles to operate latches. Since the lever is easier to operate than a knob, it is often the choice for doors in a retirement community and in homes for the aged.

The problem with a lever handle is that the spring is subjected to more strain than that in a knob. American manufacturers have done much to overcome this, but the handle at left, which the author noticed on a visit to Australia, seems to provide an ideal solution.

The springs are easy to operate yet the handle never sags. A strong post in the rose keeps all stress from the latch bolt. Through-bolts from the inside rose screw into screw posts of the outside rose, so that the outside rose shows no screw holes.

APPENDIX 1

Tables of Weights and Measures

Linear Measure

Metric System

		1 inch (in.)	2.540 centimeters (cm.)
12	inches	1 foot (ft.)	30.480 cm.
3	feet	1 yard (yd.)	0.914 meters (m.)
39.37	inches		1 m.

Square Measure

Metric System

	1 sq. in.	5.451 sq. cm.
144 sq. in.	1 sq. ft.	0.093 sq. m.
9 sq. ft.	1 sq. yd.	0.836 sq. m.
1550 sq. in.		1.0 sq. m.

Avoirdupois

Metric System

1.0	dram		1.771 grams (g.)
16.0	drams	1 ounce (oz.)	28.349 gr.
16.0	oz.	1 pound (lb.)	0.453 kilograms (kg.)
2.2046	lb.		1.0 kg.
25.0	lb.	1 quarter (qr.)	11.3 kg.
4.0	qr.	1 hundred weight (cwt.)	45.3 kg.
2,000.0	lb.	1 ton	
2,204.6	lb.		1.0 metric ton
2,240.0	lb.	1 long ton	

Circular Measure

60	seconds (sec.)	1 minute (min.)
60	minutes	1 degree
30	degrees	1 sign (of Zodiac)
90	degrees	1 quadrant
360	degrees	1 circle

Approximate Weight (Pounds) per Cubic Foot

Aluminum	162
Brass, cast	504
Brass, rolled	524
Copper, cast	542
Copper, rolled	548
Iron, cast	450
Iron, wrought	485
Lead	711
Steel	490
Zinc	437
Chestnut, dry	41
Hemlock, dry	25
Oak, white, dry	50
Pine, white, dry	25
Pine, southern yellow, dry	45

Green timber is $1\frac{1}{3}$ to $1\frac{1}{2}$ times heavier than dry timber.

Miscellaneous

3.0 in.	1 palm
4.0 in.	1 hand
6.0 in.	1 span
18.0 in.	1 cubit
1,728.0 cu. in.	1 cu. ft.
27.0 cu. ft.	1 cu. yd.
128.0 cu. ft.	1 cord
2,150.0 cu. in.	1 bushel
268.8 cu. in.	1 gallon (dry)
231.0 cu. in.	1 gallon (liquid)

1 cu. ft. water weighs 62.4 lb. and contains 7.5 gal.

APPENDIX 2
Abbreviations

Adj	Adjustable	Ga	Gauge
A.H.C.	Architectural Hardware Consultant	Galv	Galvanized
A.I.A.	American Institute of Architects	G.M.K.	Grand Master Key
Alum	Aluminum	G.S.A.	General Services Administration
A.S.A.	American Standards Association	Hdle	Handle
A.S.A.H.C.	American Society of Architectural Hardware Consultants	Hdwe	Hardware
		H.M.	Hollow metal
B.H.M.A.	Builders Hardware Manufacturers Association	Hvy	Heavy
Brkt	Bracket	Kit	Kitchen
Brze	Bronze	Lava	Lavatory
BS	Backset	N.B.H.A.	National Builders Hardware Association
C & H	Coat and hat (hooks)	N.R.P.	Non-removable hinge pin
C.S.I.	Construction Specifications Institute	Pr	Pair
Cyl	Cylinder	Rabt	Rabbeted
D.A.	Double acting (door)	Rm	Room
Dble	Double	R.S.	Reverse spring
D.H.	Double-hung (sash)	Sgle	Single
Dr	Door	Sprg	Spring
Esc	Escutcheon	S.S.	Stainless steel
Ex	Extra	Std	Standard
Ext	Exterior	TP	Thumbpiece
F.H.A.	Federal Housing Administration	U.L.	Underwriters Laboratories, Inc.
Fin	Finish	Wrt	Wrought

Hands of Doors and Casements

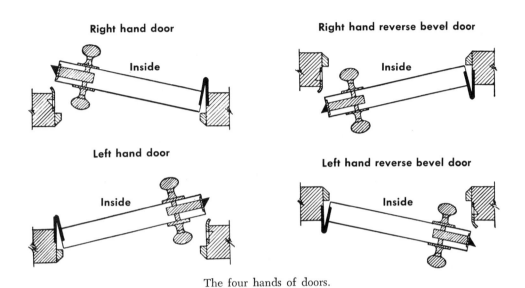

Right hand door

Inside

Right hand reverse bevel door

Inside

Left hand door

Inside

Left hand reverse bevel door

Inside

The four hands of doors.

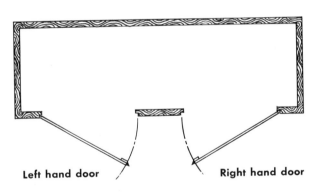

Left hand door   Right hand door

Hands of doors for cases such as cupboards, cabinets, bookcases, and refrigerators.

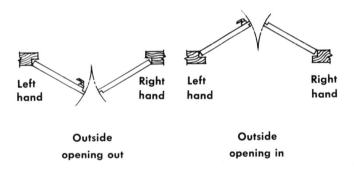

Left hand   Right hand   Left hand   Right hand

Outside opening out   **Outside opening in**

Hands for wood casement windows. Metal casement windows use the exact opposite method of handing.

Hardware Metals and Other Materials

The tremendous expansion of facilities for producing various metals, combined with important technological advances, has had an important effect upon the traditional relationships of various metals. New technological advances are sure to cause further developments.

The ever-increasing use of other materials such as wood, plastics, and ceramics also enters the field under discussion in this chapter. These materials offer attractive decorative schemes formerly unavailable in builders' hardware.

The order in which these materials are discussed in this chapter does not necessarily reflect the order of their importance. The older and long-established metals are listed first. It is the continued practice throughout this book to remain unbiased with respect to the use of the various metals and materials.

It is important, however, that the characteristics, advantages, and possible disadvantages be noted. This has been done in a generally descriptive way based on long experience. As noted above, it is acknowledged that new technological advances may well mean changes in the future.

The exact percentage composition of the following alloys varies from one manufacturer to the next, but the figures given here are typical.

Cast Bronze

Copper	85%
Zinc	5%
Lead	5%
Tin	5%

Cast Bronze is reddish. It is generally stronger than cast brass and has better wearing qualities.

It is produced by pouring the molten metal into sand molds shaped into the desired patterns.

It is highly resistant to breakage, and it withstands all the wear and tear that hardware gets in its lifetime.

Cast Brass

Copper	70%
Zinc	27½%
Lead	2½%
(No Tin)	

Cast Brass is yellowish. It is produced by the same method as Cast Bronze above. Prices of the two metals are usually the same.

Cast White Bronze

Copper	65%
Nickel	20%
Zinc	6%
Lead	5%
Tin	4%

The chief advantage of Cast White Bronze is its superior resistance to wear and corrosion. Its disadvantage is that it costs about 25% more than Cast Bronze because it is more difficult to produce.

Forged Bronze and Forged Brass

The use of Forged Bronze and Brass in place of Cast Bronze and Cast Brass has increased rapidly because of their greater tensile strength, uniformity of thickness, and greater ease of machining. Where heavy gauge (80 gauge or more) is used, forgings are generally acceptable substitutes at no difference in price, especially in such items as lock parts, knobs, and escutcheons, when items can be run in sufficient quantity to absorb the cost of producing the necessarily costly dies. It has become an industry practice to give the manufacturer the option to provide heavy forgings in lieu of cast metals as he elects.

For the same reasons lighter forgings, not less than 50 gauge, have taken an important place, having proved superior to wrought bronze and wrought brass. Made either in hot or cold forgings, they usually cost more than wrought, but have proved worth the difference.

Wrought Bronze

Copper	90%
Zinc	9%
Tin	11%

Processed by rolling large billets to the desired thickness. The thicknesses vary by product.

Wrought Brass

Copper	60 to 80%
Zinc	20 to 40%
(No tin)	

Processed like Wrought Bronze.

Cast Aluminum

Aluminum	96%
Other elements	4%

Produced from molten metal as is cast bronze. Particularly useful where acid fumes may corrode other metals, in sewage disposal plants, etc.

Other Aluminum Metals

Forged Aluminum. See comments above on Forged Bronze.

Wrought Aluminum. See comments above on Wrought Bronze.

Caution: Best used on flat plates because of possibility of denting knobs, etc.

Stainless Steel

Stainless Steel is an alloy chiefly of iron and chromium (usually 12 to 14%) and it may contain smaller percentages of other elements such as nickel and titanium. It is increasingly used for builders' hardware because it does not rust and takes a finish of high luster.

The American Iron and Steel Institute has assigned identifying type numbers to various standardized stainless steel alloys. Type No. 302 is the most popular in the builders' hardware industry; it contains about 18% chrome and 8% nickel.

Powdered Metal

The use of powdered metal is comparatively recent. Some manufacturers have installed sintering plants for this process. It offers definite savings in costs. Developments may bring it into far greater use in the future in the production of builders' hardware. The powder is pressed to shape, then sintered in a furnace. For additional strength, it is pressed further after sintering.

Wood

The use of Wood for knobs, pulls and push plates in conjunction with metal shanks and other fixtures has become popular. Also used is laminated plastic-impregnated wood that has the durability of metal. Consult manufacturers' catalogues.

Cast Iron

Cast iron is used extensively in builder's hardware. It is a ferrous metal. The rusting effect does not develop destructive results nearly as quickly as in steel.

Cast iron's lower cost, long wearing qualities, and natural lubrication offer good reasons for its use in builders' hardware. Cast iron's weakness is its brittleness and low tensile strength. A typical composition is 92% iron, with the other 8% carbon, silicon, manganese, phosphorus, and sulfur.

Malleable Iron

Malleable iron has all the good characteristics of cast iron. The iron content of malleable iron is 96 to 97%. The castings are given a special baking or annealing treatment which leaves them extremely tough and resistant to shock.

Forged Iron

Forged iron contains over 90% iron. Iron forgings are produced by hammering a red-hot bar of iron into the desired shape. In builders' hardware, forged iron's greatest use is in the manufacture of old Colonial or Spanish hardware trim.

Wrought Steel

Some cast and forged steel is used in the manufacture of builders' hardware. Screw machine parts made from steel rod are used on a wide variety of builders' hardware items.

Steel is generally stronger than iron. Ordinary carbon steel commonly used in builders' hardware chiefly contains iron, carbon, manganese, phosphorus, and sulfur.

Exposed to the elements, carbon steel is highly susceptible to rusting. It is in great use, of course, because of its lower cost. Most of the builders' hardware items made out of wrought steel are formed from flat sheets by dies in heavy presses.

There are many rust resisting finishes available, as listed under Finishes in Appendix 5. Hot galvanizing is most effective in resisting rust, but no process is completely rustproof.

Zinc

Zinc has been used in builders' hardware for many years as a coating over iron and steel to resist rust and to protect the finish. Die cast zinc is an economical base metal for manufacturing many hardware items. The ease of casting and machining, the smoothness of the metal, and good plating have popularized its use by manufacturers. Because it is non-ferrous and lower in price, it has had wide acceptance by the trade.

The softness of zinc and its tendency to freeze or crumble have restricted its use largely to non-working parts in locks. Manufacturers of zinc-die alloys emphasize that the quality of a zinc-die casting depends to the greatest degree on the purity of the zinc in the alloy.

Plastics

The plastics field in builders' hardware has grown rapidly. Bakelite, Lucite, and many other durable plastics have demonstrated their ability to compete with metal for many items, parts, and coatings. New formulas and manufacturing processes have made possible tough plastics in a variety of colors at prices that compare well with metals.

Ceramics

There are comparatively few manufacturers of this decorative trim, but there are enough who offer knobs, escutcheons and other trim to meet the special demands of some architects.

Some of the handpainted knobs are very attractive. Like glass knobs, still available, they are most decorative but both are subject to breakage.

APPENDIX 5

B.H.M.A. Standards for Finishes

The Builders Hardware Manufacturers Association (B.H.M.A.) has courageously taken the initiative in standardizing hardware specification terminology in such a way that computers can be used. The B.H.M.A. has graciously given me permission to reproduce in this Appendix their "Standard 1301, B.H.M.A. Product Standards, Section M, Materials and Finishes." (This material is copyrighted, 1969, by the Builders Hardware Manufacturers Association and is not to be reproduced without specific authorization from the B.H.M.A.)

For many years each hardware manufacturer had his own code of finishes. This proved to be chaotic as the number of manufacturers, products, and finishes increased. After a long and costly struggle, most manufacturers yielded to the inevitable and began to use the system of the Federal Bureau of Standards, with or without the prefix US (for example, US26D). They received immediate benefits for adopting this standardization.

Now the demands of computer control are rapidly forcing manufacturers to modify the system. Since a computer can handle numbers more efficiently than letters, the former US26D becomes 626, as will be seen on the following B.H.M.A. list. A number of manufacturers have not made this change, and catalogues should be consulted before specifying.

Many other variations of finishes are available that are too numerous to be included here, and selection of such finishes should be carefully checked from manufacturers' catalogues.

The term "coated" refers to a thin, tough, protective film which has taken the place of the lacquers formerly much in use. Uncoated finishes are occasionally specified, but because of small production runs, inventory costs, and overruns, they cost more than the coated finish.

The B.H.M.A. recognizes that new finishes will be developed and, accordingly, plans to update, correct, and revise their Standards on a regular basis.

In the Finish Standards, which follows the General Requirements, only finishes produced by three or more manufacturers are listed and are numbered starting with 600. Numbers 001 through 599 are reserved for individual manufacturers to use as they desire for their unique finishes.

1. GENERAL REQUIREMENTS

1.1 MATERIALS

[This brief section is not reproduced, since it has to do with a numbering system for materials related to other B.H.M.A. standards.]

1.2 FINISHES

1.2.1 There are separate numbers for finishes as they are applied to each separate base material except when brass or bronze can be used without affecting the final finish.

1.2.2 Comparative finishes shall match when viewed approximately two feet apart and three feet away on the same plane and under the same environment.

1.2.3 Samples of finishes in categories A and B together with selected samples from Category C are available for purchase at the B.H.M.A. office.

1.2.4 Category B finish samples shall be kept fresh and will be considered so if not held over six months and are kept in their original container and not handled.

1.2.5 All B.H.M.A. product types are not available in all finishes. Consult manufacturers' catalogs.

1.3 CATEGORIES

B.H.M.A. code numbers for finishes fall in one of five categories which are defined as follows:

A. Category A finishes are those that will match B.H.M.A. match plates when viewed according to the formula listed in paragraph 1.2.2.

B. Category B finishes are those that are unstable and that vary when applied to different alloys and forms of base metal. These finishes are compatible with the B.H.M.A. match plates, but it is to be understood that these finishes cannot and do not match from one alloy or form of metal to the next and from one manufacturer to the next.

C. Category C includes ornamental finishes found on all forms of metal. The metal is blackened or oxidized or relieved or highlighted, usually by hand. Aesthetically, it is not desirable that they match but they should be compatible.

D. Category D finish is a functional protective finish in which appearance is not a factor.

E. Category E finishes will be compatible in color when compared with the B.H.M.A. match plate standard having the comparable finish on brass or bronze base metal.

164

2. FINISH STANDARDS

B.H.M.A. Code	Finish Description	Base Material	Category	Nearest U.S. Equivalent
600	Primed for painting	Steel	D	USP
601	Bright japanned	Steel	D	US1B
602	Cadmium plated	Steel	D	US2C
603	Zinc plated	Steel	D	US2G
604	Zinc plated and dichromate sealed	Steel	D	
605	Bright brass, clear coated	Brass	A	US3
606	Satin brass, clear coated	Brass	A	US4
607	Oxidized satin brass, oil rubbed	Brass	B	
608	Oxidized satin brass, relieved, clear coated	Brass	C	
609	Satin brass, blackened, satin relieved, clear coated	Brass	C	US5
610	Satin brass, blackened, bright relieved, clear coated	Brass	C	US7
611	Bright bronze, clear coated	Bronze	A	US9
612	Satin bronze, clear coated	Bronze	A	US10
613	Oxidized satin bronze, oil rubbed	Bronze	B	US10B
614	Oxidized satin bronze, relieved, clear coated	Bronze	C	
615	Oxidized satin bronze, relieved, waxed	Bronze	C	
616	Satin bronze, blackened, satin relieved, clear coated	Bronze	C	US11
617	Dark oxidized satin bronze, bright relieved, clear coated	Bronze	C	US13
618	Bright nickel plated, clear coated	Brass, Bronze	A	US14
619	Satin nickel plated, clear coated	Brass, Bronze	A	US15
620	Satin nickel plated, blackened, satin relieved, clear coated	Brass, Bronze	C	US15A
621	Nickel plated, blackened, matte relieved, clear coated	Brass, Bronze	C	US17A
622	Flat black coated	Brass, Bronze	A	US19
623	Light oxidized bright bronze, clear coated	Bronze	C	US20
624	Dark oxidized, statuary bronze, clear coated	Bronze	C	US20A
625	Bright chromium plated	Brass, Bronze	A	US26
626	Satin chromium plated	Brass, Bronze	A	US26D
627	Satin aluminum, clear coated	Aluminum	A	US27
628	Satin aluminum, clear anodized	Aluminum	A	US28
629	Bright stainless steel	Stainless steel 300 Series	A	US32
630	Satin stainless steel	Stainless steel 300 Series	A	US32D
631	Flat black coated	Steel	E	US19
632	Plated bright brass, clear coated	Steel	E	US3
633	Plated satin brass, clear coated	Steel	E	US4
634	Plated oxidized satin brass, oil rubbed	Steel	B	
635	Plated oxidized satin brass, relieved, clear coated	Steel	C	
636	Plated satin brass, blackened, bright relieved, clear coated	Steel	C	US7
637	Plated bright bronze, clear coated	Steel	E	US9
638	Plated satin brass, blackened, satin relieved, clear coated	Steel	C	US5
639	Plated satin bronze, clear coated	Steel	E	US10
640	Plated oxidized satin bronze, oil rubbed	Steel	B	US10B
641	Plated oxidized satin bronze, relieved, clear coated	Steel	C	
642	Plated oxidized satin bronze, relieved, waxed	Steel	C	
643	Plated satin bronze, blackened, satin relieved, clear coated	Steel	C	US11
644	Plated dark oxidized satin bronze, bright relieved, clear coated	Steel	C	US13
645	Bright nickel plated, clear coated	Steel	E	US14
646	Satin nickel plated, clear coated	Steel	E	US15
647	Satin nickel plated, blackened, satin relieved, clear coated	Steel	C	US15A
648	Nickel plated, blackened, matte relieved, clear coated	Steel	C	US17A
649	Plated light oxidized bright bronze, clear coated	Steel	C	US20
650	Plated dark oxidized statuary bronze, clear coated	Steel	C	US20A
651	Bright chromium plated	Steel	E	US26
652	Satin chromium plated	Steel	E	US26D

2. FINISH STANDARDS (continued)

B.H.M.A. Code	Finish Description	Base Material	Category	Nearest U.S. Equivalent
653	Bright stainless steel	Stainless steel 400 Series	D	
654	Satin stainless steel	Stainless steel 400 Series	D	
655	Light oxidized satin bronze, bright relieved, clear coated	Bronze	C	US13
656	Plated light oxidized satin bronze, bright relieved, clear coated	Steel	C	US13
657	Plated dark oxidized copper, satin relieved, clear coated	Steel	C	
658	Plated dark oxidized copper, bright relieved, clear coated	Steel	C	
659	Plated light oxidized copper, satin relieved, clear coated	Steel	C	
660	Plated light oxidized copper, bright relieved, clear coated	Steel	C	
661	Plated oxidized satin copper, relieved, clear coated	Steel	C	
662	Plated satin brass, browned, satin relieved, clear coated	Steel	C	
663	Plated zinc with clear chromate seal	Steel	D	
664	Plated cadmium with clear chromate seal	Steel	D	
665	Plated cadmium with iridescent dichromate	Steel	D	
666	Plated bright brass, clear coated	Aluminum	E	US3
667	Plated satin brass, clear coated	Aluminum	E	US4
668	Plated satin bronze, clear coated	Aluminum	E	US10
669	Bright nickel plated	Aluminum	E	US14
670	Satin nickel plated	Aluminum	E	US15
671	Flat black coated	Aluminum	E	US19
672	Bright chromium plated	Aluminum	E	US26
673	Aluminum, clear coated	Aluminum	D	
674	Primed for painting	Zinc	D	USP
675	Dichromate sealed	Zinc	D	
676	Flat black coated	Zinc	A	US19
677	Plated bright brass, clear coated	Zinc	E	US3
678	Plated satin brass, clear coated	Zinc	E	US4
679	Plated bright bronze, clear coated	Zinc	E	US9
680	Plated satin bronze, clear coated	Zinc	E	US10
681	Bright chromium plated	Zinc	E	US26
682	Satin chromium plated	Zinc	E	US26D
683	Plated oxidized satin brass, oil rubbed	Zinc	B	
684	Black chrome, bright	Brass, Bronze	C	
685	Black chrome, satin	Brass, Bronze	C	
686	Black chrome, bright	Steel	C	
687	Black chrome, satin	Steel	C	
688	Satin aluminum, gold anodized	Aluminum	E	US4

APPENDIX 6

Glossary

A

Active Door (in a pair of doors). The leaf that opens first and the one to which the lock is applied.

Adjustable Ball Hinge. A hinge so designed that, when the door is closed, only a ball-type knuckle is exposed. The hinge has an adjustment for vertical control within limited scope.

A.H.C. Indicates a qualified member of the American Society of Architectural Hardware Consultants. This may be preceded by "D" indicating that the member has been honored as "Distinguished," or by an "H" indicating that the member has been honored as an "Honorary" member by the Society for exceptional service to the Society. The H.A.H.C. may or may not have been a distinguished or regular A.H.C.

Anti-Friction Latch Bolt. The latch bolt of a lock equipped with a device designed to reduce friction when the bolt starts to engage and the lock strike.

Architectural Hardware. Finish Hardware, not including rough hardware. Both types make up **Builders' Hardware.**

Armor Plate. A plate similar to a kick plate but covering the door to a height usually 40 inches or more from the bottom.

Armored Front. A plate secured to the lock front by machine screws.

Astragal. A molding applied to the meeting edges of pairs of doors for protection against weather conditions.

Auxiliary Latch. A supplementary latch which automatically deadlocks the main latch bolt when the door is closed.

Auxiliary Spring. A device containing a hub and a spring to prevent sagging of lever handles. It is usually installed in the lock.

Auxiliary Spring Rose. A rose containing a built-in hub and a strong spring to prevent the sagging of a lever handle.

B

Back Check. A feature in hydraulic door closers which slows the opening speed of the door.

Back Plate (mailbox). The inside plate that finishes off the opening cut for a letter drop.

Back Plate (rim cylinder). A small plate applied to the inside of a door through which the tail piece of the rim cylinder passes and to which connecting screws attach that hold the cylinder in place.

Backset (of a lock). The horizontal distance from the face of the lock to the center of the knob, hub, keyhole, or cylinder. On locks with a beveled face, this distance is measured from the center of the lock face. On rabbeted doors, it is measured from the lower step at the center of the lock face.

Ball-Bearing Hinge. A hinge equipped with ball bearings between the hinge knuckles to reduce friction.

Bevel (of a door). The angle of the lock edge in relation to the face of the lock stile. Standard bevel is ⅛ inch in 2 in. If otherwise detailed, it must be so noted in ordering locks.

Bevel (of a lock). The slant at the end of a latch bolt. Doors opening in have a regular bevel; reverse bevel for doors opening out.

Bevel (of a lock front). The angle of a mortise lock face to make it flush with an angled edge of the door.

Bit (of a key). The projecting blade which is cut in a manner to actuate the tumblers and the bolt of a lock.

Bit Key Lock. A lock with lever tumblers operated by a key having a wing blade bitted to fit the lock.

Bitting. The cuts on the blade of a key which operates the tumblers.

Bolt (of a door). A bar to prevent a door or any movable part from opening.

Bored Lock, or **Bored Latch.** A lock or latch mortised into drilled openings. A tubular or cylindrical lock.

Bottom Bolt. A bolt designed for use on the bottom of a door only.

Box Strike. A strike which provides a complete housing to enclose the bolt openings.

Builders' Hardware. All hardware used in building construction, both finish and rough.

Butt Hinge, or **Butt.** A hinge applied to the butt edge of a door and mortised into the frame.

C

Cabin Door Hook. A hook and staple, each with a heavy plate for attaching. Generally used on marine installations.

Cabinet Lock. A small lock for use on cabinet work or furniture.

Cam (of a cylinder lock). A rotating piece attached to the end of the cylinder plug to operate the locking mechanism.

Cane Bolt. A heavy bolt with the top bent at right angles; used at the bottom of a door.

Casement Adjuster. A device for holding a casement window open or shut.

Casement Fastener. A catch used to fasten a casement window shut.

Casement Hinge. A hinge to swing a casement window. The term is often used to describe a hinge designed to throw the sash out far enough to permit cleaning the outside of the glass from the inside of the room on an outward-swinging casement.

Ceiling Hook. A hook that fastens to the ceiling or under the side of a shelf.

Chain Bolt. A vertical bolt applied at the top of a door and retracted by pulling a chain.

Chain Door Fastener. A device which permits sliding a chain into a plate on the door, allowing the door to be opened slightly for conversation without intrusion.

Change Key. A key cut to operate only one of a set of locks.

Changes (key). The different bittings or tumbler arrangements in a series of locks.

Checking Hinge. A hinge combining a spring for closing and a compression chamber in which the liquid or air escapes slowly, thus retarding the closing action.

Closet Set. A lock or latch set having a knob outside and a thumb turn inside.

Closet Spindle. A spindle having a turn that is used in place of a knob, usually used on the inside of closet doors.

Coat and Hat Hook. A hook with two or more prongs; usually with a short prong for the coat and a longer prong for the hat.

Combined Escutcheon. An escutcheon cut for both knob and keyhole or cylinder.

Communicating Door Lock. A lock having a latch bolt operated by knobs and a deadbolt operated by a turn each side. Frequently such locks have a "split" bolt so that a turn on either side locks against the other.

Concealed Hinge. A hinge so constructed that no parts are exposed when the door is closed.

Continuous Hinge, or **Piano Hinge.** A hinge extending the length of the moving part to which it is applied.

Conventional Lock. The older type of mortised lock, inserted into a rectangular hole in the edge of the door.

Co-ordinator. A device used on pairs of doors, usually in connection with panic devices, consisting of two arms to regulate the proper closing of the inactive leaf before the leaf having the astragal can close.

Cremone Bolt. A device, of surface application, that, by a turn of knob or lever handle, locks a door or sash into the frame top and bottom.

Cup Escutcheon. A door plate, for use on sliding doors, having a recessed panel to afford finger hold and to contain a flush ring and a keyhole, all being flush with the surface of the plate.

Cupboard Turn. A small spring catch for fastening light doors and operated by a rotating knob or handle.

Cylinder (of a lock). The housing containing the tumbler mechanism and the keyway, which can be actuated only by the correct key.

Cylinder Lock. A lock with both keyhole and tumbler mechanism in a cylinder separate from the case.

Cylinder Ring. A collar or washer placed under the head of a cylinder to enable a long cylinder to be used on thin doors.

Cylinder Screw. The set screw that holds a cylinder in place and prevents the cylinder from being turned after installation.

Cylindrical (locks and latches). A term used to describe locks with a cylindrical case which has a separate latch bolt case that fits into the cylindrical lock case.

D

Deadbolt. A lock bolt having no spring action which is operated by a key or a turn knob.

Dead Latch. A spring-bolt latch in which the bolt is deadlocked against end pressure, but may be retracted by a knob and/or a key.

Deadlock. A lock having a dead bolt only.

Door Closer, or **Door Check.** A device, not a hinge, combining a spring for closing and a compression chamber in which the liquid or air escapes slowly, thus retarding the closing action to prevent the slamming of the door.

Door-Closer Bracket. A device whereby a door closer may be installed without being applied directly to the door.

Door Holder. A device for fastening a door in an open position.

Door Opener. Same as **Electric Strike.**

Door Pivot. A pivot designed to fit into the floor and mortised into the heel of a door with a guide pivot at the head. No springs.

Door Silencer. A strip of rubber mortised into the frame of a door to cushion its closing.

Door Stop. A device to limit the opening swing of a door.

Double-Acting Spring Hinge. A hinge permitting the door to swing in either direction and return to a closed position.

Double-Throw Bolt. A bolt that can be projected beyond its normal position, thus giving extra security.

Drawer Roller. A device used to ease the sliding of a drawer open or shut, usually with a metal or fiber wheel rolling on a metal track.

Drawer Slides. A series of telescoping slides that support a drawer, permitting easy operation.

Drivers. The upper set of pins in a pin tumbler cylinder, which, activated by the springs, project into the plug until raised by the key.

Drop Escutcheon, or **Drop Key Plate.** An escutcheon with a pivoted covering for the keyhole.

Drop Ring. A ring handle that operates a bolt and hangs in a dropped position when not in use.

Dummy Trim. Non-functioning finish hardware; as, dummy knobs, dummy studs.

Dust Proof Strike. A strike with a spring plunger that completely fills the bolt hole when the door is open.

Dutch Door. A door with two leaves, one hung over the other; usually equipped so that both leaves can be opened independently.

Dutch Door Bolt. A vertical bolt for locking together leaves of a Dutch door. Compare **Quadrant.**

E

Easy Spring Lock. A lock which uses a soft spring to operate the latch and a heavier spring to operate the knob hub with a positive action.

Edge Pull. A pull mortised into the edge of a sliding door that slides into a pocket.

Elbow Catch. A pivoted fastening usually used to fasten the inactive door of a pair of cupboard doors and which engages a strike.

Electric Strike, or **Door Opener.** An electrical device that replaces a regular lock strike and allows opening of a door by means of a push button from any convenient location.

Escutcheon. A shield, or plate, to protect wood, or for ornament, such as the metal plate around a keyhole.

Espagnolette. A fastening rod for French windows, with hooks top and bottom plus a hinged handle locking the casement at the center. In one turn the handle operates all three locking positions.

Exit Device, or **Panic Bolt,** or **Fire-Exit Bolt.** A cross bar that, when pressed, unlocks and opens a door.

Extension Bolt. A flush bolt in which the connection between bolt head and operating mechanism is by means of a rod inserted through a hole bored in the thickness of the door.

Extension Link. A metal device that can be linked to the latch of a cylindrical lock to increase the backset.

F

Face (of a lock). The plate surface which shows in the edge of a door after installation.

Finish Hardware. Hardware that, in itself, is of a finished appearance, which may be considered as a part of the decorative treatment of a room or a building.

Fire-Exit Bolt. See Exit Device.

Floor Closer. A floor pivot or hinge with checking action.

Floor Hinge. A pivot hinge set in a floor. It may be spring type only or may be combined with liquid control for quiet closing.

Flush Bolt. A door bolt that, when applied, is flush with the face or edge of the door.

Flush Cup Pull. A door pull mortised into a sliding door.

Flush Ring. A door pull mortised into a door, having a drop ring that folds flat into a cup.

Foot Bolt. A type of bolt applied at the bottom of a door. The bolt head is usually held up by a spring when the door is unbolted.

French Door. A door with glass panes throughout its length, usually with narrow stiles.

French Door Lock. A mortise lock usually equipped with a lever handle, necessary because of the narrow backset.

French Window. A side-hinged window, glass-paneled, extending to the floor.

Friction Catch. A catch or a holder that engages a strike and is held by friction.

Friction Hinge. A hinge designed to hold a door at any desired position by means of friction control incorporated in its knuckle.

Front (of a lock). The plate through which the latching or locking bolts project. (See **Face.**)

G

Grand Master Key. A key that operates a given number of **Change Key** locks which also are master keyed under two or more **Master Key** systems.

Guard Bar. One of two or more cross bars fastened to a door to protect glass or screen.

H

Handed (of lock, door, etc.). Designed for right-hand or left-hand use but not both.

Harmon Hinge. A hinge that swings a door open into a pocket at right angles to the frame.

Hinge Plate. An ornamental plate butted against the hinge or stop to give the effect of a strap hinge.

Horizontal Spring Hinge. A spring hinge mortised horizontally into the bottom rail of a door and fastened to the floor using a pivot at the head.

Hotel Lock. A lock with special functions for guestroom doors.

Hub. The part of a lock through which the spindle passes to actuate the mechanism.

I

Inactive Door. That leaf of a pair of doors that is bolted when closed and to which the lock strike is fastened to receive the latch of the active door.

Indicator Button. A device used in connection with a hotel lock to indicate whether or not the room is occupied.

Integral Lock. A term used in Federal specifications to describe a type of mortise lock produced by only one manufacturer.

J

Jamb. An upright piece forming the side of an opening.

K

Keeper. The strike of a lock, the opening that keeps a latch bolt in position.

Key Plate. A small plate or escutcheon having only a keyhole.

Keyway. The aperture, in cylinder locks, which receives the key and closely engaged with it throughout its length.

Kick Plate. A protective plate applied on the lower rail of a door, especially a swinging door.

Knob Latch. A device having a spring bolt operated by a knob or handle at all times (not one actuated by a key).

Knob Shank. The projecting stem of a knob into which the spindle is fastened.

Knuckle. Any of the joining parts of a hinge through which the pin passes.

L

Latch Bolt. A beveled-headed spring bolt, usually operated by a knob or lever handle.

Lever Handle. A horizontal handle for operating the latch bolt of a lock.

Lever Tumbler. The locking part of a **Bit Key Lock**, generally flat, having a pivoting motion when actuated by the bit of a key.

Lip of a Strike. The protecting part on which the **Latch Bolt** rides.

Lock Set. A lock, complete with trim, such as knobs (or handles), and escutcheons.

M

Magnetic Catch. A cupboard catch that uses a magnetized strike to hold the door closed.

Mailbox Chute. A lining of the opening through a door behind the letterbox plate, usually inclined downward.

Mailbox Hood. A cover attached to the inside of a door to conceal the opening through the door and to guide mail downward.

Mailbox Plate. A plate with a slot to allow the passage of mail.

Master Key. A key that operates a given number of **Change Key** locks.

Mop Plate. A plate narrower than a **Kick Plate**, fastened to the bottom of a door to protect it.

Mortise Bolt. A door bolt designed to be mortised into a door, not applied to its surface.

Mortise Lock. A lock designed to be mortised into a door, not applied to its surface.

Mullion. A fixed or movable partition dividing an opening vertically.

N

Night Latch. An auxiliary lock having a spring bolt operated from the outside by a key and from the inside by a thumb turn.

Non-Ferrous. Nonrusting; containing no iron.

O

Olive Knuckle Hinge. A hinge that shows an oval-shaped knuckle when the door is closed.

Overhead Concealed Closer. A closer concealed in the frame header with an arm connecting with the door at the top rail.

P

Panic Bolt. See **Exit Device**.

Paracentric. A term used in connection with pin-tumbler cylinder locks having projections on the sides of the keyway that extend beyond the vertical center line of the keyway to hinder picking.

Passage Set. A latch set with knobs on both sides and no locking feature.

Piano Hinge. Same as **Continuous Hinge.**

Pin Tumblers. Small sliding pins in a **Cylinder Lock**, working against coil springs and preventing the cylinder plug from rotating until raised to the proper height by the bitting of the key.

Plug (of a cylinder lock). The round part containing the keyway and rotated by the key to transmit motion to the bolt.

Preassembled Lock. A lock set constructed so that its mechanism, knobs, and escutcheons form a permanent complete lock assembly as a unit.

Privacy Set. A tubular or cylindrical lock used on bathroom and bedroom doors, having an inside push or turn button to lock the outside knob and usually an emergency key function which will unlock the set from the outside.

Push Button (of a door). A button in the center of a knob that locks a door when depressed and unlocks it when released. Usually same function as **Turn Button.**

Push Plate. A plate applied to the lock stile to protect the door.

Q

Quadrant (or Dutch door quadrant). A quadrant-shaped device that pivots about its center to fasten together the leaves of a Dutch door. Compare **Dutch Door Bolt.**

R

Rabbet. A groove, as on the edge, or face, of one of a pair of doors or casement windows, which receives a projecting edge of the other door or window, which has been rabbeted on the opposite side. Half of each edge projects about ½ in. beyond the other half.

Rabbeted Lock (or Latch). A lock whose face conforms to the rabbet on the edge of a door.

Rail (of a door). A horizontal member which joins the stiles. There are usually three rails, top, bottom, and center (lock rail).

Reinforcement Unit. A metal box designed to reinforce a metal door in which a cylindrical lock is to be used.

Reversible Lock. A lock which, by reversing the latch bolt, may be used either hand. On certain types of locks, other parts must also be changed, but the lock is readily reversible.

Rim Lock. A lock applied to the surface of a door, not mortised into it.

Rose, or **Rosette.** A plate with a hole for receiving the shank of a door knob.

Rounded Front. The front of a lock or bolt conforming to the rounded edge of a double-acting door. The standard radius is 4 in.

S

Sash Balance. A spring device used to counterbalance the weight of a window sash or other vertical sliding part.

Sash Center. A transom support comprising a pivot and a socket for the pivot.

Sash Chain, or **Sash Cord.** A chain for use with sliding sash, attached to the sash and sash weight.

Sash-Chain Iron. A small metal holder inserted in the edge of the sash to which sash chain or cord is attached.

Sash Fast. A fastener attached to the meeting rail of sashes, used to lock a double-hung window.

Sash Lift. A flush hook or bar applied to the lower sash, by which it may be raised or lowered.

Sash Lock. A fastening with a locking device controlled by a key to secure sash.

Sash Pivot. Synonymous with **Sash Center.**

Sash Pole. A wood or metal pole to which a sash-pole hook is attached.

Sash-Pole Hook. A metal hook attached to a wooden or metal pole used to lower or raise a transom or sash beyond hand reach.

Sash Pulley. A pulley mortised into the frame of a double-hung sash frame over which the sash cord or chain passes.

Sash Socket. A metal plate containing a hole or cup to receive a sash-pole hook.

Sash Weight. A weight used to balance sliding sash, usually of cast iron or, if conditions require, of lead.

Secret Gate Latch. A latch operated by a concealed button or other device; usually used on office gates.

Semi-Concealed Closer. A door closer mortised into the top rail of a door with the barrel partially extending beyond the surface of the door.

Shank (of a knob). The projecting stem of a knob into which the spindle is fastened.

Shutter Adjuster. A swinging arm for adjusting and securing shutters in the desired position.

Shutter Bar, or **Shutter Bolt.** A fastening to bolt shutters closed.

Shutter Dog, or **Turnbuckle.** An ornamental device to hold shutter open.

Shutter Operator, or **Shutter Worker.** A device for opening or closing a shutter from inside without opening window.

Signal Sash Fastener. A sash-fastening device to lock double-hung windows which are beyond reach from the floor. It has a ring for a sash-pole hook. When locked, the ring lever is down; when the ring lever is up, it signals by its upright position that the window is unlocked.

Spacing. The distance between the center of a knob hub and a keyhole, a cylinder hole or a turn-knob hub, or of an escutcheon. In a mortise handle lock, the distance from the bottom of the trip to the center of the cylinder hole.

Spindle. The bar, usually of square section, that connects door knobs and operates latch.

Spring Balance. A device to keep sash windows from falling. When window is up, spring is unstretched.

Spring Bolt. A bolt retracted by pressure and shot by a spring when the pressure is released.

Spring Hinge. A hinge containing one or more springs to close a door. It may be either single- or double-acting.

Stile. In a door or sash, one of the two upright members.

Stool (of a window) or **Window Stool.** The flat piece corresponding to the sill of a door, against which the window shuts. The narrow shelf fitted on the inside against the actual sill.

Stop (of a lock). One of a pair of buttons in the face of a lock to lock or unlock outside knob or thumbpiece. An inside button on a night latch to hold bolt retracted.

Strap Hinge. A surface hinge fastened by long metal flaps.

Strike. The metal lip on the jamb struck by the latch bolt when the door is closed; also, a **Keeper.**

T

Template Hardware. Hardware that is made to template; that is, each piece exactly matches the master template as to spacing of all holes and dimensions.

Thimble. The socket or bearing attached to an escutcheon plate in which the end of the knob shank rotates.

Three-Point Mortise-Bolt Lock. A device required on "A" label Underwriters fire doors to lock the active door at three points.

Threshold. A piece of metal that lies under a door, usually covering the joining place of two floor materials.

Thumbpiece. The small pivoted part above a door handle that operates a latch bolt.

Thumb Turn. The part on a lock turned by thumb and finger to operate a dead bolt.

Transom Catch. A fastening applied to a transom and having a ring by which the latch bolt is retracted.

Transom Chain. A short chain used to limit the swing of a transom; usually provided at each end with a plate for attachment.

Transom Lift. A vertically operated device attached to door frame and transom by which the transom may be opened or closed.

Trim. Finish Hardware.

Tubular Lock. A lock having a case that requires a bored (round) hole rather than a rectangular mortise. The face plate is attached to the lock case as a unit.

Tumbler. A movable obstruction in a lock, consisting of a pin, lever, or the like, which must be moved by a key to lock or unlock.

Turnbuckle. Same as **Shutter Dog.**

Turn Button. A button in the center of a knob that locks or unlocks a door by being turned. Same function as **Push Button.**

Two-Point Lock. A device required on "A" label Underwriters fire doors to lock the inactive door of a pair of doors at top and bottom.

U

Unit Lock. A lock set constructed so that its mechanism, knobs, and escutcheons are permanently combined as a unit. Synonymous with **Preassembled Lock.**

Universal. Serving for both left-hand and right-hand use without change.